Published by Islam and Christianity in Prophecy Seminars, Emmett, Idaho 83617

An earlier edition was previously published by the Review and Herald Publishing Association in 2011.

The author is open to discussing translation and publication into other languages. Books may be purchased in bulk. For details email newsletter@IslamAndChristianity.org or contact through our website:IslamAndChristianity.org.

For more information on this and other related topics, visit our website at IslamAndChristianity.org.

Editing and interior layout by Lorna M. Hartman
Cover art and interior art copyright © Steve Creitz

Printed in the USA

ISBN 978-0-9976890-0-6

ISLAM AND CHRISTIANITY IN PROPHECY

TABLE OF CONTENTS

Introduction
SOME THINGS TO KNOW ABOUT THIS BOOK

My Approach to Prophecy

I am a big-picture forest person, not a tree person. I study the trends and avoid getting bogged down in the details. After being immersed in history and Bible prophecy for more than 30 years, I've come to have a feel for it.

In 2002 I had an "aha" moment, an epiphany of sorts, about the central meaning of Daniel 11. Following that "aha" moment I spent several years testing my findings, and I have now, I believe, confirmed them after checking sources and consulting with scholars and researchers.

Now that current events have proven the first edition accurate, this revised edition will be even clearer. I've also made revisions to be more detailed and technically accurate than in the first edition.

I am indebted to all who have challenged my conclusions, as they have led to a continued study that has proven this understanding of the Daniel 11 prophecy to be accurate.

I got into this study during the 1970s as a freshman in college. Since I didn't enjoy writing, I decided that if I had to do a composition paper, I would write about something that I like—Bible prophecy.

As I studied the various methods of prophetic interpretation, I discovered that the way of the Reformers (Luther, Calvin, the Wesleys, and others) for understanding Bible prophecy, known as historicism, is much more accurate and true to the Bible text than the methods used by most prophecy teachers today.

Historicism is a method of interpretation based on the idea that biblical predictions, instead of something reserved solely for the future, have not only been fulfilled throughout history but continue to be fulfilled today.

Because of my study, this book is built on history and Scripture, illuminated by the Reformers' understanding of prophetic interpretation.

The resulting picture is clear. Our world is experiencing great change. Are you ready for the worsening holy war that has already begun to engulf this world? Or for what will come after it? Islam and Christianity will show you what to expect. That knowledge will give you the chance to survive both spiritually and physically.

The prophecies that God placed in the Bible have proved reliable since the beginning of human history. Bible prophecy helps people to know with certainty what events are coming and causes them to believe when they see the predicted events actually happening.

This book does not attempt to explain every prophecy in the Bible. Rather, it presents a commonsense big picture of where the human race has come from and where it is going next. Nor does it seek to be politically correct.

My goal is to be biblically correct—faithful to the Bible text. It is not my goal to offend you, but if I do, I hope you will take the time to find out for yourself whether what I say is true to the Bible.

If you do conclude that the book's message and conclusions agree with the Bible, I hope you will be open to making changes in your life that will bring you into harmony with God and His words.

That is the purpose of Bible prophecy: to help each of us be prepared for the future. The prophecy cannot help us if we don't act on it.

How Much Do You Know Already?

While the more you know about the Bible, the easier it will be to connect some of the ideas I present to your general understanding of God's Word, don't be concerned if you have little Bible knowledge. This book explains the prophecies of Daniel step by step.

Who is the Intended Audience of the Book?

The great news about the Daniel prophecies concerning the end of the world is that the truth fits all people. Assuming you and I are still alive when the end of the world comes, we can live through the most catastrophic times without fear or uncertainty and come out safely (at least spiritually) on the other side.

You do not have to be surprised by world events as they happen. Nor do you need to be overwhelmed by anxiety and bewilderment. Great trouble will fill the time ahead, but God tells us clearly what is coming and what to do in the face of it.

The Best Place to Start

If you have not read the book of Daniel all the way through, now is a good time to do it. Even if you've read it before, you will appreciate the review. Though you may not understand everything you read, keep going and read through it. Then, when you read Islam and Christianity in Prophecy, the book of Daniel will become clearer to you.

Basic Terms

I will use some terms frequently in this book. Here are the most common ones and their meanings:

- The Bible: the Old and New Testaments of the sacred Scriptures, the written Word of God
- Bible prophecy: predictions about the future, given by God to individuals, who wrote them down in Scripture
- Geopolitical: political aspects of nations, especially having to do with international relations, as influenced by geography
- Spiritual: the religious aspects of nations or political powers
- The king of the North: geopolitical powers in prophecy that come against Israel from the north
- The king of the South: geopolitical powers in prophecy that attack Israel from the south
- The papacy: the ecclesiastical system of governance in the Roman Catholic Church that is headed by the pope
- Islam: the religion of Muslims, a monotheistic faith regarded as revealed through Muhammad as the prophet of Allah
- The Reformation: the sixteenth-century religious movement that rejected or modified some Roman Catholic doctrines and practices, and resulted in the creation of Protestant churches
- The Reformers: the leaders of the Protestant Reformation

The Key Bible Text of the Book

If you have just read the book of Daniel again, you may be wondering why succeeding chapters appear to repeat some parts of the prophecies. Daniel 2, 7, and 8 seem to be talking about the same powers and events, but with details added or omitted.

What you need to know is that the chapters are layers, each one adding more detail than the previous chapter. Daniel 11 provides the road map you need to understand the prophecies.

It is a sequential guide to all of the prophecies described in previous chapters of Daniel—and even for those in the book of Revelation.

All Doom and Gloom?

End-time scenarios turn off many people. Why even talk about the end of the world as we know it? Why spread fear and anger and sadness, they say, when we could be looking for the good in the world and making a positive difference?

Think about this: the study of Bible prophecy is a both/and activity. A faithful and accurate take on Bible prophecy shows us what is really happening in our world, prompts us to take positive action now, and brings to light the promises of much better things to come.

It raises the questions, Why look to the future for better things to come? Why not just work for the good of people in the world today?

Bible prophecy has a both/and application here as well. Good and evil are at war in the world. The only way to avoid that reality is to pretend it isn't there.

Working for the good of people in the world today is extremely important—a must-do—but it must be done in the context of a world in the grip of spiritual and physical conflict.

It is a giant mistake for anyone to live in denial of the spiritual and political aspects of our world. Rather, it is extremely important for us to understand what God has revealed.

Bible prophecy lifts the veil from what will happen in the near future. Today's complicated realities, both good and bad, find an explanation in the revelations of the prophet Daniel and other Bible writers.

Let's Find the Truth

In Islam and Christianity in Prophecy we are on a quest for truth. Not my truth or your truth. Not the truth of one church or one religion, nor of one political ideology or political party. Not liberal truth or conservative truth. We are looking for Bible truth—the truth that God gave to all people.

Why is that important? God's Word in the Bible transcends all human manipulation. And your life depends on it! Follow God and His Word, and you will live. Ignore it, twist it, misrepresent it, neglect it, and you will not survive the coming trouble. So let's find the truth in Bible prophecy.

Chapter 1

MODERN "HOLY WAR"

People no longer trust their leaders and governments, a sad reality in our world today. However, God has told us what to expect in the future, and unlike world leaders, He has a perfect track record of honesty.

The mayhem portrayed in movie thrillers is sometimes eerily similar to the visions described by the Bible prophets in several places. The Bible has the advantage of being reliable in its predictions, however. As we look into the prophecies in the books of Daniel and Revelation, we will uncover the plain truth about what is in store for our world.

Introducing Daniel

The statesman Daniel was one of the most important Bible prophets. Prime minister of two world empires, he began his civic career in his youth, about 605 B.C., when taken into exile in Babylon from the tiny country of Judah. His captors trained him to serve in the court of Nebuchadnezzar, the new emperor of Babylon.

Through his long career Daniel endeared himself to the kings he served because he had a relationship with his God that gave him access to reliable knowledge and wisdom, and his integrity was unshakable.

God entrusted him with prophecies about the future. His first one, recorded in Daniel 2, explains Nebuchadnezzar's dream about a giant statue. The later prophecies, revealed in Daniel 7 and 8, build on that first prophecy like layers on a cake, adding more detail to the prophecies. The frosting on the cake is Daniel 11. That chapter defines and explains in sequential order the prophecies of world history from Daniel's time to the end of the world.

Islam and Christianity

I believe that the prophecies of Daniel predict three holy "wars" between Islam and Western Christianity. In the sense used here, "war" means a lengthy conflict between two broad powers in the world. The first war was the Arab expansion of Islam and the Christian Crusades from A.D. 1095 to 1291. The second was the growth of the Islamic Ottoman Empire during the period of the Reformation and following, roughly A.D. 1360 to 1840.[1]

These first two major Christian/Islamic "wars" have already happened, and the third holy war is just beginning. In the third and final holy war, radical Islam attacks Western Christianity. Western Christianity, including the United States and Europe, counterattacks. How can we know that the third war will happen? And what will it look like? We will explore the biblical evidence in this book.

But I am not the only one who has come to this conclusion. Others have also noticed similar trends from history and current events. Boris Johnson, in his 2008 British Broadcasting Corporation documentary After Rome: Holy War and Conquest, sees a north-south split of the Roman Empire and continuing conflict between Islam and Christianity.[2]

Samuel P. Huntington in his major Foreign Affairs article in 1993 indicated that the coming conflicts are likely to be between civilizations, such as the Christian West and Islam.[3] Many news commentators have alluded to a possible holy war.

A Prophecy of the Third Holy War

Daniel 11 gives the prophecy predicting the third holy war. To understand what the chapter says, keep in mind that the king of the North represents Western Christianity and the king of the South represents Islam. The "Glorious Land" (Dan. 11:41) and "the glorious holy mountain" (verse 45) are names for the land of Israel and/or Jerusalem.

In places where the words "he" or "him" are not clearly connected to one of the kings, I have indicated the correct king in brackets.

---

1   *The historical basis of this chapter comes from a variety of sources, but any reputable book of world history will bear it out.*
2   *Boris Johnson, "After Rome: Holy War and Conquest," directed by Grace Chapman and Francis Hanley, two-part series aired Nov. 29 and Dec. 6, 2008 (London: BBC, 2008).*
3   *See Samuel P. Huntington, "The Clash of Civilizations?", Foreign Affairs 72, no. 3 (Summer 1993): 22-49.*

"At the time of the end the king of the South shall attack him [the king of the North]; and the king of the North shall come against him [the king of the South] like a whirlwind, with chariots, horsemen, and with many ships; and he [the king of the North] shall enter the countries, overwhelm them, and pass through.

"He [the king of the North] shall also enter the Glorious Land, and many countries shall be overthrown; but these shall escape from his hand: Edom, Moab, and the prominent people of Ammon.

"He [the king of the North] shall stretch out his hand against the countries, and the land of Egypt shall not escape. He shall have power over the treasures of gold and silver, and over all the precious things of Egypt; also the Libyans and Ethiopians shall follow at his heels.

"But news from the east and the north shall trouble him [the king of the North]; therefore he shall go out with great fury to destroy and annihilate many. And he [the king of the North] shall plant the tents of his palace between the seas and the glorious holy mountain; yet he [the king of the North] shall come to his end, and no one will help him" (Daniel 11:40-45).[4]

The third war will result in the destruction of Islam as we know it, a change that will likely be much more dramatic and pivotal than the Crusades of the Middle Ages or World Wars I and II. As depicted in Daniel 11, the third holy war will dramatically alter the world and our freedoms as we have known them.

It is then, in the aftermath of the third war, that God will rescue a small part of Christianity as well as a small part of Islam. These are those who are truly following God and His book the Bible.

Please note that the prophecy and its interpretation is neither anti-Muslim nor anti-Christian. Rather, it is a straightforward prediction of what will happen in the future.

Daniel 11: A Sequential Prophecy

The entire prophecy that includes predictions of the three major conflicts between Christianity and Islam appear in Daniel 11:2-12:3. It starts in the time of Daniel (seventh-century B.C.), moves in a straightforward way through human history, and concludes with the end of the world and God's people living with Him

---

4   *The Daniel 11 prophecy with detailed explanation appears in Appendix B, with Bible texts on the left and interpretation on the right.*

forever after the return of Jesus Christ and the resurrection. Because this chapter of Daniel is sequential, it gives us a timeline of major events in history. Many of the predicted events have already occurred, so in this book we will check them against the historical record. The final events of Daniel 11 have begun to be fulfilled with some as yet unfulfilled.

Although most Bible scholars have considered Daniel 11 a difficult passage, many of them are reaching conclusions similar to those presented here. It has been my experience that once people learn certain keys of interpretation, the Daniel 11 prophecy will become clear to most. See appendix A "Contextual Hermeneutics" for a detailed explanation of the keys of interpretation.

People in the world today worry about the possibility of nuclear war. Let me set your mind at ease: I am certain that nuclear war will not destroy the human race. How do I know that? When Jesus returns to earth, the prophet tells us in Revelation 1:7 that human beings will be alive to see His coming. No all-out nuclear war will annihilate humanity.

That does not rule out limited nuclear war, however. The United States has already used such weapons against Japan in 1945, and they could be used again by any group in the future.

Many are concerned about terrorism. They wonder, Where will it hit next? The Bible does not say where it will happen next, but it does, I believe, tell us that the Islamic south will be pushing against or attacking the Christian North. So we can expect continued terrorism until the Christian and moderate Muslim powers destroy radical Islam.

The Signs to Watch For

The Bible talks about signs that will indicate the progression of these events. Some, the Bible says, will increase in intensity and frequency as the time of Jesus Christ's coming gets close, and therefore no one needs to be surprised by the events as they happen.

Scripture compares the increasing intensity to the contractions of a woman giving birth: "Concerning the times and the seasons, . . . you yourselves know perfectly that the day of the Lord so comes as a thief in the night.

"For when they say, 'Peace and safety!' then sudden destruction comes upon them, as labor pains upon a pregnant woman. And they shall not escape. But you

13

. . . are not in darkness, so that this Day should overtake you as a thief " (1 Thessalonians 5:1-4). No one needs to be surprised by either the turbulent events that lead up to the return of Jesus Christ or the Second Coming itself. But we must be watching for the signs.

When Jesus lived on earth during the early first century A.D., He explained some of the signs: "As He sat on the Mount of Olives, the disciples came to Him privately, saying, 'Tell us, when will these things be? And what will be the sign of Your coming, and of the end of the age?'

"And Jesus answered and said to them: 'Take heed that no one deceives you. For many will come in My name, saying, "I am the Christ," and will deceive many. And you will hear of wars and rumors of wars. See that you are not troubled; for all these things must come to pass, but the end is not yet'" (Matthew 24:3-6).

History has witnessed countless wars through the centuries as well as frequent rumors of impending or potential ones. It is important for us to establish a general picture of the present world situation.

Recent history shows that the tension between the Islamic world and other powers has been growing for many decades. The flashpoints are familiar to anyone who keeps track of world news.

As an example, notice a typical report about Iran and Israel from November 2008: "Senior Tehran officials are recommending a preemptive strike against Israel to prevent an Israeli attack on Iran's nuclear reactors, a senior Islamic Republic official told foreign diplomats two weeks ago in London.

"The official, Dr. Seyed G. Safavi, said recent threats by Israeli authorities strengthened this position, but that as of yet, a preemptive strike has not been integrated into Iranian policy."[5]

Iran suggested that it might launch a preemptive attack on Israel because Israel had declared that it might attack Iran before Iran could get a nuclear weapon to strike Israel. Each side seeks to preempt a preemptive attack! That's the kind of world we live in today—one full of wars and continuing rumors of wars.

The rumors are there, but we want to figure out whether we live in a time of increasing "labor pains." Are the pressures mounting in frequency and strength?

---

5   Source: www.haaretz.com/news/top-iran-officials-recommend-preemptive-strike-against- israel-1.255799.

Labor pains start out soft and slow and get more and more intense until the birth. We are seeing indications that history's labor pains are growing more severe.

A Word of Caution

People have been looking at and evaluating the signs and rumors of wars for a long time. One of the dangers of focusing on such events in the news is that it's easy to jump to the conclusion that the ones apparent right now represent the very intense labor pains just before the birth. But are they really?

The book *Heralds of the Morning*, written by Asa Oscar Tait and published in several editions at the end of the nineteenth century, shows what happens when a student of prophecy believes that events in his or her day represent those final labor pains. *Heralds of the Morning* includes a long chapter titled "And the Nations Were Angry." It describes in great detail the capabilities of the United States military during the 1890s.

The author writes: "The prophetic declaration is that the war spirit will prevail over the whole world; and what may be seen among the nations today? Does the outlook indicate a universal peace? Are not the greatest armies being hastily gathered, and the most marvelous implements of war being forged, that could ever have been conceived in the wildest realm of imaginative fancy?"[6]

Further on, he adds: "The weapons with which Napoleon and the great generals of all former times fought were mere toys when compared with the weapons that are now being prepared."[7] And marveling at the many guns of his time, he observed: "In 1861 Dr. R. J. Gatling invented the gun that bears his name, and the ingenious mechanism of this weapon enables it to fire from 600 to 1,200 shots per minute."[8]

But today the United States has gone far beyond the destructive capability of the late nineteenth century, including such devices as smart bombs. A pilot in an airplane several miles above the earth's surface can by remote control drop a bomb down a vent stack into a bunker. The military has missiles that can hit anywhere in the world to within a couple feet of the target and devastate vast areas. We are no longer talking about just rapid-firing guns.

---

6   Asa Oscar Tait, Heralds of the Morning (Oakland, Calif.: Pacific Press., 1899), pp. 183, 184.
7   Ibid., pp. 186, 187.
8   Ibid., p. 187.

What is my point? Be careful in looking at such things and using them to announce, "Jesus will be here in a very short time, because this sign is being fulfilled." Many people have made that mistake. Christ Himself said: "Nation will rise against nation, and kingdom against kingdom. And there will be famines, pestilences, and earthquakes in various places. All these are the beginning of sorrows" (Matthew 24:7, 8).

He did not say that such events indicate His immediate return, but rather that they were just the beginning of the signs. The wars are preliminary birth pains. We need to be looking at what is going on around us and be getting ready, but there are some things in Scripture that are more solid indicators than the "wars and rumors of wars."

Famines, diseases, and earthquakes in various places are sadly commonplace in the world. Can we find anything that helps to measure whether the intensity of such catastrophes is increasing?

Consider, for example, this news release: "New research compiled by Australian scientist Dr. Tom Chalko shows that global seismic activity on Earth is now five times more energetic than it was just 20 years ago. The research proves that destructive ability of earthquakes on Earth increases alarmingly fast and that this trend is set to continue. …

"The analysis of more than 386,000 earthquakes between 1973 and 2007 recorded on the U.S. Geological Survey database proved that the global annual energy of earthquakes on Earth began increasing very fast since 1990."[9]

The point of looking at such signs is not that we are all the way there, but rather that we are getting closer and that the labor pains are intensifying. Sooner or later the final event is going to happen—Jesus will return.

Continuing in Matthew 24, we discover more of the signs: "Then they will deliver you up to tribulation and kill you, and you will be hated by all nations for My name's sake. And then many will be offended, will betray one another, and will hate one another.

"Then many false prophets will rise up and deceive many. And because lawlessness will abound, the love of many will grow cold. But he who endures to the end shall be saved. And this gospel of the kingdom will be preached in all the world as a witness to all the nations, and then the end will come" (verses 9-14).

---

9   www.cbsnews.com/stories/2008/06/18/tech/main4191556.shtml.

What is the major sign of the return of Jesus? The gospel truth about Jesus being communicated to all the world. That's the big one! Watch for that one.

A Message for You

The words of Jesus declare that those who endure to the end will be saved. It means that we might go through some hard times. The labor pains might be tough to take. But if we hang in there, we will receive something really good at the end: a new life.

When the gospel has gone to the whole world, then we get to spend eternity with Jesus. That is something really good.

The good news about Jesus Christ is now spreading across the world in a multitude of ways right now—through the Internet, through radio, through individual people with great courage on the ground in areas where it is not easy to share the gospel.

Who Are the Real Christians?

God in 2 Timothy 3:1-4 reveals more about what the situation will be like at the end of the world: "But know this, that in the last day"—meaning near the end of time—"perilous times will come: For men will be lovers of themselves, lovers of money, boasters, proud, blasphemers, disobedient to parents, unthankful, unholy, unloving, unforgiving, slanderers, without self-control, brutal, despisers of good, traitors, headstrong, haughty, lovers of pleasure rather than lovers of God."

While it sounds like the world of today, it's not referring to the society or culture in which we live. If we keep reading, we find that verse 5 speaks of people "having a form of godliness but denying its power. And from such people turn away!"

Unfortunately, Paul is talking about the Christian church! Proud, blasphemers, lovers of pleasure, growing cold in their love—those verses describe people who have a form of godliness and claim to be Christians but are really not.

How can that be possible? Consider the findings of George Barna, the Christian researcher. He found that 62 percent of Protestants say they are "born again" and 22 percent of Catholics say they are "born again."

By "born again" he simply means that "a person has a relationship with Christ that causes them to believe that they have been forgiven of their sins and expect to live with Him forever." That's a pretty simple definition. But Barna's survey found that only 62 percent of Protestants and 22 percent of Catholics consider themselves born again.

In a more recent study,[10] Barna asked how many of these people have a biblical worldview. He settled on a minimum of six beliefs that make up a biblical world-view. They included:

- Absolute moral truth exists.
- The Bible is totally accurate in all of the principles it teaches.
- Satan is a real being or force, not merely symbolic.
- People cannot earn their way into heaven by trying to be good or doing good works.
- Jesus Christ lived a sinless life on earth.
- God is the all-knowing, all-powerful Creator of the world who still rules the universe today.

How many born-again Christians actually affirmed all six concepts? Only 9 percent! So, among people who profess to be Christian, only about 5 out of 100 are born again and have a biblical worldview. It's probably safe to say that some of them claim it but don't really live it, so the real figure is probably worse.

Barna sums it up this way: "Although most Americans consider themselves to be Christian and say they know the content of the Bible, less than one out of ten Americans demonstrate such knowledge through their actions." This reminds me of what Mahatma Gandhi said: "I like your Christ. I do not like your Christians. Your Christians are so unlike your Christ."

Now you may be one who has given up on the Christian church because you met some of those who weren't really Christian, and you said, "Forget it!" But I want to encourage you: Don't give up. Keep digging into God's Word. Keep looking for a real, true Christian who follows God's Word, has a biblical worldview, and trusts in Jesus Christ so that you can see what a real Christian is like.

The apostle Paul said something important to Christians in 1 Corinthians 10:31: "Therefore, whether you eat or drink, or whatever you do, do all to the glory of God." If you are a Christian, make sure you are doing that, because if you are not, you are going to lead somebody else to reject Christianity.

---

10   www.barna.org/barna-update/article/21-transformation/252-barna-survey-exam-ines- changes-in-worldview-among-christians-over-the-past-13-years.

The Time for Understanding Is Now

The end of the Daniel 11 prophecy, which actually appears in Daniel 12, says: "But you, Daniel, shut up the words, and seal the book until the time of the end; many shall run to and fro, and knowledge shall increase" (verse 4).

God said the prophecy wouldn't be understood for a long while, or, as verse 4 states, "until the time of the end." Therefore, you can expect the book of Daniel to be fully comprehended right about the time period indicated in Daniel 11:40.

As I was working on this volume, someone shared study materials with me on the book of Daniel. Interestingly, they did not include chapter 11 at all. Why? Because many have considered it a very difficult chapter to interpret. But at the end of the prophecy of Daniel 11 (which, as I said, runs into chapter 12), the angel presenting the vision declares that it will be comprehended (Daniel 12:4).

That really excites me, because people are beginning to grasp Daniel 11, and that puts us right about the time of verse 40 in Daniel 11. Since the first printing of this book Daniel 11:40 has begun to be fulfilled just as expected!

Daniel 11 takes us through the same empires as those found in the statue prophecy of Daniel 2. As we will see, it starts in Daniel's day and works step by step through the Persian Empire, the Greek Empire, the time of Christ, the Roman Empire, and right up to a final struggle between the kings of the North and South. Finally, it shows Jesus rescuing His people, describes a resurrection, and then declares that God's people will live with Him forever.

It is the only prophecy in the Bible with that much detail, beginning far back in history—about 535 B.C.—and continuing all the way to the return of Christ. In some ways Daniel 11 also acts like a filing system. We can take all of the other prophecies of Daniel and those from other books of the Bible, and find where each of them fits in the Daniel 11 sequence. Although it's not that difficult to understand, God did not open people's minds on it until recently.

How the Filing System Works

Daniel 11:2 says: "Now I will tell you the truth: Behold, three more kings will arise in Persia." Daniel was its prime minister at the time, and so this verse indicates that the prophecy begins in his era. "Three more kings will arise in Persia, and the fourth shall be far richer than them all; by his strength, through his riches, he shall stir up all against the realm of Greece."

This led to the downfall of the fourth king as the king of the North. When Xerxes (called Ahasuerus in the Bible) did that, the Greeks defeated him in battle. We have here a switch from the Persian to the Greek Empire, and later Alexander takes control.

Daniel 11 does not stay with one political power, but tracks the succeeding powers as the prophecies advance through time. This transition sets up a pattern for similar prophetic progressions elsewhere in the chapter. Whenever the current world power challenges the next rising power and loses, the focus will shift to the new power as the king of the North, even though the old power may continue for some time in a weakened state. In the case of Persia, a number of additional kings reigned after Greece entered the scene.

Verses 3 and 4: "Then a mighty king shall arise, who shall rule with great dominion, and do according to his will. And when he has arisen, his kingdom shall be broken up and divided toward the four winds of heaven, but not among his posterity nor according to his dominion with which he ruled; for his kingdom shall be uprooted, even for others besides these."

Not only do we have a shift from Persia to Greece, but verse 4 says that the new kingdom will fragment into four segments. When Alexander the Great died at age 32, four of his generals split up his empire into four primary Greek or Hellenistic kingdoms. God's prophecies are right on the mark.

Now I want to demonstrate how the Daniel 11 "filing system" works. We will look at some other chapters in Daniel to show how to expand our understanding of chapter 11.

In Daniel 2 King Nebuchadnezzar had a dream one night, and during his dream he saw something amazing. Then he woke up and forgot the dream. Puzzled, he summoned his counselors and said, "Tell me the dream, and I will give you great riches. Don't tell me the dream, and you're dead."

"You want us to tell you what you dreamed last night?" they asked. "Oh, king, nobody does that."

"But you are going to," their ruler retorted.

Why? The counselors claimed to have a connection with the gods. Thus they could interpret dreams, because the gods would explain to them what the dreams meant.

And so, if the gods sent the dreams and the interpretation, surely the counselors should be able to tell Nebuchadnezzar what the dream had been. Basically the king was saying, "If you can't do this, then you are a bunch of frauds, and you're done."

Since the wise men still hedged, the king sent soldiers to round them up and execute them all. The troops came to Daniel's house (he had not been invited to the meeting) and knocked on his door. When he inquired what was going on, they told him.

Requesting some additional time from Nebuchadnezzar, Daniel assured the king that his God could reveal to Daniel what the dream had been.

The prophet returned home, and with his friends Meshach, Shadrach, and Abed-nego, he had a serious prayer meeting. In essence they were saying, "God, either give us the dream or we are dead!"

The Lord showed Daniel the dream, and so the young man went back to the court and announced, "King, here is the dream you had. You were thinking about the future, and you dreamed about a statue with a head of gold, chest of silver, belly and thighs of brass, legs of iron, and feet of iron and clay. As you looked at that, a rock that was cut out without hands came crashing down on the statue and destroyed it. The statue just blew away as dust in the wind, and then the Rock took over the whole world.

"Here's the interpretation," Daniel announced to the king. "You are the head of gold—Babylon. After you will rise another kingdom, one inferior to you." (This was actually Medo-Persia.) "And then a third power will take over." By the time we get to Daniel 11 the book of Daniel actually identifies most of the powers by name. But in Daniel 2 the prophet named only Babylon and then symbolically described the rest.

Continuing, Daniel said, "King, after the third one will come a very strong kingdom with legs of iron." This was Rome. History tells us that when it began to decline, it wasn't conquered as a whole. Instead, it fell apart, and remnants of the Roman Empire remained afterward. As time passed it went from being the Roman Empire to the various countries of Europe, North Africa, and the Middle East.

We are still living in that time of divided Europe and other areas of the former Roman Empire, a condition that will continue until the second coming of Jesus Christ.

The prophecy predicts four major empires, and after them, a collection of weaker countries that nobody would be able to reunite. If you look at the most important family trees of Europe, for example, "they [would] mingle with the seed of men," as Daniel 2:43 puts it. The leading families of the nations intermarried, trying to keep peace between the different parts of the region. Then they would have a family feud and go to war anyway! It didn't work, just as Daniel said it wouldn't.

Several emperors and conquerors tried to unite Europe and hold it together, but nobody could. Some of the fragments of other former parts of the Roman Empire also tried to unite, such as Egypt and Syria under Gamal Abdel Nasser (president of Egypt) during the twentieth century, but eventually failed. Daniel said that no one would be able to unite Europe after the Roman Empire, and nobody has.

That puts us down in the "toenails" of time. We are right down at the end somewhere, during which those "labor pains" are becoming more intense.

In Daniel 7 the prophet goes over the same material, only this time the prophecy depicts the powers as animals. Those four beasts are God's cartoons.

We use animals in cartoons all the time. Americans depict Democrats as donkeys and Republicans as elephants. You can glance at a political cartoon and know right away what it is talking about.

Daniel starts out portraying Babylon as a lion with eagle's wings. If you had entered the processional way in Babylon, you would have seen blue-tiled walls with animals on them.[11] They are beautiful, and on the walls are lions with wings. The winged lion was a symbol of Babylon in Daniel's day. Everybody knew what the prophet was talking about when he mentioned the lion with eagle's wings.

Following that in the vision was a bear, which represented Medo-Persia. It was humped up on one side. What did that mean? That one side would be more powerful. This was the case in that the Persians were the stronger element of the Medo-Persian coalition. The first king was a Mede, but after that, the Persians took control.

Next emerged Greece, depicted by a leopard that rapidly conquered the world that the people of the Bible knew. The leopard had four heads. After the death of Alexander the Great, his kingdom split into four major segments. Again, the detail is correct.

---

11   *You can walk through those gates today, but you can't go to Babylon to do it. You have to visit the Pergamon Museum in Berlin, Germany. The Germans took the gate down piece by piece, transported it to their country, and rebuilt it.*

Later in Daniel 7 a unique and fearsome beast with 10 horns comes up, which represents Rome. These are important points to keep in mind as we go through Daniel 11.

I am not going to give every last detail of the history in Daniel 11. Anyone not especially interested in history would get bored and fall asleep. For the complete list of historical events and corresponding verses in Daniel 11, see Appendix B.

Kings of the North and South

While there seems to be in Daniel's prophecies a direct correlation between an animal or beast symbol and a particular power, apparently that is not always the case in Daniel 11.

It employs the terms "king of the North" and "king of the South" for different powers at different times, depending on which nations controlled the areas to the north and south of Israel and could make incursions into it from those directions.

For instance, Daniel 11:4-19 talks about Alexander's kingdom and how it split four ways, but then it focuses on only two of them. The two that it concentrates on are called the king of the North (the black arrow) and the king of the South (the gray arrow). One of the powers invaded from the north of Jerusalem, and the other attacked from the south.

This is not the first designation of the king of the North in prophecy. The first empire so named was Babylon, according to the prophet Jeremiah.

Now the Babylonian Empire lay mostly to the east of Jerusalem, so why would anyone refer to Babylon in the east as a kingdom of the north? Because when the Babylonian army approached Israel, it had to march northwest around the desert regions and then down to Jerusalem from the north. No army commander would be foolish enough to cut through the desert.

At this point we can say from history that in Daniel 11, the king of the North is a power that would invade Jerusalem from the north. And we can conclude that the king of the South would be a power coming from the south of Israel.

In Daniel 11:4 and following, we begin to see that the imagery of the king of the North and the king of the South applied to the time of the Greeks. The armies of Alexander the Great marched around by land from the west and entered Jerusalem from the north. After his empire split up, the two powers north and south of Israel comprised the dynasties of two of Alexander's generals, Ptolemy and Seleucus.

Ptolemy was made governor of Egypt, but later declared it the Ptolemaic kingdom. Calling himself pharaoh, he took the title of Ptolemy I.

Seleucus, given the governorship of what had been Babylonia, proved even more ambitious. In less than 10 years he conquered a vast territory from the middle of present-day Turkey east to the Indus River, the western frontier of India, creating the Seleucid Empire.

In relation to Jerusalem, the Seleucid Empire lay to the north and the Ptolemaic kingdom to the south. If the two powers got into a fight, who found themselves caught in the middle? Jerusalem. As it happened, Ptolemy I took over the area around Jerusalem in violation of an agreement that had given the territory to Seleucus. That prompted a series of six conflicts called the Syrian Wars.

Seleucus' grandson Antiochus II tried to take back the territories of Israel, Judah, and Syria in the second Syrian War, and Ptolemy II, the son of Ptolemy I, fought to keep them. In an attempt to make peace, Ptolemy II sent his daughter Berenice to marry Antiochus II. So Antiochus II divorced his wife, Laodice, and sent her into exile. With his new wife, Queen Berenice, Antiochus II had a son.

Ptolemy II died and was succeeded by his eldest son, Ptolemy III. Up in the Seleucid Empire, Antiochus II thought, Berenice's father is gone, and so he dumped her and again took up with his first wife, Laodice.

Soon after that, Antiochus II died (likely poisoned by his angry first wife). She then declared her son Seleucus II the new emperor and succeeded in having Berenice and her son poisoned.

Consider how accurately Daniel 11:5, 6 depicts the events: "Then the king of the South shall become strong, as well as one of his princes; and he shall gain power over him and have dominion. His dominion shall be a great dominion.

"And at the end of some years they shall join forces, for the daughter of the king of the South shall go to the king of the North to make an agreement; but she shall not retain the power of her authority, and neither he nor his authority shall stand;

but she shall be given up, with those who brought her, and with him who begot her, and with him who strengthened her in those times."

Isn't that exactly what happened to Berenice and her son? The authority of Antiochus II did not last, and Berenice did not retain her power, and she was given up, along with those who brought her to the Seleucid court.

Ptolemy III, Berenice's brother, was extremely upset about her poisoning. The marriage was supposed to be a peace treaty. So Ptolemy III marched back up through Judea, fought a battle, and won. Then the conflict swung back and forth for some time. (No need to describe all of those encounters here.) Daniel 11:7-9 draws the overall picture:

"But from a branch of her [Berenice's] roots one shall arise in his place, who shall come with an army, enter the fortress of the king of the North, and deal with them and prevail. And he shall also carry their gods captive to Egypt, with their princes and their precious articles of silver and gold; and he shall continue more years than the king of the North. Then the king of the North shall come to the kingdom of the king of the South, but shall return to his own land."

Daniel 11:7 declares: "From a branch of her roots one shall arise in his place." This points back to the root, Ptolemy I, and the succeeding kings are each a different branch from Ptolemy I. The passage clearly shows the symbolism of "a branch of her roots."

In verses 17-19 Antiochus III tried to do the same thing as Ptolemy II. He thought that with a marriage, he could establish peace: "He shall also set his face to enter with the strength of his whole kingdom, and upright ones with him; thus shall he do. And he shall give him the daughter of women to destroy it; but she shall not stand with him, or be for him.

"After this he shall turn his face to the coastlands, and shall take many. But a ruler shall bring the reproach against them to an end; and with the reproach removed, he shall turn back on him. Then he shall turn his face toward the fortress of his own land; but he shall stumble and fall, and not be found."

Let's see if, once again, the prophecy matches history. Antiochus III, the Seleucid king in the north, said, "OK, I'm going to send my daughter down to Egypt to marry a Ptolemy, to make a peace treaty." He sent his daughter, by the name of Cleopatra I, down to the south, where she married the king of the South but had no intention of being true to her father or husband.

Assuming control of the Ptolemy government, she then played the Seleucids and the Romans (the new power emerging in Europe) against each other. With Cleopatra in the south, Antiochus III turned against the western powers and was defeated by the Roman commander Lucius Cornelius Scipio Asiaticus in 190 B.C. Antiochus III died while trying to plunder a pagan temple near Susa (187 B.C.) just a year after signing peace accords with Rome (188 B.C.). Thus, as Scripture says, he stumbled and was found no more.

The role of the king of the North now switched to Rome. As biblical scholar Roy Gane has pointed out,[12] when a ruler from the current kingdom (Greece, in this case) attacks the rising kingdom and loses, the prophetic focus will switch to the new emerging kingdom (now Rome).

The Rise of Rome

In verses 20-22 we come to the Roman phase. After Antiochus III's time, the Romans gained power in Europe and the Middle East. And here we find mention of the prince of the covenant.

Some people ask me, "How can you be sure there is a change from the Greeks to the Romans?" Daniel's prophecies of chapters 2 and 7 say that a series of powers would emerge: Babylon, Medo-Persia, Greece, Rome, and a divided former Roman Empire.

One after another, these kingdoms represent the king of the North from Daniel's era all the way through to the time of the end. They each occupy Jerusalem/Israel from the north.

The book of Jeremiah repeatedly refers to the Babylonian invasion of Jerusalem as coming from the north. Jeremiah 50:9 also declares that Babylon's conqueror will arrive from the north. This makes Medo- Persia the second king of the North.

Then Daniel 11 calls the Seleucids, a part of the Greek Empire, as the king of the North, and introduces another part of the empire, the Ptolemaic kingdom, as a new power from the south. Finally, Rome, the fourth major power from Daniel 2 and 7, also advances from the north as it occupies Jerusalem. Our conclusion, then, is that the powers of Daniel 2 and 7 all attack Jerusalem from the north, and each is correctly identified as the king of the North.

---

12   "The Un-Manifestation of Antiochus IV Epiphanes in Daniel 11:1-22." This can be found on the resources page of www.IslamAndChristianity.org.

Jesus, the Center of Prophecy

We need to go back now and look at Daniel 11:20-22 to revisit the time of Rome and the prince of the covenant. Again we are examining the match between the prophecy and what actually happened in history.

"There shall arise in his place [the Greek king of the North] one who imposes taxes on the glorious kingdom; but within a few days he shall be destroyed, but not in anger or in battle.

"And in his place shall arise a vile person, to whom they will not give the honor of royalty; but he shall come in peaceably, and seize the kingdom by intrigue. With the force of a flood they shall be swept away from before him and be broken, and also the prince of the covenant."

At the beginning of this passage we find someone in power imposing taxes on the "glorious kingdom," which is Israel. We find confirmation of such taxation in Luke 2:1: "And it came to pass in those days that a decree went out from Caesar Augustus [the Roman emperor] that all the world should be registered [taxed]."

Here you have a link from the New Testament to Daniel 11. The birth of Jesus happened when that person taxed the "glorious kingdom." Jesus was broken (killed) during the time of the Roman Empire. Jesus is the prince of the covenant spoken of in Daniel 11:22.

Now we go to another part of Daniel that expands on what the prince of the covenant does when He arrives. Daniel 9 contains a prophecy about the prince of the covenant, who will put an end to sin and bring in righteousness. Who does that? Jesus Christ!

Daniel 9:24-27 announces: "Seventy weeks are determined for your people and for your holy city, to finish the transgression, to make an end of sins, to make reconciliation for iniquity, to bring in everlasting righteousness, to seal up vision and prophecy, and to anoint the Most Holy.

"Know therefore and understand, that from the going forth of the command to restore and build Jerusalem until Messiah the Prince, there shall be seven weeks and sixty-two weeks; the street shall be built again, and the wall, even in troublesome times. And after the sixty-two weeks Messiah shall be cut off, but not for Himself; and the people of the prince who is to come shall destroy the city and the sanctuary. The end of it shall be with a flood, and till the end of the war desolations are determined.

"Then he shall confirm a covenant with many for one week; but in the middle of the week he shall bring an end to sacrifice and offering. And on the wing of abominations shall be one who makes desolate, even until the consummation, which is determined, is poured out on the desolate."

The prophecy needs some explanation. First of all, in Ezekiel 4:6 and in Numbers 14:34 we find a principle for interpreting time prophecies, which states that a prophetic day equals a year. Keep this in mind whenever you run into a time prophecy. It works very well in Daniel 9.

"Seventy weeks are determined for your people." How many days in 70 weeks? 7 x 70 = 490 days. Applying the principle of a day for a year, we have 490 years. And so, "from the going forth of the command to restore and build Jerusalem until Messiah the Prince" (the prince of the covenant) there elapses 62 weeks, or 483 years.

Notice that the verse says there are seven weeks and 62 weeks, and the Messiah comes after the 62. The seven weeks represented the first jubilee cycle of 49 years of rebuilding the Temple and city, and the 62 weeks symbolized the long time period from the rebuilding of the Temple and city until the coming of the Messiah. Add those together, and they total 483 years to Messiah the Prince.

Did that actually happen? The book of Ezra announces the decree that authorized the rebuilding of Jerusalem. Archaeology has pinned that date to 457 B.C. Doing the math (457 B.C. plus 490 years) brings us to A.D. 34. If we use the 483 years, that brings us to A.D. 27. (Don't forget that in going from B.C. to A.D., you have to add one year, because there was no zero year.)

According to the prophecy, then, Jesus the Messiah, the prince of the covenant, should enter the picture in A.D. 27, and the time of probation for the Israelite nation should be over in A.D. 34. What happened in A.D. 27? Jesus began His ministry. Here is what Luke recorded: "Now in the fifteenth year of the reign of Tiberius Caesar," "when all the people were baptized, it came to pass that Jesus also was baptized; and while He prayed, the heaven was opened" (Luke 3:1, 21).

When Jesus is baptized, He comes up out of the water, the Holy Spirit descends on Him, anointing Him for ministry, and He begins the ministry of the Messiah. Luke pinpoints the anointing of Messiah the Prince at the fifteenth year of Tiberius Caesar, which was A.D. 27.[13]

---

13   Seventh-day Adventist Bible Commentary *(Review and Herald Publishing Association, Revised 1976), Vol. 4, p. 853.*

What else does this tell us? If we count the Passover cycles in the Gospel of John, we find three and a half Passover cycles during Jesus' ministry, which meant that He died in or about A.D. 31. Daniel 9:27 declares, "Then he shall confirm a covenant with many for one week; but in the middle of the week he shall bring an end to sacrifice and offering."

If you are a Christian, have you offered a sacrifice recently? Killed a lamb to atone for your sins? Why not? Because Jesus is the Lamb of God. He died on the cross for our sins. Jesus brought an end to sacrifice—that is why you are not offering them.

Mark 15:38 records the end of sacrifice this way: "The veil of the temple was torn in two from top to bottom." When Jesus said, "It is finished" on the cross, an unseen hand from heaven grabbed that huge Temple veil and ripped it apart.

From God's perspective, sacrifices no longer mattered, because Jesus, the Lamb of God, had just died to take away your sins and mine and every sin that has ever been committed on earth, for all who will let Him remove their sins from them. Jesus put an end to sacrifices.

Yes, the Jewish priests still offered them for a few more years before the destruction of the Temple, but from heaven's perspective, they ceased when Jesus said, "It is finished."

When Jesus left this earth and went back to heaven, the angels told His disciples to work first in Jerusalem, next in Judea, then in Samaria, and finally the uttermost parts of the world. Why did He tell them to focus on Judea first? Because, according to the prophecy, three and a half years still remained for the nation to decide if it would fully accept Jesus and His gift.

At the end of those three and a half years, the religious leaders of Judea stoned Stephen to death (read about it in Acts 7). Saul, who had actively participated in the execution, went out to persecute Christians. Jesus called to him from heaven, knocked him down with a bright light, and asked why he was persecuting Him.

When Saul saw the wrong he was doing, Jesus said to him, "Depart, for I will send you from here to the Gentiles." The time period was up—the 70 weeks were over. The gospel now also went to non-Jews, not primarily Jews.

Without question Jews can still be saved in God's kingdom. But the special focus on them as a nation was gone—conversion was now for anyone, Jew or gentile, who would accept Jesus Christ. The prophecy of Daniel 9 was completely fulfilled in the ministry of Jesus Christ, and that is the prophecy alluded to in verses 20-22 of Daniel 11.

Who is really the center point of prophecy? In Daniel 11, Jesus dies right in the middle of verse 22. After His resurrection, Jesus said to the two He met on the road to Emmaus: "Don't you know that all those prophecies from the Old Testament point to Me?" (See Luke 24:13-27.) Jesus is the one who ties it all together.

Some people wonder if Christians should even study Daniel 11 because it is in the Old Testament. But Jesus said that all those prophecies pointed to Him.

Don't shortchange your study by throwing out or neglecting any part of the Bible. It's true that we don't need to offer sacrifices anymore, but all of the Bible points to Jesus Christ. You can be sure of this: If you know all about Bible prophecy and don't know Jesus, you will have missed both its meaning and its fulfillment.

Chapter 2

THE KING OF THE NORTH: ROMAN TO HOLY ROMAN EMPIRE

In chapter 1 we read an overview of Daniel 11 through 12:4 from the time of the prophet Daniel to the end of sin and suffering. We found that the kings of the North and South go through phases of conflict.

The first phase was the struggle between the Greek Ptolemies and the Greek Seleucids, and then Rome came from the north. As we got up to verses 20-22 we saw that the prince of the covenant is Jesus Christ. Daniel 9 expanded on that, giving us a time frame for when His ministry would begin, the dates for His baptism and His death, and a description of how He would bring an end to sacrifice. Jesus is the ultimate sacrifice for sin, and that makes Him the focal point of Bible prophecy.

When Jesus lived on earth, the pagan phase of the Roman Empire was the king of the North. We saw that power also depicted in the legs of iron in the statue of Daniel 2. Because the legs of iron turn into feet of iron and clay, there is some continuation of the iron into the feet.

In a match to this prophecy, Daniel 7 explains how the attention turns from the pagan Roman Empire as it changes from a beast with iron teeth and claws to a focus on the beast's 10 horns that develop after it. The 10 horns of the beast rise in Europe after the breakup of the western Roman Empire, and a little horn comes up after that.

Daniel 2, 7, and 8 are parallel prophecies with Daniel 11. They mean that the king of the North, after the breakup of the Roman Empire, will be the same as the feet of iron and clay in Daniel 2 and the same as the little horn of Daniel 7 and 8.

31

Most Bible commentators believe that the little horn of Daniel 7 and 8, the "Man of Sin" in 2 Thessalonians 2, and the beast of Revelation 13 are all the same power that emerges from within the western Roman Empire—an entity often called the antichrist.

The commentators do not all agree on exactly what or who this power is, but most Bible commentary and prophecy books of today agree that the three Bible references refer to the same agency. The power described in those texts is the same as the king of the North appearing after the Roman Empire in Daniel 11.

Among the descriptions in 2 Thessalonians, Daniel, and Revelation are 15 specific characteristics that reveal the identity of the little horn/king of the North/man of sin/antichrist power. Let's examine the characteristics and see which historical power matches up with all 15.

In this chapter and in the rest of the book I will refer to the antichrist, the little horn, and the king of the North interchangeably as the same power.

We have already learned that when the current king of the North attacks the new rising power, the focus changes to the new or rising king of the North. When Greek Antiochus III attacked Rome, and the Roman commander Scipio defeated him, Rome became the new king of the North, focusing on the following great world leader Augustus and the caesars who followed.

In Daniel 11:22, when the Romans attack Jesus at the cross and lose at the resurrection, we should expect that a new great world leader will arise: a leader with connections to Jesus because Jesus wins, and to Rome because of the link to Rome through the iron legs and the horns in Daniel 2, 7, and 8.

First Characteristic

The antichrist power will arise from the Roman Empire and will last until Jesus delivers His people.

Jesus dies in Daniel 11:22, and then in verse 23, a new king of the North rises that will last until verse 45 at its destruction when Jesus returns.

"And after the league is made with him he shall act deceitfully, for he shall come up and become strong with a small number of people … yet he shall come to his end, and no one will help him. And at that time your people shall be delivered…" (Daniel 11:23, 45; 12:1).

In Daniel 7 we have the "little horn" that spans history from the breakup of Rome to God's kingdom being established.

"I was considering the horns, and there was another horn, a little one, coming up among them and last till it is destroyed by flame … I watched then because of the sound of the pompous words which the horn was speaking; I watched till the beast was slain, and its body destroyed and given to the burning flame" (Daniel 7:8, 11).

Based on the parallel quote from 2 Thessalonians, this flame is the coming of Jesus. The Man of Sin in 2 Thessalonians spans the first century when it is being held in check until it later comes out in the open and lasts until it is destroyed at the coming of Jesus. According to 2 Thessalonians 2:1-3, the antichrist power rises before the return of Jesus, when He gathers His believers.

"Now, brethren, concerning the coming of our Lord Jesus Christ and our gathering together to Him, we ask you not to be soon shaken in mind or troubled, either by spirit or by word or by letter, as if from us, as though the day of Christ had come. Let no one deceive you by any means; for that Day will not come unless the falling away comes first, and the Man of Sin is revealed, the son of perdition."

The antichrist will manifest itself before Jesus returns. The Man of Sin must appear, and then Jesus will come. Remember the sequence, because that is important in determining the identity of this power. 2 Thessalonians 2:7, 8 says, "For the mystery of lawlessness is already at work; only He who now restrains will do so until He is taken out of the way. And then the lawless one will be revealed, whom the Lord will consume with the breath of His mouth and destroy with the brightness of His coming."

The Beast of Revelation 13 also spans from the breakup of Rome till God's kingdom is set up. "I saw a beast rising up out of the sea, having seven heads and ten horns ... and on his heads a blasphemous name. Now the beast which I saw was like a leopard, like a bear, and like a lion. The dragon gave him his power, his throne, and great authority" (Daniel 7 imagery).

"And I saw the beast, the kings of the earth, and their armies, gathered together to make war against Him who sat on the horse and against His army. Then the beast was captured, and with him the false prophet who worked signs in his presence, by which he deceived those who received he mark of the beast and those who worshiped his image. These two were cast alive into the lake of fire burning with brimstone."

Who, then, is this king of the North, little horn, Man of Sin, beast power that spans from the first century when it is being held in check, later comes out in the open, and lasts until it is destroyed at the coming of Jesus?

Luther, Calvin, Wycliffe, and the Wesleys taught that it was the Roman Catholic papal system (its ecclesiastical structure), and I agree with them.

That does not mean the king of the North is the Roman Catholic membership. When God calls those within every fallen church "My people" in Revelation 18:4, that applies to people within the Catholic Church as well.

We can expect many Roman Catholic people to be in heaven, because for centuries it has had faithful Christians within it. That will continue to be the case until just before the end of the world.

It is the papal system—the governmental structure and teachings of the Roman Catholic Church—that have some very serious problems with Scripture. The church places the authority of tradition ahead of that of Scripture, and anytime something is placed ahead of Scripture, dangerous things can happen.

Does papal Rome fit? It is linked to both Rome and to Jesus. The Christian church in the first century was already seeing the beginning of a system of ideas that valued tradition above Scripture. Paul was fighting it, and he said it would be held back.

Who restrained it during the apostle's day? The pagan Roman Empire had iron fisted control, and because it was persecuting Christians, it inadvertently blocked many of those errors.

As soon as Christianity became acceptable in the empire and no longer faced persecution, errors rushed in, and aspects of paganism crept into the church. Christianity became mixed with other traditions.

So the problem of "the mystery of lawlessness," as Paul called it, had already begun in the first century. Papal Rome claims the papacy started with Peter and is still in existence.

Since this power had already emerged in the time of the early church, Paul could write about it. This makes papal Rome the leading contender to fulfill this characteristic of starting from the early church and lasting to the coming of Jesus. Please note that this must be an antichrist system, not a single man, because it lasts for 2,000 years (so far).

Second Characteristic

The king of the North antichrist power will be deceitful.

Daniel 11:23 says, "And after the league is made with him he shall act deceitfully." This is fulfilled when Constantine decides to fight under the sign of the cross in A.D. 312, thus attempting to unite Rome with Christianity. In the process, pagan and Christian teachings were merged.

The coin of Constantine pictured (minted about A.D. 316) illustrates this league or merger. Note the sun god "Sol" in the center, with the sun from pagan sun worship on the right and the Christian cross on the left.

The first part of the deceit is the passing of a merged pagan/Christian religion as true Christianity. The second part of the deceit came after Constantine moved the capital from the city of Rome to Constantinople.

The papacy then obtained "The Donation of Constantine," now known to be a forged decree by which the emperor Constantine the Great supposedly transferred to the papacy authority over the city of Rome and the western Roman Empire. This decree was used for centuries to prove the authority of the Pope. If the papacy based its claim to power on a forged document, then they did so with deceit.

The Man of Sin is also deceitful, as shown by 2 Thessalonians 2:9,10: "The coming of the lawless one is according to the working of Satan, with all power, signs, and lying wonders, and with all unrighteous deception among those who perish, because they did not receive the love of the truth, that they might be saved."

Third Characteristic

It is a small but powerful kingdom.

Scripture mentions several times that it is small. "For he shall come up and become strong with a small number of people" (Daniel 11:23). "There was another horn, a little one, coming up among them" (Daniel 7:8).

While it will be a smaller or younger power, it will have vast influence. While today Vatican City has a land mass of about 110 acres (tiny compared to previous papal territory), it has power far beyond its size. Small kingdom, large power. This matches all of the descriptions in Daniel, 2 Thessalonians, and Revelation.

Furthermore, in Daniel 11:23, 24 we find that the next power that represents the king of the North lacks an army and acquires the kingdom through intrigue.

While the passage does not specifically name any entity, we do know that the papacy originally possessed no military forces, but rather had the city of Rome left to it when Emperor Constantine moved away. The legs of iron gave way to the feet of iron and clay.

Fourth Characteristic

It is peaceable but becomes rich.

Daniel 11:24 says, "He shall enter peaceably, even into the richest places of the province; and he shall do what his fathers have not done, nor his forefathers: he shall disperse among them the plunder, spoil, and riches; and he shall devise his plans against the strongholds."

If you were to visit the Vatican, or nearly any cathedral, you would quickly realize that the papacy has become rich. The construction of St Peter's Cathedral was largely financed by the sale of indulgences by people like Tetzel in the time of Martin Luther. Tetzel told people their loved ones would be freed from purgatory as soon as their coin dropped into the box.

The papacy was also able to influence the naming of kings and of policies of the European nations by alternatively offering blessings to those who cooperated with them and the threat of excommunication to leaders and their people who opposed them or their policies.

Fifth Characteristic

The system has a human being as its head.

Daniel 11 identifies the king of the North as the leader of a geopolitical and religious power. In describing the little horn, Daniel 7:8 states, "There, in this horn, were eyes like the eyes of a man, and a mouth speaking pompous words." Revelation 13:8 follows suit: "All who dwell on the earth will worship him, whose names have not been written in the Book of Life of the Lamb slain from the foundation of the world." Finally, 2 Thessalonians 2:3 says about the Man of Sin, "That day will not come unless the falling away comes first, and the Man of Sin is revealed."

Almost all Bible scholars view the antichrist power as led by a man. Does the papacy have a human being at its head? Clearly, it is the individual called the pope. Considered the supreme leader of the Roman Catholic church, the pope's word is law within it.

Sixth Characteristic

The king of the North leads in attacks against the king of the South.

Daniel 11 describes three such conflicts. The first is described in Daniel 11:25: "He shall stir up his power and his courage against the king of the South with a great army." This was fulfilled when Pope Urban II called for war against Muslims in the Holy Land and the Christian nations of Europe started the crusades because of the threat of Islam.

The second conflict is mentioned in verse 29, which says: "At the appointed time he shall return and go toward the south; but it shall not be like the former or the latter." This was fulfilled when Pope Pius V organized the "Holy League" to fight against the spread of Islam. Once again, the Christian nations followed because the threat of Islam.

Verse 40 says that there will be a final conflict between the Kings of the North and the South. At this point the world is once again following the papacy because of the threat of a radical or violent Islam. (More on the third conflict later in this book.)

Seventh Characteristic

The antichrist power has a limited time of 1,260-day or year supremacy.

Daniel 11:24 says: "Only for a time." Daniel 7:25 give the time element: "Then the saints shall be given into his hand for a time and times and half a time."

How do we get 1,260 days out of that? We take "time" as one year, and "times" (the Hebrew word means "two") for two more years, for a total of three. "Half a time" is the half year to finish it. That all adds up to three and a half years.

In Revelation 12:14 we find this time period mentioned again. "The woman was given two wings of a great eagle, that she might fly into the wilderness to her place, where she is nourished for a time and times and half a time, from the presence of the serpent."

There you have "times" again, but does it really signify three and a half years? Revelation gives the figure in a different way in still another verse, Revelation 12:6: "The woman fled into the wilderness, where she has a place prepared by God, that they should feed her there one thousand two hundred and sixty days." The same woman goes to the same place for the specified period of time. One thousand two hundred and sixty days equals three and a half years.

But the book of Revelation describes it a third way just to make sure we get it. "He [the antichrist] was given a mouth speaking great things and blasphemies, and he was given authority to continue for forty-two months" (Rev. 13:5).

How many years is 42 months? Three and a half years. And 42 months times 30 equals 1,260, which means the years had only 360 days, indicating that they were symbolic years, not literal. All of these references have the same three-and-a-half-year time prophecy, which equals 1,260 years using the prophetic day = year principle. The antichrist receives authority for the 1,260 years, and then its power ceases.

In A.D. 533 Justinian declared the pope to be the head of all the Christianity in the empire. The Code of Justinian, book 1, title 1, proclaims the bishop of Rome as "head of all the holy churches" and "head of all the holy priests of God."

The year of key prophetic importance, however, is A.D. 538. In that year Justinian defeated the Ostrogoths, who had held Italy and brought Rome under his protection. "Vigilius … ascended the papal chair under the military protection of [General] Belisarius (538-554)."[1]

It removed the last of the three Arian tribes that had stood in the way of papal authority. Now the little horn had gained religious and political power across the empire, and the pope was the generally acknowledged and undisputed leader of the Christian church.

From A.D. 538, 1,260 years takes us to A.D. 1798. That year, the Napoleonic general Louis-Alexandre Berthier and his French Republican troops entered Italy

---

1   *Philip Schaff,* History of the Christian Church *(New York: Scribner, 1867), vol. 3, p. 327.*

and invaded the Vatican. Berthier proclaimed a Roman republic. Napoleon abolished the papal states (those areas directly under the control of the pope). (The papal states were temporarily reconstituted several times until they were finally incorporated into a unified Italy in 1870.)

When Pope Pius VI refused to surrender, Berthier arrested him and carried him off to France, where the pope died in captivity. The world thought that the papacy as a political power had met its end.

Eighth Characteristic

The king of the North/little horn would take upon itself to change God's law.

In Daniel 11:28, 30 and 31 it says he is "against the Covenant," while in 7:25 "[He] shall intend to change times and laws."

Daniel 11:28, 30, and 32 state that the king of the North would be against God's covenant. In other words, it would think to change or do away with God's law. Has that happened?

Here is what Ferraris' eighteenth-century Ecclesiastical Dictionary says: "The Pope is of so great authority and power that he is able to modify, declare, or interpret even divine laws. The Pope can modify divine law, since his power is not of man but of God, and he acts as vicegerent of God upon earth with most ample power of binding and loosing his sheep."[2]

Based on that claim, the pope can alter God's Word whenever he wants to. That is why the Catholic Church announces that its authority and traditions can supersede God's written Word.

I believe in sola scriptura (the Bible only) as the primary guide for life. I listen to other people, but I always test what they present by the Bible. Make it a habit to check everything. Ask yourself, "What does the Bible really say?" Always be sure that what people teach about Scripture actually reflects the message of the Bible.

Has the Roman Catholic Church changed times and laws? To answer, first let us consider a simple example. Peter Geiermann's Convert's Catechism of Catholic Doctrine discusses the Ten Commandments: "The First Commandment is: I am

---

2 *Translated from the Latin in* Lucius Ferraris.

the Lord thy God; thou shalt not have strange gods before Me."[3] If you were reading along in Exodus 20, you would find that, yes, that is the first commandment.

Then the catechism continues: "The Second Commandment is: Thou shalt not take the name of the Lord thy God in vain."[4]

Whoops! If you are reading along in your Bible, you will see that what should be the second commandment appears in Exodus 20:4. It states that we should not bow down to images.

The catechism's list of the Ten Commandments ignores the verse, not stressing it as a separate commandment. Why would the church do that? If you have been in a Roman Catholic cathedral, you will have seen the statues lining the walls. People bow and pray before them.

Perhaps the church's teaching glosses over the injunction because of this. It is still there in the explanation of the first commandment, but it is not treated as a separate commandment. So in the catechism the first commandment is "I am the Lord thy God; thou shalt not have strange gods before Me." The second one is "Thou shalt not take the name of the Lord thy God in vain."

From that point on, the commandment list in this catechism is off by one from the traditional Protestant list, until you get to the tenth commandment.

The earlier Catholics had to split the commandment against coveting into two commandments in order to make 10 separate commandments. But let us look at what is clearly the most extreme example. Here's what the same catechism says:

"Q. What is the Third Commandment?
A. The Third Commandment is: Remember that thou keep holy the Sabbath day.

Q. Which is the Sabbath day?
A. Saturday is the Sabbath day.

Q. Why do we observe Sunday instead of Saturday?
A. We observe Sunday instead of Saturday because the Catholic Church transferred the solemnity from Saturday to Sunday …

---

3   *Peter Geiermann,* The Convert's Catechism of Catholic Doctrine *(St. Louis: Herder Book Co., 1946), p. 48.*
4   *Ibid., p. 49.*

Q. By what authority did the Church substitute Sunday for Saturday?

A. The Church substituted Sunday for Saturday by the plenitude of that divine power which Jesus Christ bestowed upon her."[5]

The church claims authority over Scripture so that it has the ability to change divine law. But I do not believe that any human institution has such power. Daniel said that the little-horn power would alter times and laws. The examples cited here fit the prophecy.

Ninth Characteristic

The antichrist would speak "great words," or blasphemy.

What is blasphemy? Jesus helps us understand it. While He was on earth, He said, "Before Abraham was, I Am" (John 8:58). God is the "I Am" of Scripture. But then, according to John 10:31, "The Jews took up stones again to stone Him," because they thought He was claiming to be God. Blasphemy happens when a person claims to be God, but is not. The catch for Jesus' accusers was that He really is God.

Jesus faced another accusation of blasphemy in Mark 2:5-7. "When Jesus saw their faith, He said to the paralytic, 'Son, your sins are forgiven you.' But some of the scribes were sitting there and reasoning in their hearts, 'Why does this Man speak blasphemies like this? Who can forgive sins but God alone?'"

Blasphemy happens when a sinful human being claims a prerogative limited only to God. Only God can forgive sin.

In Daniel 11:36, 37 the king of the North blasphemes: "Then the king shall do according to his own will: he shall exalt and magnify himself above every god, shall speak blasphemies against the God of gods, He shall regard neither the God of his fathers nor the desire of women, nor regard any god; for he shall exalt himself above them all."

Daniel 7:8 refers to "a mouth speaking pompous words," verse 20 mentions "a mouth which spoke pompous words," and verse 25 declares that "he shall speak pompous words against the Most High."

In 2 Thessalonians 2:4 we find someone "who opposes and exalts himself above all that is called God or that is worshiped, so that he sits as God in the temple of

---

5   *Ibid.*, p. 50.

God, showing himself that he is God." And Revelation 13:5 describes a being who "was given a mouth speaking great things and blasphemies."

The Man of Sin claims the prerogatives or attributes of God. The little horn speaks pompous words against God. Revelation combines the two types of speech—the pompous words and the blasphemy. You can see from these descriptions how Bible commentators see this power as the same entity: because it repeatedly displays the same characteristics.

We have already seen in Mark 2 and John 10 that blasphemy is either someone putting themselves in the place of God when they are not, or claiming to be able to forgive sin, which is solely a divine prerogative.

Let's see what the Roman Catholic Church leadership says about its own authority and abilities in these areas. The following are quotations from Roman Catholic materials. They are not from people who have an ax to grind against that church.

"The Pope is of so great dignity and so exalted, that he is not mere man, but as it were, God, and the vicar of God … The Pope is called the most holy because he is rightfully presumed to be such. He is, likewise, the divine monarch, and supreme emperor, and king of kings. Hence the Pope is crowned with a triple crown as king of heaven and of earth and of hell."[6]

Look at the names for the pope listed here: divine monarch, supreme emperor, and king of kings! But Jesus Christ is the real King of kings in Scripture, so in essence the quotation attributes to the pope characteristics limited to Jesus Christ alone. When anyone claims that a human being has divine prerogatives when they are not God, then that declaration meets the biblical definition of blasphemy.

Another statement from the same article in Prompta Bibliotheca says: "The Pope is as it were God on earth, Sole sovereign of all the faithful of Christ, chief king of kings, having a plentitude of unbroken power, entrusted by the omnipotent God to govern the earthly and heavenly kingdoms."[7]

Here he is chief king of kings. That would put him above Jesus, if Jesus is the King of kings. And then it says, "God on earth." You have noticed, I am sure, that popes come and go. They die, and therefore are not God—but that is the claim.

---

6   *Translated from the Latin in F. Lucius Ferraris, "Papa, Articulus II,"* Prompta Bibliotheca: Canonica, Juridica, Moralis, Theologica, Ascetica, Polemica, Rubristica, Historica *(Paris: J. P. Migne, 1858), vol. 5, pp. 25. Retrieved from http://www.aloha.net/~mikesch/prompta.htm.*
7   *Ibid.*

The book *On the Authority of the Councils* declares, "All names which in the Scriptures are applied to Christ, by virtue of the which it is established that He is over the church, all the same names are applied to the Pope."[8]

You get the overall drift with these words: "Thou art the shepherd, thou art the physician, thou art the director, thou art the husbandman, finally thou art another God on earth."[9]

In a 1984 article in the *Los Angeles Times* entitled "No Forgiveness 'Directly From God,' Pope Says," Don Schanche wrote: "Rebutting a belief widely shared by Protestants and a growing number of Roman Catholics, Pope John Paul II on Tuesday dismissed the 'widespread idea that one can obtain forgiveness directly from God' and exhorted Catholics to confess more often to their priest."[10]

What, then, is the Catholic Church's teaching on forgiveness? That you must obtain it from a priest.

Another source for the church's claims about the power of the priests is Michael Müller: "Seek where you will, throughout heaven and earth, and you will find but one created being who can forgive the sinner, who can free him from the chains of sin and hell: and that extraordinary being is the priest, the Catholic priest. . . . Yes, the priest not only declares that the sinner is forgiven, but he really forgives him. The priest raises his hand, he pronounces the words of absolution, and in an instant, quick as a flash of light, the chains of hell are burst asunder, and the sinner becomes a child of God. So great is the power of the priest, that the judgments of heaven itself are subject to his decision."[11]

If this were true, it would place great power into the hands of a human being. But Mark 2:7 indicates that if a person claims they can forgive sin, it is blasphemy, because only God can do that.

Furthermore, Catholic doctrine not only teaches that the priest forgives sins but that God has to do what the priest tells Him to do. Think of it this way: If you are

---

8   On the Authority of the Councils, *book 2, chap. 17.*

9   *Philippe Labbe and Gabriel Cossart,* History of the Councils, *Vol. XIV, col. 109.*

10   *Abstract available at http://pqasb.pqarchiver.com/latimes/access/675039382. html?dids=675039382:675039382&FMT=ABS&FMTS=ABS:AI&type=historic&date=Dec+12%2C+1984&author=DON+A+SCHANCHE&pub=Los+Angeles+-Times+(1886-Current+File)&edition=&startpage=B11&desc=No+Forgiveness+%27Directly+-From+God%2C%27+Pope+Says.*

11   *Michael Müller,* God, the Teacher of Mankind *(New York: Benziger Brothers, 1882), vol. 6, p. 332.*

friends with the priest and the priest forgives you, then God has to do the same, even if you did not mean it. If, on the other hand, you are enemies with the priest and ask to be forgiven, and he says, "No, I will not forgive you," then, according to the doctrine, God cannot forgive you either. That teaching has brought untold trouble through the centuries.

Thankfully, as the Scripture says, any one of us can go to Jesus, confess our sins, and know that we are forgiven and thus have eternal life. I am thrilled that God's Word is simple and straightforward on that, and that we do not have to seek forgiveness through a human being.

Tenth Characteristic

The king of the North would persecute the saints, or God's people.

In Daniel 11: 32, 33 it says: "The people who know their God shall be strong, and carry out great exploits. And those of the people who understand shall instruct many; yet for many days they shall fall by sword and flame, by captivity and plundering."

Speaking of the little horn, Daniel 7:25 says, "[He] shall persecute the saints of the Most High." Revelation 13:7 states, "It was granted to him to make war with the saints and to overcome them." One of its hallmarks is that the antichrist would attack God's people

Those who truly followed God's word were attacked because they did not hold the same Christian beliefs as the papal religious authorities did. Through the centuries, millions have faced suffering and death because they disagreed with church positions. If you believed that you should have the Bible in your own language and be able to read it, for example, you could die by the sword or be burned at the stake.

In a 1994 letter Pope John Paul II acknowledged the history of persecution by the church. He wrote that a "painful chapter of history to which the sons and daughters of the Church must return with a spirit of repentance is that of the acquiescence given, especially in certain centuries, to intolerance and even the use of violence in the service of truth."[12]

---

12   *"Apostolic Letter Tertio Millennio adveniente of His Holiness Pope John Paul II, to the Bishops, Clergy, and Lay Faithful on Preparation for the Jubilee of the Year 2000." Available online at www.vatican.va/holy_father/john_paul_ii/apost_letters/documents/hf_jp-ii_apl_10111994_tertio-millennio-adveniente_en.html.*

In March 2000 John Paul urged forgiveness for centuries of wrongs that the Roman Catholic Church had perpetrated on others. In a day-long ceremony called the "Day of Forgiveness," he and seven senior church leaders read prayers that asked forgiveness for the Crusades, the Inquisitions, forced conversions, and acts committed against women, indigenous peoples, and Jews, among other things.

"We humbly ask for forgiveness for the part that each of us with his or her behaviors has played in such evils, thus contributing to disrupting the face of the church," John Paul said.[13]

Clarifying the purpose of the prayers, the pope said the next day: "The Church does not cease to implore God's forgiveness for the sins of her members."[14]

Do such persecuting practices continue today? I have experienced it myself. In South America I presented some Bible lectures, which upset the local Catholic priest. He sent some police officers with automatic rifles to our hotel in the middle of the night. That is not a fun way to wake up, finding armed police officers inside your hotel room. Such things still happen.

Eleventh Characteristic

The little horn, or antichrist entity, would receive a deadly wound, and later it would come back to life, but now with great worldwide power.

Revelation 13:3 explains: "I saw one of his heads as if it had been mortally wounded, and his deadly wound was healed. And all the world marveled and followed the beast." One of the marks of the beast power portrayed here is that it will recover from a deadly wound and have a global following.

As successor to the Roman Empire, the papacy had both political and religious power until 1798 and then received a "deadly wound." The Bible also says the wound would be healed, and the antichrist would then hold power until the end of time.

This king of the North will continue until the coming of Jesus Christ, and unless we can find another entity that replaces the king of the South, Islam will maintain its influence until almost the end as well.

---

13   Quoted in the CNN "Sunday Morning News" transcript for March 12, 2000. http://transcripts.cnn.com/TRANSCRIPTS/0003/12/sm.06.html.

14   Pope John Paul, Angelus, March 12, 2000. Quoted in Growth in Agreement III, ed. Jeffrey Gros, Thomas F. Best, and Lorelei F. Fuchs, (Geneva: WCC Publications, 2007), p. 255.

Revelation 13:3 describes the healing of the deadly wound. "I saw one of his heads as if it had been mortally wounded, and his deadly wound was healed. And all the world marveled and followed the beast."

Newspapers around the world reported a remarkable development in 1929. The *San Francisco Chronicle* of February 12, 1929, put it this way: "The Roman question tonight was a thing of the past and the Vatican was at peace with Italy. The formal accomplishment of this today was the exchange of signatures in the historic Palace of St. John Lateran by two noteworthy plenipotentiaries, Cardinal Gasparri for Pope Pius XI and Premier Mussolini for King Victor Emmanuel III.

"In affixing their autographs to this memorable document, healing the wound which has festered since 1870, extreme cordiality was displayed on both sides."[15]

Revelation says that the wound would be healed. The *San Francisco Chronicle* actually used the words "healing the wound." From 1798 until 1929 the papacy had been in trouble. It had not been in control of Vatican City itself since 1870.

Not until 1929 did the church regain jurisdiction of even this small territory. The treaty with the Italian government in 1929 was of utmost importance to the church, because now it once again had political authority of its own.

From that time on, the power of the papacy began to recover. In the twentieth century John Paul II was a major mover in restoring its authority. His death brought together almost every national leader in the world for his funeral, along with the president of the United States and several past presidents.[16]

Now, Pope Francis is taking the world leadership to the next level. In the fall of 2016 Francis visited the United Nations, triggering a media frenzy.

The Huffington Post stated, "But shrewdly, methodically and with a showman's flair, the soft-spoken, 78-year-old Argentinian Jesuit priest named Jorge Mario Bergoglio—Pope Francis—showed Thursday that he is running to become president of the planet."[17]

---

15   *San Francisco Chronicle, Feb. 12, 1929, 1. Retrieved from http://biblelight.net/ lateran1.gif.*

16   *Daniel 11:40-45 covers the time period we are talking about here, after the healing of the deadly wound, when the papacy is resurgent, until the papacy's destruction. We will study that in detail in a later chapter.*

17   *Huffington Post, "Pope Francis Wants To Be President Of The World", September 24, 2015.*

Twelfth Characteristic

It would be unlike all the other kingdoms preceding it.

"The ten horns are ten kings who shall arise from this kingdom. And another shall rise after them; he shall be different from the first ones" (Daniel 7:24).

Think back to Babylon, Medo-Persia, Greece, and Rome. They were all primarily political entities, but the papacy is primarily religious in nature, and only secondarily political, with its followers supplying the military power. It is diverse or different from the previous kingdoms because it is primarily a religious power. Through the course of Daniel 11:23-45, the king of the North takes on religious characteristics. Again this matches up with the references in Daniel, 2 Thessalonians, and Revelation.

Thirteenth Characteristic

The antichrist surfaces among the 10 horns, which means it rises from somewhere in the European part of the former Roman Empire.

Daniel 7:8 says, "I was considering the [10] horns, and there was another horn, a little one, coming up among them."

The 10 horns are kingdoms that developed out of the breakup of the Roman Empire. The following 10 were the major tribes: Ostrogoths, Visigoths, Vandals, Alemanni, Burgundians, Franks, Lombards, Anglo-Saxons, Suevi, and Heruli. As the old empire fell apart, these tribes took over. The little horn—the antichrist—rose from among them. The little horn power would uproot three of the 10 horn powers formed out of the Roman Empire.

"There was another horn, a little one, coming up among them, before whom three of the first horns were plucked out by the roots" (verse 8). Verse 24 adds, "And shall subdue three kings."

Three powers would be deposed to make room for the little-horn power. The emperor Justinian subjugated the Heruli, the Vandals, and the Ostrogoths for a very simple reason. Although they had accepted Christianity, they followed the teachings of Arius.

Emperor Justinian believed that Arian theology was heretical and unorthodox, and he issued edicts that forbade anyone in his empire to espouse Arius' views.

His armies conquered the three tribes to enforce his decrees. Their destruction made the papacy the leader of Christianity and gave it full rein in Europe.

Fourteenth Characteristic

The least important of the characteristics, in my opinion, but the most widely popularized, is the number 666.

"Let him who has understanding calculate the number of the beast, for it is the number of a man: His number is 666" (Revelation 13:18).

I have heard all kinds of ideas about 666, such as "It's a credit card, or a bar code." It is none of those things. The issue is something else far more important and fundamental.

What is the number 666? Many Protestants have seen in the title "Vicarius Filii Dei" a name attributed to the pope that might match the number. I have read a whole book written on just that title.[18] It records the times that the Catholic Church's own documents employ the words "Vicarius Filii Dei."

Vicarius Filii Dei means vicar, or representative, of the Son of God. The letters in the name can be seen as Roman numerals, and the conversion from letters to Roman numerals looks like this:

VICARIVS: V = 5, I = 1, C = 100, A = 0, R = 0, I = 1, V = 5, S = 0. (Latin has no U; a V was used in its place.)
FILII: F = 0, I = 1, L = 50, I = 1, I = 1.
DEI: D = 500, E = zero, I = 1.

The numbers of the name equal 666. The sum works as follows:

VICARIVS FILII DEI = 5 + 1 + 100 + 1 + 5 + 1 + 50 + 1 + 1 + 500 + 1 = 666.

Through the years people have tried to figure out if the numeric value of the letters of some prominent leader's name represents 666. But it does not matter what the numbers of any name add up to if the other characteristics do not match.

If *all* the other characteristics correspond to a particular person, only then is it worth checking the numbers of their name.

---

18   *Jerry A. Stevens,* Vicarius Filii Dei *(Berrien Springs, Mich.: Adventists Affirm, 2009).*

Fifteenth Characteristic

The antichrist would receive the "dragon's" throne.

"The dragon gave him his power, his throne, and great authority" (Revelation 13:2). The dragon in Revelation symbolizes Satan, but it also represents a power that he worked through. "The dragon stood before the woman who was ready to give birth, to devour her Child as soon as it was born" (Revelation 12:4).

The Child born to the woman ends up ruling the world with a "rod of iron," as King of kings, and He is taken up to heaven to be with God. Who fits that description? Jesus Christ.

After Jesus' birth, Herod tried to kill Him. As a vassal king, Herod was part of the Roman government, and he sent soldiers into Bethlehem to kill the infant boys in an attempt to kill Jesus. Since Herod ruled under the authority of Rome, it is the nondescript, dragon-like power that Satan was working through. We can expect that the Roman power would give the little horn some kind of seat or throne.

In the first and second centuries A.D., Rome became recognized as an important center of Christianity, especially because of its association with the apostolic tradition of Peter and Paul.

Gradually the Roman church manifested authority over other churches. Pope Leo the Great declared in A.D. 445: "The care of the universal Church should converge towards Peter's one seat, and nothing anywhere should be separated from its Head."[19]

After Emperor Constantine built a new capital for the Roman Empire and named it Constantinople, he spent little time in Rome. In his absence, the head of the Roman church became the leader of Christianity and increasingly enjoyed civic power in Rome as well.

As one scholar noted: "The Roman church pushed its way into the place of the Western empire, of which it is 'the actual continuation.' Thus the empire did not perish; it only changed its form. The pope became Caesar's successor."[20]

---

19   *Leo, bishop of the city of Rome, letter to Anastasius, bishop of Thessalonica. www. newA.D.vent.org/fathers/3604014.htm.*

20   *Le Roy E. Froom,* The Prophetic Faith of Our Fathers *(Washington D.C.: Review and Herald Pub. Assn., 1950), vol. 1, p. 498.*

In the power vacuum resulting from the collapse of the Roman Empire, the former capital city of Rome continued to exercise great authority, but the one in the seat of power was the pope. The Bible says the beast would receive the seat of the dragon, and that, too, was fulfilled.

The Church's Reaction

What did the papacy do in response to being cast as the antichrist by the Protestant Reformers? One example is the reaction of Luis De Alcasar, a priest during the Counter-Reformation, who came up with a concept now called *preterism*.

Alcasar said that the books of Daniel and Revelation focus on the past. The prophecies are not about the papacy when they describe the little horn. Instead, Daniel foretells the activity of Antiochus Epiphanes IV, a Seleucid king ruling before the time of Jesus. The book of Revelation is not talking about the papacy when it portrays the beast, but rather points to the Roman emperor Nero.

A second response came from Francisco Ribera, a Jesuit priest, who created the concept termed *futurism*. He taught that Daniel and Revelation have no current application to the papacy. The prophecies will all be fulfilled in the future, when an individual will appear as the antichrist just before the second coming of Jesus. Therefore, he said, the papacy is not the little horn or the beast power or the Man of Sin.

The Vatican 100-lira coin pictured here was minted in the late 1950s and early 1960s. Look at it closely. Do you know what *Vaticano* means? It comes from a Latin root meaning "prophecy." I have to wonder about the art department that created this coin. When they placed the woman with a cup in one hand and a cross in the other, I imagine they were thinking about Ephesians 5:23-27, which

speaks of the church as the bride of Christ. Or perhaps they were looking at Revelation 12:1-6 and verse 17, which describes a pure woman, dressed in white, representing God's people. This must be what they had in mind.

Unfortunately, another woman also appears in the book of Revelation. Revelation 17:3-6 states: "Then the angel carried me away in the Spirit into a wilderness. There I saw a woman sitting on a scarlet beast that was covered with blasphemous names and had seven heads and ten horns. The woman was dressed in purple and scarlet, and was glittering with gold, precious stones and pearls. She held a golden cup in her hand, filled with abominable things and the filth of her adulteries. The name written on her forehead was a mystery:

BABYLON THE GREAT
THE MOTHER OF PROSTITUTES
AND OF THE ABOMINATIONS OF THE EARTH.

I saw that the woman was drunk with the blood of God's holy people, the blood of those who bore testimony to Jesus" (NIV).

Of great interest here is that the pure woman of Revelation 12 hid in the wilderness. The woman in Revelation 17 is found in the wilderness, but she is no longer a pure woman, dressed in white. She now wears scarlet. The woman is an adulterer.

God's bride (His people) was supposed to remain true to Him, but instead mixed paganism and Christianity together. The church comes out of this time period as a scarlet woman—a harlot. God's people have fallen away from Him.

The woman on the coin has a cup in her hand. Which one of the women in Revelation is a better match to the image on the Vatican coin? It's not the woman with nothing in her hands, but rather the one holding a cup full of abominations.

Not only that, but the woman with the cup was dressed in scarlet. Ironically, what are the papal colors? Usually scarlet over white. In the prophecy, the woman started out with clothing of white that became scarlet.

King of the North

In Daniel 11:23-45 we read about the time period of the Roman Catholic Church's reign as the king of the North. Verse 23 says: "And after the league is made with him he shall act deceitfully, for he shall come up and become strong with a small number of people."

As we noted previously, the Vatican took control of Western Europe without an army of its own. The Roman emperor Constantine simply moved away from Rome to Constantinople and left the papacy in the power vacuum created by his departure. Here is the beginning of the Vatican in control. The end of verse 24 announces, " ... but only for a time." We also learned earlier that according to Daniel and Revelation the papacy would have a 1,260 day/year rule—it was only for a time.

During the 1,260 years, the papacy as the king of the North engaged in battles with the king of the South. "He shall stir up his power and his courage against the king of the South with a great army. And the king of the South shall be stirred up to battle with a very great and mighty army; but he shall not stand, for they shall devise plans against him. Yes, those who eat of the portion of his delicacies shall destroy him; his army shall be swept away, and many shall fall down slain. Both these kings' hearts shall be bent on evil, and they shall speak lies at the same table; but it shall not prosper, for the end will still be at the appointed time" (verses 25-27).

These encounters—several major crusades and many minor ones—went on for several centuries. Large armies took part, and the casualties were high.

When the papal armies were successful, they would return with relics, and they would use those to deceive people into worshipping them instead of worshipping according to God's Word.

"While returning to his land with great riches, his heart shall be moved against the holy covenant; so he shall do damage and return to his own land" (verse 28). Europe was greatly enriched by all the booty the armies brought back and all the knowledge and ideas they learned about the East from their incursions into the Holy Land.

Verses 30 indicated a naval battle: "For ships from Cyprus shall come against him; therefore he shall be grieved, and return in rage against the holy covenant, and do damage. So he shall return and show regard for those who forsake the holy covenant. "

Pope Pius V best represents the actions depicted here. During his time as pope, the Ottoman Turks had control of the eastern end of the Mediterranean Sea. Pius brought together the Holy League of 1571. The Fleet of the Holy League sailed towards Cyprus with the intent of fighting the Ottoman army there and driving it off the island. However, the fleet of the Holy League never got there!

The Ottoman fleet, which had embarked from Istanbul, took positions off the coast of Cyprus, where it landed an invasion force of at least 30,000 men and ultimately captured the entire island. Meanwhile, the Ottoman fleet sailed on to its western outpost at Lapanto and blocked the fleet of the Holy League. The Ottoman fleet was destroyed, but the Christians were unable to take advantage of this victory. The sacrifice of the Ottoman fleet stopped the fleet of the Holy League from going on to Cyprus, and the Ottomans held on to their prize.[21]

Because of his political victories in gathering Europe together to slow the spread of Islam, Pius V gained power, and he used that influence to ramp up the Inquisition and to enforce the liturgical Mass throughout Europe.

Daniel 11:31 describes the papacy gaining military power, in the pre-Reformation period, while verse 32 and following describe how they use that power to attack Christians during the Reformation period (see appendix F on the "Times of Daniel 11 and 12"): "And forces shall be mustered by him, and they shall defile the sanctuary fortress; then they shall take away the daily sacrifices, and place there the abomination of desolation.

"Those who do wickedly against the covenant he shall corrupt with flattery; but the people who know their God shall be strong, and carry out great exploits. And those of the people who understand shall instruct many; yet for many days they shall fall by sword and flame, by captivity and plundering."

During the Reformation came the reawakening of personal Bible study. People began to trust in Scripture again rather than in religious traditions. Many in the Roman Catholic Church opposed those who desired to put the Bible into common languages.

Verse 33 says, "Those of the people who understand shall instruct many," but as a result, the king of the North would destroy by the sword and the flame. The papal powers would come in with the sword and destroy whole cities that had gone against Roman Catholicism and its teachings. They would take the leaders and burn them at the stake, something we find clearly described in Daniel.

"Now when they fall, they shall be aided with a little help; but many shall join with them by intrigue. And some of those of understanding shall fall, to refine them, purge them, and make them white, until the time of the end; because it is still for the appointed time" (verses 34, 35).

God appointed the Reformation to take place sometime during the 1,260 years of the papal power's dominance. The Lord also promises in these verses that at the time of the end, He will resurrect those who were faithful to Him.

---

21   A Military History of the Western World, *Major General J.F.C. Fuller Funk and Wagnalls Company, New York, 1954, Vol1 pp. 559-579*

Verse 36: "Then the king shall do according to his own will: he shall exalt and magnify himself above every god, shall speak blasphemies against the God of gods, and shall prosper till the wrath has been accomplished; for what has been determined shall be done."

The power that speaks blasphemy will dominate until the "wrath has been accomplished." Later in the chapter on the plagues we will see that the seven last plagues are God's wrath. The book of Revelation depicts how the beast power is destroyed at the end of the plagues.

By now you understand that all of these prophecies come together and point to one and only one power: the papal system. The prophecies do not point to the Roman Catholic people, many of whom are true Christians. Because of this, we share God's truth to everyone with kindness and love.

Chapter 3

THE ACTORS AND POWERS OF THE TIME OF THE END

" At the time of the end the king of the South shall attack him; and the king of the North shall come against him like a whirlwind, with chariots, horsemen, and with many ships; and he shall enter the countries, overwhelm them, and pass through. He shall also enter the Glorious Land, and many countries shall be overthrown; but these shall escape from his hand: Edom, Moab, and the prominent people of Ammon. He shall stretch out his hand against the countries, and the land of Egypt shall not escape. He shall have power over the treasures of gold and silver, and over all the precious things of Egypt; also the Libyans and Ethiopians shall follow at his heels" (Daniel 11:40-43).

The Players

This book takes the position that from the breakup of the Roman Empire to the end of time, most, if not all, of the symbols/players are both geopolitical and religious powers. We can see the dual role through the geopolitical and religious aspects of the prophecy, through other passages of Scripture, and in the record of history. Let us define some of the prophecy's elements.

The king of the North: Geopolitically, the king of the North is the papal-led Christianity that emerged in the former Roman Empire and that attack Israel from the north during the Crusades. Religiously, it also opposed any group that rejected the concept of allowing church traditions to overrule Scripture.

The king of the South: Geopolitically, the king of the South is the Islamic powers that conquered the southern part of the former Roman Empire and invaded Israel from the south. Religiously, it also opposed Christianity and the divinity of Jesus.

The Glorious Land and the glorious holy mountain: Geopolitically, this would be Israel and Jerusalem. Religiously, the New Testament indicates that true Christians are included in Israel, as they are the sons of Abraham and citizens of God's true people.

Many countries: the Islamic nations defeated by the king of the North and mostly not mentioned by name in the prophecy, though it does specifically name Egypt, Libya, and Ethiopia (most likely the ancient region south of modern Egypt that includes Sudan, Ethiopia, and more).

Edom, Moab, and Ammon: Geopolitically, these regions now make up part of western Jordan. Historically they are related to Abraham and were once a part of the Davidic kingdom. This book takes the position that, religiously speaking, they represent the people within Islam who are true believers in God, trust in Jesus as Savior, and do not follow the king of the North at the end.

Egypt: Geopolitically, this is the nation of Egypt, and it will be overthrown in the third and final conflict between Christianity and Islam. Religiously, Egypt and the many countries represent those who take up radical Islam and would prefer death to following any form of Christianity. I suggest this indicates that during the third and final conflict Egypt will radicalize in opposition to the "Christian" nations.

Libya and Ethiopia: Geopolitically, they represent the nations of Libya and Ethiopia (though see note under number 4 above). If we consider their ancient boundaries instead of the modern ones, the two countries would take up most of north Africa. They represent moderate Muslims who are not willing to die for Islam but would rather follow the king of the North than be overthrown or destroyed.

It is important to keep in mind that throughout our examination of the Daniel 11 prophecy, the players in the prophecy, whether countries or powers or individuals, have both a geopolitical and religious definition that comes into play and affects the outcome. Both roles must be acknowledged and interpreted in order for us to understand what God has revealed.

Chapter 4
THE UNITED STATES IN BIBLE PROPHECY

A wide range of beliefs exists about the United States and its potential role in biblical prophecy. Some people see America in the end-time prophecies, and others don't. Take, for instance, the author Joel Rosenberg. In his novel Dead Heat he gets rid of the United States so that it is not a player at the end of time.

His method for wiping out the United States goes something like this: The Republican National Convention is in session in Los Angeles during a rocky, tumultuous period in history. The president has already served two terms, and he wants his vice president to be elected. The president walks out on the stage at the convention to give a speech and pass his mantle to the vice president.

Suddenly there is a warning. Before anyone can get the president into a safe room, a nuclear missile hits the convention center and destroys the elected government. Simultaneously, missiles launched from container ships off the East Coast strike Washington, D.C., causing chaos on both coasts of the United States and wiping the country out as a political and military player for the end times.[1]

Why did Rosenberg get rid of the United States as part of his ideas about the end times? He did not find any role for the United States in Bible prophecy, so in his novel, he had to get rid of the nation in some way.

But since I do see the United States in Bible prophecy, it leads me to some very different conclusions about end-time events. I believe that what I have found is in harmony with the Bible and the teaching of the Reformers. I'm going to show you how one of them, John Wesley, was pointing in the same direction that I look.

---

1   *Joel Rosenberg, Dead Heat (Tyndale, 2008).*

I love the United States. Having traveled outside of the country many times, I always appreciate getting back home. When the airplane touches down, I know a couple things for sure: I have religious freedom again, by and large, and I have police officers that are normally more honest than corrupt—something that is not always true in other parts of the world. And then I also have plumbing that works and water I can drink.

Now, I cannot give you extremely detailed specifics about the United States in prophecy, because the Bible simply doesn't provide them. Instead, Scripture gives a general outline. The more specific and detailed students try to be in explaining prophecy, the more likely they are going to be wrong, because the Bible does not give those specifics. I am going to stick to what the Bible says and try not to go much beyond that.

2 Peter 1:19 declares: "We also have the prophetic word made more sure, which you do well to heed as a light that shines in a dark place, until the day dawns and the morning star rises in your hearts."

What could be better than when Jesus brings a whole new day to our world at His second coming, when He puts away sin and suffering once and for all? In the meantime, God's prophetic Word is a good light to follow as the guide for life.

So far we have seen that Daniel 11 covers the time of the prophet Daniel all the way to the end of sin and suffering, and we have noticed that the kings of the North and the South go through phases. The clashes between North and South started with Greece and then switched to Rome by the time Jesus was on earth as the prince of the covenant.

We saw that the identity of the king of the North in Daniel 11:23 and following is the same as the little horn, the man of sin, and the beast power of the book of Revelation.

Those four terms or images are different symbols representing the same power: the papacy. All share common characteristics, and the description of each of the four symbols added a little more information not given in the others.

The papal power arises after the pagan Roman Empire, and it will perish at the coming of Jesus Christ. It holds power during the time period in between. Furthermore, the pagan Roman Empire becomes those entities represented by the legs of iron changing to the iron and clay in the feet, powers that last until the coming of Jesus Christ.

Think about this, though. Does the fact that the beast of Revelation is the papacy mean that Roman Catholics are bad somehow? No! Countless true Christians belong to the Roman Catholic Church. The Bible has a problem with the papacy and its teachings, not with the Catholic people. Revelation 18:4 says: "Come out of her, my people." God sees faithful Catholics as His people "within," until just before the very end, when He calls them out.

In Daniel 11:25-31 we saw that the papacy is the king of the North during the Crusades against Islam, and Islam in prophetic terms has become the king of the South. Verses 32-39 dealt with the Reformation. The Reformers were strong for God and stood up for Him. Some were put in prison, killed by the sword, and burned at the stake.

Daniel 11:40-45, the section that we are now examining, describes the papacy after the healing of the deadly wound it received in 1798. That process, as we saw earlier, began in 1929 with the Lateran Treaty between the state of Italy and the Vatican, signed by Benito Mussolini.

As a result, the passage outlines the time of the papacy's resurgence to power, from the healing of the deadly wound until its destruction at the return of Christ. Now we are going to slow down and spend several chapters just on these five verses, 40-45.

Allies of the Papacy

Daniel 11:40, 41 says: "At the time of the end the king of the South shall attack him; and the king of the North shall come against him like a whirlwind, with chariots, horsemen, and with many ships; and he shall enter the countries, overwhelm them, and pass through. He shall also enter the Glorious Land, and many countries shall be overthrown."

If the king of the North is the papacy at the time of the end, who does the Bible say will be its allies? That's an important question. In the final conflict, who stands with the papacy and who doesn't? Where does the papacy get military power, since it does not have its own? Even the Vatican must "borrow" the Swiss Guard. The police force from the surrounding city of Rome patrols St. Peter's Square.

Verse 41 continues by saying that some would "escape from his hand," apparently referring to areas of the southern kingdom that the king of the South controls.

These parts escape: "Edom, Moab, and the prominent people of Ammon." We will explore what that might mean in chapter 7.

Continuing in Daniel 11: "He [the king of the North] shall stretch out his hand against the countries, and the land of Egypt shall not escape. He shall have power over the treasures of gold and silver, and over all the precious things of Egypt; also the Libyans and Ethiopians shall follow at his heels. But news from the east and the north shall trouble him; therefore he shall go out with great fury to destroy and annihilate many" (verses 42-44).

Where does the papacy get its military? That's where we find the role of the United States. Revelation 13:1-10 describes the rise of the papacy through the symbolism of the beast power. In verses 11-17, the prophecy depicts the beast's helper, the one who is the strong arm (or police force) of the world, if you will.

Let's see what Revelation 13:11-17 says about the helper of the beast power: "Then I saw another beast coming up out of the earth, and he had two horns like a lamb and spoke like a dragon. And he exercises all the authority of the first beast [the papacy] in his presence, and causes the earth and those who dwell in it to worship the first beast [the papacy], whose deadly wound was healed" (verses 11-13).

Daniel 11:40 and following describe the time period after the wound to the first beast. The papacy appears to go down in Daniel 11, and it drops out of sight. Then it resurfaces at the time of the end. Likewise, the book of Revelation reveals that the beast receives a deadly wound and then comes back when the wound is healed. So Revelation 13, speaking of the second beast, is talking about the time of the end:

"He [the second beast] performs great signs, so that he even makes fire come down from heaven on the earth in the sight of men. And he deceives those who dwell on the earth by those signs which he was granted to do in the sight of the beast, telling those who dwell on the earth to make an image to the beast who was wounded by the sword and lived.

"He was granted power to give breath to the image of the beast, that the image of the beast should both speak and cause as many as would not worship the image of the beast to be killed. He causes all, both small and great, rich and poor, free and slave, to receive a mark on their right hand or on their foreheads, and that no one may buy or sell except one who has the mark or the name of the beast, or the number of his name" (verses 14-17).

Who or what is the second beast power? Notice that it seeks to police the world. It forces humanity to follow the leading of the first beast.

Rise of the Second Beast Power

Keep a couple of characteristics in mind. The second beast rises out of the earth, while the first one emerged from the sea. The first and second beast have different origins. Revelation 17:15 says: "And he said to me, 'The waters which you saw, where the harlot sits, are peoples, multitudes, nations, and tongues.'"

The harlot is sitting on the first beast, which came out of water. The water represents lots of people and different nationalities. The beast that the harlot is riding—the first beast power—has traits of a lion, a leopard, and a bear, and it has the horns from a nondescript beast. Those are the creatures of Daniel 7 and 8 that appeared out of the sea. That's telling you the beast power had its origin in the Mediterranean Basin, the cradle of civilization—the sea of humanity.

The second beast power does not come up from that source. It emerges from "the earth," which apparently symbolizes a place with relatively few people. It's not the heavily populated Old World.

A second characteristic is that the beast with lamblike horns in Revelation 13 does not have crowns on its horns. That suggests that it does not have kings as the Old World kingdoms did.

Also, it is "like a lamb," possibly lamblike or Christlike-peace-loving. But it ends up speaking like a dragon. It has the "might makes right" attitude that pagan Rome, papal Rome, and Satan had: they have the power, so they are right. In other words: "You had better do it our way, or else!"

The second beast surfaces after the healing of the fatal wound of the first beast. The period of papal supremacy stood from A.D. 538 to 1798. Keep those dates in mind, because the second beast is going to be a player after that second date.

In 1754 John Wesley had no question in his mind that the papacy was the first beast of Revelation 13, and when thinking about the second beast of Revelation 13, he said this: "He [the second beast] is not yet come, though he can not be far off; for he is to appear at the end of the forty-two months of the first beast."[2]

---

2   *John Wesley,* Explanatory Notes Upon the New Testament *(London: Epworth Press, 1929), p. 1010.*

So in 1754 Wesley believed that the second beast was about to surface on the scene. I have a lot of respect for his confidence to look only at future Bible prophecy without having history behind him, and yet to be able to conclude what was coming!

Is this second beast the United States? I believe it is. It makes its appearance after the first beast receives the "deadly wound." That was in 1798. The United States began to gain power about the same time.

You might protest, "The United States Declaration of Independence was in 1776." The prophecy doesn't say the second beast was born on an exact date— just that it comes into existence about the same time. The United States was no world power at the beginning.

For a parallel, look at the papacy. It was in existence before 538, but it did not have its full power before then. The Bible does not necessarily go by the beginning date of an entity's existence. It focuses on when the beast acquires its power. About 1798 the United States arrives on the scene and grows in power after that time. And it emerges from the "earth," in an area with relatively few people.

The United States took its place as a world player at the time of World War II, soon after 1929, when the papacy recovered its sovereignty of Vatican City. Thus America had begun as a nation about the time the papal power received its wound, and it gained global influence right about the time the wound was healed. So we have some good matches on this prophecy.

Revelation 13:11 says the second beast power has its origin in the "earth." The United States definitely did not come up out of the Old World. If we look at other options besides the United States in the New World, we have Canada, South America, and Australia. Which one of them is playing police officer of the world today—the apparent role of the second beast of Revelation 13?

Today the United States is the primary power seeking to maintain peace and order in international affairs. It has no crown and no king. Americans have been very clear about not wanting a monarch.

Has the United States been lamblike or peace-loving? It depends on how you look at it. The nation has been pretty rough on other countries in some of the wars in the past 100 years.

But there is something unique about the United States, something different than other powers before it. When the United States wins a war, it rebuilds the enemy's lost infrastructure and gives back the country! Japan and Germany offer prime examples. These countries are now some of the primary economic competitors of the United States. The United States is a very different kind of nation. It is peace-loving in a particular way. If you leave the United States alone, it by and large does not bother you. But according to the prophecy, it becomes the world's police officer and ends up "speaking like a dragon."

Lamblike could also mean Christlike. We could possibly say that the United States is a Christlike or Christ-connected nation. To much of the non-Christian world, the United States represents Christianity. That also is a match to the second beast.

Here is the catch, though—when the Islamic world looks at the United States, it focuses on Hollywood and the rest of American culture and concludes, "That's what Christianity is." No wonder Islam has a warped view of Christianity.

Fall of Religious Freedom

Revelation 13 says that the second beast would "speak like a dragon." In legislation, "speech" simply means "expressing in legislation," which eventually involves enforcement. Right now the U.S. still has good laws that provide religious freedom, but these laws have been eroding. You know how things have gone: we experience a few acts of terrorism, and we then hurriedly give up certain rights. Call it the Patriot Act or anything else—society can become dangerous as we lose our rights. Religious rights and national safety find themselves in constant tension.

Could religious repression emerge in the United States? I hear people saying they want to make or remake America as a Christian nation. It sounds like a good idea to some, but I hope it does not happen. Robert Grant, director of Christian Voice, said: "If Christians unite, we can do anything. We could pass any law or any amendment. And that's exactly what we intend to do."[3]

Here's the question: Whose version of Christianity would be enforced by law if the United States formally became a Christian nation?

Back in medieval times, the papacy decided what form of Christianity was acceptable and then persecuted all who held dissenting views. I would rather have the U.S. as a nation of complete religious liberty, in which each one of us can

---

3   In Roland R. Hegstad, "Down the Road to a Christian Republic," Liberty, May/June 1980, p. 4.

share as we believe and are not restricted by any church's or politician's definition of what it means to be a Christian. I do not trust politicians or church leaders to decide who or what a true Christian is. That would be real trouble!

W. A. Criswell, a Baptist pastor, said on the CBS Evening News, "I believe this notion of the separation of church and state was the figment of some infidel's imagination."

Baptists used to be in favor of the separation of church and state. Back at the founding of the United States the denomination was among the primary players that brought about separation of church and state. But Criswell has said it was a figment of some infidel's imagination. He seems to be implying that the early Baptist founders were infidels, but I agree with the early Baptists. Separation is a good idea.

Unfortunately, most of the people seated on the United States Supreme Court in the twenty-first century would agree with Justice William Rehnquist that "the 'wall of separation between church and state' is a metaphor based on bad history, a metaphor which has proved useless as a guide to judging. It should be frankly and explicitly abandoned."[4]

That is a dangerous thought for the United States Supreme Court to have. But the prophecy said that a time will come when the United States would "speak like a dragon" and force people to worship in a certain way, which is something the nation has not yet done. I encourage you to resist that trend. We are now in a volatile period of religious liberty in the U.S.A.

Wesley hinted at the coming of the second beast in the 1750s, but the first time I'm aware that someone named the United States as the second beast was in the early 1850s. J. N. Andrews, a Bible scholar, wrote that the United States is the second lamblike beast in Revelation 13.[5]

Think of the courage it took to make that statement in his day. Before the Civil War, when the United States was at risk of falling apart and splitting down the middle, he said (and I paraphrase), "The United States is going to be the worldwide player to enforce the wishes of the papacy." Just as many do today, some thought that America was not going to survive at that time. But Andrews pro-

---

4   *Wallace v. Jaffree, 472 U.S. 38 (1985)*, at 107 (Rehnquist, J., dissenting opinion).
5   J. N. Andrews, *"Thoughts on Revelation XIII and XIV," Second Advent Review and Sabbath Herald*, May 19, 1851, pp. 81-86.

claimed, based on Bible prophecy, that the United States was the second beast power from Revelation 13:11-17.

Signs and Wonders

Most of the world views the United States as Christian and as the powerhouse, not so much of Catholicism, but of Protestantism. You might wonder if the United States and the papacy would ever work together. But they already have. The two powers may have contributed to a major change of history by working together in Europe.

Here is a quote from *Time* magazine: "'This was one of the great secret alliances of all time.' . . . Reagan and the pope agreed to undertake a clandestine campaign to hasten the dissolution of the Communist empire. . . . Step by reluctant step, the Soviets and the Communist government of Poland bowed to the moral, economic, and political pressure imposed by the pope and the president" (Feb. 24, 1992).

Pope John Paul II and President Ronald Reagan met together and laid their plans. They both supported the labor unions in Poland against the Communist government. Reagan instigated an arms race that hastened the fall of the Soviet Union. He also armed and funded the Mujahedin in Afghanistan to turn it into a "Soviet Vietnam." Unfortunately for the U.S., one of those trained at that time was a man named Osama bin Laden.

Through these combined efforts, Reagan and the pope were able to bring down Communism. Nobody knew about their agreement when it was happening. Not until after the fall of Communism did Time magazine break the story. Could the United States and the papacy work together to change the world? They already have. And I believe they are again.

Some people say, "What about Revelation 13 saying the second beast calls fire down from heaven? Is that referring to the United States using nuclear weapons?" I have heard people suggest that, but I don't agree.

Revelation 13:13, 14 says: "He [the United States] performs great signs, so that he even makes fire come down from heaven on the earth in the sight of men. And he deceives those who dwell on the earth by those signs which he was granted to do in the sight of the beast."

Do nuclear weapons deceive people or kill them? They kill them. So I do not believe the fire refers to nuclear weaponry. I think there is a better answer.

Fire Comes Down

Is it possible that fire would flash down from heaven? Think back to other times in the Scriptures that someone summoned fire from heaven. In all of those instances it was done to demonstrate who the true God was, the one who should be worshipped.

1 Kings 18 reports an encounter on Mount Carmel between the God of heaven and the pagan god Baal. Elijah was on God's side. On Baal's side was the king of Israel, much of the Israelite nation, and 450 prophets of Baal.

Three years of famine had desolated the land because Elijah had said, "There won't be any rain until I say so." The nation was in serious trouble from the lack of dew or rain. Think about how your town would look with no rain for three years. It would be devastating.

After three years Elijah showed up and said, "OK, let's meet on Mount Carmel for a showdown." Once the nation had gathered there, he said to the prophets of Baal, "Here's the deal. You build an altar and put a sacrifice on it. I'll build an altar and put a sacrifice on mine. Then we'll see which deity can rain fire down from heaven and burn up the sacrifice. The real God can send fire from heaven. That's the test."

The priests of Baal didn't have much of a choice. Everybody was there, and they didn't want to lose face, so they agreed. They built an altar and placed a sacrifice on it, and the 450 prophets started yelling and cutting themselves to get Baal's attention.

Elijah had a sense of humor. As he stood nearby, he said, "Hey, shout a little louder. Your god must be asleep." They did, but to no avail. He suggested, "Baal must be on vacation! Shout louder!" After awhile, he announced, "Now it's my turn. Be quiet." Erecting his altar, he set his sacrifice on it. He had a trench dug around the altar and water poured over it, filling the trench with water.

Finally, he said, "OK, Lord. Show them who is God." Flash! Fire from heaven! It burned up the sacrifice, consumed the rocks, and vaporized the water.

And the nation of Israel responded, "The God of Elijah is the real God." There was a showdown, and the God of heaven won.

According to Revelation 13 another confrontation will take place at the end, but God has already warned that this time around He's not answering with fire—at least not till later. The counterfeit power will do that. Do not be deceived by the counterfeit.

In Acts 2 we also find a story about fire from heaven, and it is even more appropriate to Revelation 13. On the day of Pentecost, tongues of fire settled on the heads of the disciples. As a result of being filled with the Holy Spirit, they went out and worked "signs and wonders" to take the gospel to the world.

Compare this to the lamblike beast, or second beast of Revelation 13. It performs signs and wonders to deceive people into false worship instead of the true worship of Jesus Christ. People follow the one who claims to be in the place of Jesus Christ.

What have we seen that the papacy has claimed? It has claimed to be in the place of Jesus on earth. So be careful. At the end, those who profess to work through the Holy Spirit will perform "signs and wonders," counterfeit miracles, possibly even bringing fire down from the sky, which will lead people to follow the beast.

2 Thessalonians 2:9-12 gives this warning, using the phrase "the lawless one" for the papal / king of the North power: "The coming of the lawless one is according to the working of Satan, with all power, signs, and lying wonders, and with all unrighteous deception among those who perish" (verses 9, 10).

Those who listen to the lawless one are going to die "because they did not receive the love of the truth." Jesus said that His Word is truth. You either believe God's Word, the Bible, and base everything on that, and not on tradition, or you will be deceived and perish.

The passage in 2 Thessalonians concludes: "And for this reason God will send them strong delusion, that they should believe the lie,that they all may be condemned who did not believe the truth but had pleasure in unrighteousness" (verses 11, 12).

God says in His Word that He is going to let Satan look as though he is performing real miracles. But if you are reading the Word, you also know the truth. When the false powers throw a curveball and try to take you away from what God declares, you can say, "No, I know what God's Word teaches, and I am going to stick with God's truth!"

Why does God allow such a counterfeit? It separates those who are true believers from those who are not. Right before Jesus returns a clear dividing line will emerge between those who are truly following God's Word and those who accept tradition—be it Islamic, Christian, Buddhist, or anything else. If you do not let God and His Word guide you, you will be sorted into a group that follows tradition instead. That's why God said He would allow "strong delusion"—false wonders and signs and miracles.

The False Prophet

You don't find the lamblike horned beast mentioned after Revelation 13 because the name of the power changes. The lamblike beast power is still there, but it is now under a different name. The new name is the false prophet, and it is also the United States.

If Revelation 13 describes the United States, then the "false prophet" is the same power. Here's how we know that. Revelation 19:20 is a quote right out of Revelation 13: "Then the beast was captured, and with him the false prophet who worked signs in his presence, by which he deceived those who received the mark of the beast and those who worshiped his image."

In Revelation 19 the second beast works signs and wonders, deceives people, and forces them to worship the beast. Same actions, same beast.

Revelation 19:20 continues: "These two were cast alive into the lake of fire burning with brimstone." The papacy is destroyed at the coming of Jesus Christ, and the second beast, his right-hand helper, perishes at the same time.

The name change has a reason behind it. The United States is pushing a false prophetic message—one already being presented by many Christians in the United States. If you are speaking like or for Satan the Dragon, you are a false prophet.

A little while back I saw a headline: "The Demise of the United States as a World Power." According to the broad outline of the prophecy, the United States remains in power until Jesus Christ comes and destroys it with fire at the very end.

The U.S. will not disappear before then. That is not to say that it will not go through some rocky times. It probably will. But the U.S. will survive as the major world power right up until the end.

If the U.S. is in decline, then we are likely to be close to the end when Jesus rescues His people. I might add that a superpower in decline can be more dangerous than one at its zenith. The former tends to get more volatile.

A False Trinity

We are looking at three powers—the dragon, the beast, and the false prophet. A false trinity. We call God the Father, God the Son, and God the Holy Spirit the Trinity. You might be aware that some people question whether there really is a Trinity of the Father, the Son, and the Holy Spirit. But I believe that the Bible teaches exactly that.

When He was on earth, Jesus was baptized, and at the same time the Holy Spirit descended as a dove. As Jesus emerged from the water, the Father said, "This is My beloved Son" (Matthew 3:17). Here all three members of the Trinity are active in the same verse.

Here is another reason I believe in the true Trinity: Satan has a counterfeit one. If you have never noticed it before, look at how interesting this counterfeit trinity is.

TRUE TRINITY	FALSE TRINITY
Father	Dragon
Gives power and authority	
Son	Beast
3 1/2-year—1,260-day/year—fatal wound—revives with power	
Holy Spirit	False prophet
Fire from heaven—signs, wonders, and miracles—enables work of the "Son"	

Down the left-hand column of the table you see the true Trinity, while down the right-hand column you find the false trinity. According to Scriptures, in the true Trinity, God the Father gives power and authority to the Son (John 5:19-30; Matthew 28:18). In the false trinity, the dragon extends power and authority to the beast (Revelation 13:4).

Remember, the beast power—the papacy—claims to be Jesus Christ on earth. The papacy gets its power from the dragon, Satan. So if you follow the beast, you place yourself under the control of the dragon. And if you worship the beast, you are really worshipping the dragon.

The dragon was, in a symbolic way, Rome, but according to Revelation, it was ultimately Satan. So Satan is the powerhouse—he gives authority to the others in the false trinity. But God the Father, the true powerhouse, bestows the authority in the true Trinity.

Parallel Prophecies

Jesus Christ the Son had a three-and-a-half-year ministry as described in Daniel 9 and the Gospels. Three and a half years equals 1,260 days, or 42 months. According to Bible prophecy and history, the beast power had a 1,260-day/year reign and then received a fatal wound. Jesus had a three-and-a-half-year ministry and died on the cross. He also had a fatal wound.

What happens to Jesus right after His crucifixion? In a short time, He is resurrected. All of the world should be worshipping Him, but it does not. The beast, on the other hand, at the end of the 1,260 days/years, received a fatal wound when the French seized the pope in 1798. The French took him to France where he died in captivity. But with the Lateran Treaty in 1929, papal power received resurrection and a new life.

This kind of parallel imagery is not coincidence, but most Bible scholars and prophecy students have missed it. Why? Because most of them follow one of the two prophetic methods that emerged during the Counter-Reformation (preterism and futurism). They gave up the historicist method of interpretation as employed by the Reformers. If you stick with the Reformers' method, though, you will be like John Wesley and see things coming before they happen!

We have seen the parallel of the Father and the Son, the dragon and the beast. The final Trinity parallel is the Holy Spirit. In Acts 2 the Holy Spirit arrives with fire from heaven, working signs and wonders, enabling the work of the Son, Jesus Christ. The Holy Spirit lifts up Jesus Christ and spreads the gospel to the world.

In the false trinity, the false prophet emerges on the scene and works false signs, wonders, and miracles to cause people to worship the beast. When they worship the beast, they are really worshipping Satan. That's a counterfeit!

The Christian Counterfeit

I challenge you to dig into God's Word. Make sure that what you are doing and what you believe is based on the Bible and not on some kind of counterfeit. The counterfeit is strong, and it seeks, by and large, to deceive Christians.

Some people say, "You have got to be kidding me! How can the beast power, the antichrist power, arise from within the Christian church?" That's exactly where 2 Thessalonians said it would emerge—in the temple of God (2 Thessalonians 2:4).

The temple in the New Testament is the church (Ephesians 2:20-22). In Revelation the beast power takes over the role of the pure woman, the pure church. Revelation 12 declares that the pure woman hides in the wilderness. In Revelation 17, John looks and sees the church now coming out of the wilderness as a harlot. Christianity changes.

Remember that according to George Barna, the majority of Christians today apparently do not hold biblical worldviews. That tells you that the majority are vulnerable to following the false prophet. A few signs and wonders, and they are deceived! Many of them are already following the beast, and the deception will just finish them off. It will continue until the very end of the time of the plagues.

People often ask me, "How could the United States become dragon-like?" Dragon-like speech and actions could come from either the political left or the political right. Wherever I go in the U.S., audiences are telling me they have been losing liberties over the last 15 years. We already know intuitively that the U.S. is changing, and not for the better. Both sides have been taking liberties and neither side has been giving them back.

I conclude that the change of the United States into a persecuting power could come from the religious right, the political right, or the political left. But I'm not so worried about figuring out who will be in office at that time or which group might cause the change. Instead, I'm watching the ongoing intensification of the conflict between papal-led Christianity and Islam.

The Islamic state already sees the U.S. as the enforcer for Rome. "Jihadi John said: 'To Obama, the dog of Rome. Today we are slaughtering the soldiers of Bashar and tomorrow we will be slaughtering your soldiers and with Allah's permission we will break this final and last crusade and the Islamic State will soon, like your puppet David Cameron said, begin to slaughter your people on your streets.'"[6]

The role of the United States as the second beast makes more sense to me than anything else I can find—a lot more than the nation being blown away by nuclear weapons and not being a power at the end of time. The papacy must have a military arm, and the prophecy tells us that the U.S. will be the primary military arm.

---

6   *London Telegraph, November 17, 2014.*

Chapter 5
THE ROLE OF EUROPE AND CHINA

Besides the United States, the papacy has other allies. In Daniel 11:40 the king of the South attacks, and the king of the North responds with a huge military operation that decimates the South. Who are the rest of the papacy's allies? Revelation 17:7-14 tells us:

"But the angel said to me, 'Why did you marvel? I will tell you the mystery of the woman and of the beast that carries her, which has the seven heads and the ten horns. The beast that you saw was, and is not, and will ascend out of the bottomless pit and go to perdition. And those who dwell on the earth will marvel, whose names are not written in the Book of Life from the foundation of the world, when they see the beast that was, and is not, and yet is.

"'Here is the mind which has wisdom: The seven heads are seven mountains on which the woman sits There are also seven kings. Five have fallen, one is, and the other has not yet come. And when he comes, he must continue a short time. And the beast that was, and is not, is himself also the eighth, and is of the seven, and is going to perdition.[1]

And the ten horns which you saw are ten kings who have received no kingdom as yet, but they receive authority for one hour as kings with the beast. These are of one mind, and they will give their power and authority to the beast. These will make war with the Lamb, and the Lamb will overcome them, for He is Lord of lords and King of kings; and those who are with Him are called, chosen, and faithful.'"

---

1   *The seven kings are Babylon, Persia, Greece, Rome, the papacy, France (ends papal rule in 1798 and is described in Revelation 11), U.S. (Revelation 13), and finally the papacy again, which comes back with the U.S. at the end.*

Both Jesus the Son of God and the papacy, the beast power, claim to be King of kings and Lord of lords. But only one can be. Thus one is true, and the other is false.

Revelation 17 mentions that "those seven heads were seven hills" on which the woman sits with her throne. The city widely known as the "city of seven hills" is Rome.

The passage also said that 10 kings would give their power and authority over to the beast for a short time at the end. In Daniel 7, the 10 horns represented the European area the papacy ruled over following the breakup of the Roman empire. At the end of time, although Europe is never truly united under one ruler, a period comes when the 10 powers are working together in such a way that they can give their power and authority to the beast. I believe that I am watching that develop as the European Union continues to evolve, and they have a common concern as regards the spread of violent Islam.

What do we have if we put the kings of Christian Europe (the 10 horns of Revelation 17) together with the United States (Revelation 13's beast with lamblike horns)? It is plain and simple. We have a prophetic description of NATO—the U.S. and Western Christian Europe—that will hand its power and its military might over to the papacy and be directed by the papacy in the third and final conflict between Islam and papal-led Christianity.

In case you are thinking we've just gone looking for a possible description of NATO, remember that Bible prophecy shows that at the time of the end there will be a strong papacy, a strong United States, and European powers willing to give power over to the papacy. I believe this third and final conflict has already begun. I will explain this in more detail in Chapter 8.

If we keep our eyes open, we can see this conflict developing, and we can better know how to handle life in what may be the toughest period in human history. Europe is concerned with radical Islamic terrorism and mass Muslim immigration. The far right anti-immigration anti-Islam parties are rapidly gaining power across Europe. Most of these European nations have already joined the coalition against the Islamic State (radical Islam).

The little horn, or beast, had 1,260 years of power, lost its power, and then recovered it. Clearly we are in the "toenails of time" right before Jesus returns. We cannot know how long this final conflict will last. But by calling it a whirlwind, Daniel hints that it will be relatively short. I do know this: we are headed in the direction that the prophecy foretells. All that was predicted and that is now history was fulfilled exactly as foretold. So you can trust the prophecy of what is yet to come. I certainly do.

What would unite Europe, the United States, and the papacy? The biggest enemy that those three powers have is radical Islam. Daniel 11:40 tells us what unites those powers. "At the time of the end, the king of the South shall attack him."

Let's take the imagery out of it for a moment. For the previous 20 verses of Daniel 11, the king of the South was Islam. Then verse 40 declares: "At the time of the end the king of the South [Islam] shall attack him [the papacy and its Christian alliance]; and the king of the North [the papacy and its alliance] shall come against him [Islam] like a whirlwind, with chariots, horsemen, and with many ships; and he [the papal alliance] shall enter the countries, overwhelm them, and pass through."

The passage goes on to describe the destruction that follows. According to Daniel 11, it is aggressive behavior by Islam that unites the papal alliance.

What would bring Europe, the United States, and the papacy into one massive coalition? It is Islam pushing hard against them: nuclear weapons somewhere, an attack on Israel, or massive terrorism in Europe. All kinds of things could do it. I don't know all the details, but according to the prophecy, that's what will happen.

Are the powers of the papal alliance united yet? Only partially. I don't believe that what happened on September 11, 2001, fulfilled Daniel 11:40. But I do believe that it was a warning or a sample of what awaits us. Interestingly, when the United States retaliated and entered Iraq, it was the papacy that tried to hold the United States back from that war. However, on August 7, 2014 the papacy called for military action against the Islamic state. I will describe the details in Chapter 8.

Daniel 11 describes what happens when the war between the Christian West (in the book of Daniel, the king of the North) and Islam changes from political to holy war, and that's when the time of the end is unleashed. We should note that for radical Islam it is already a holy war. Just think what it will be like when both sides view it that way!

China

Another question people sometimes ask me is "What about China?" The only place I can perhaps see a role for China is in Revelation 18. When the papacy and the United States and the 10 kings perish, a certain group stands in the distance, watching and crying because they've lost their markets. Who is becoming the new economic powerhouse in the world? China.

Revelation 18:3 says: "For all the nations have drunk of the wine of the wrath of her fornication, the kings of the earth have committed fornication with her, and the merchants of the earth have become rich through the abundance of her luxury." Earlier, we described NATO as the military might of the king of the North. Who are the customers of China? NATO countries. The Eastern merchants have gotten rich off the Western world.

Verse 11: "And the merchants of the earth will weep and mourn over her, for no one buys their merchandise anymore." When things go bad for the Christian empire, things don't go well for the merchants. They weep because no one is in a position to buy anymore.

Which side would China take if there were a showdown between Islam and Christianity? Well, which side represents their major market? I expect that they will side with them. The Chinese have a lot invested in the United States. If they turn against America, the United States could write off its debt to the Chinese. Europe could do the same. "And all the world follows the beast," Revelation 13:3 states, because that is seemingly in their best interest.

What about Russia? Russia has a Christian history and now considers itself the protector of Orthodox Christianity in the Middle East[2], and it also faces an Islamic threat.

We can see how the powers of the world are jostling together. According to prophecy the papacy is the primary beast, the United States is the second-most-important player, and then the rest of the world will support them. What was the major challenge to Christian powers in the past? Islam. And who contends against Christian powers today? Militant Islam.

---

2   *Frontpage Magazine, October 7, 2015. "Russia Declares 'Holy War' on Islamic State While Obama Sides with Christian Murdering 'Freedom Fighters'."*

Chapter 6

THE ROLE OF ISRAEL IN PROPHECY

One of the keys to understanding Daniel 11 is knowing whether a power is attacking Israel from the north or the south. Israel is always the country in the middle.

We will look at some of the implications from the Old and New Testament for understanding Israel in Bible prophecy. What does it mean when in the description of the third and final conflict Daniel 11:41 and 45 talk about "the Glorious Land"?

Verse 41: "He shall also enter the Glorious Land, and many countries shall be overthrown." "He" is the king of the North advancing into Israel. Verse 45: "And he shall plant the tents of his palace between the seas and the glorious holy mountain."

Geographically, we do find a mountain between the Dead Sea and the Mediterranean Sea—the mountain where Jerusalem sits. So when the verse says "between the seas and the glorious holy mountain," I believe it is talking about Israel and/or Jerusalem.

Previously we have gone to other parts of the Bible, especially Revelation, to understand elements of the prophecies of Daniel, and we find that Revelation explains Israel as well. Revelation 7:1 states: "After these things I saw four angels standing at the four corners of the earth, holding the four winds of the earth, that the wind should not blow on the earth, on the sea, or on any tree."

Have you ever wondered why we don't have more terrorist attacks than we do? Or why the world doesn't spin out of control? If I were a terrorist, I could think of all kinds of ideas that would cause massive death and destruction. But many of their plans get stopped, and some of them simply fall apart. Why? God declares that He is holding back the winds of trouble until a certain time when He lets them blow. I don't know how long it will be before He releases those winds. We have no time prophecy that tells us. But it will happen when God and His people are ready.

Revelation 7:2, 3: "Then I saw another angel ascending from the east, having the seal of the living God. And he cried with a loud voice to the four angels to whom it was granted to harm the earth and the sea, saying, 'Do not harm the earth, the sea, or the trees till we have sealed the servants of our God on their foreheads.'" Keep in mind that seal, or distinguishing mark, on their foreheads. It will come up again later.

A List of Tribes

In Revelation 7:4-8, we find a list of the 12 tribes of Israel:

"And I heard the number of those who were sealed. One hundred and forty-four thousand of all the tribes of the children of Israel were sealed:
of the tribe of Judah twelve thousand were sealed;
of the tribe of Reuben twelve thousand were sealed;
of the tribe of Gad twelve thousand were sealed;
of the tribe of Asher twelve thousand were sealed;
of the tribe of Naphtali twelve thousand were sealed;
of the tribe of Manasseh twelve thousand were sealed;
of the tribe of Simeon twelve thousand were sealed;
of the tribe of Levi twelve thousand were sealed;
of the tribe of Issachar twelve thousand were sealed;
of the tribe of Zebulun twelve thousand were sealed;
of the tribe of Joseph twelve thousand were sealed;
of the tribe of Benjamin twelve thousand were sealed."

To understand this list, we need to get some context in Revelation 14, where we find the 144,000 mentioned again.

"Then I looked, and behold, a Lamb standing on Mount Zion, and with Him one hundred and forty-four thousand, having His Father's name written on their foreheads. And I heard a voice from heaven, like the voice of many waters, and like the voice of loud thunder. And I heard the sound of harpists playing their harps. And they sang as it were a new song before the throne, before the four living creatures, and the elders; and no one could learn that song except the hundred and forty-four thousand who were redeemed from the earth. These are the ones who were not defiled with women, for they are virgins. These are the ones who follow the Lamb wherever He goes. These were redeemed from among men, being first fruits to God and to the Lamb. And in their mouth was found no deceit, for they are without fault before the throne of God" (Revelation 14:1-5).

Here are the servants of God, 144,000 people, categorized as the 12 tribes of Israel. The list raises many questions. What is its purpose? Why does each tribe have exactly 12,000? Are they a literal group of people, or are they symbolic of something? And what does this tell us about Israel at the time of the end?

To begin answering these questions, we need to resolve some apparent problems with the list of tribes. Look at the table below to see how the Bible cites the tribes elsewhere.

Genesis 49	Ezekiel 48	Revelation 7
Reuben	Reuben	Reuben
Simeon	Simeon	Simeon
Levi	Manasseh	Levi
Judah	Judah	Judah
Zebulun	Zebulun	Zebulun
Issachar	Issachar	Issachar
Dan	Dan	Manasseh
Gad	Gad	Gad
Asher	Asher	Asher
Naphtali	Naphtali	Naphtali
Joseph	Ephraim	Joseph
Benjamin	Benjamin	Benjamin

The first column comes from Genesis 49, describing the beginning of the nation of Israel. The second column is from Ezekiel 48, and the last column appears in Revelation 7—both of which are end-time scenarios. One would assume that Ezekiel and Revelation would agree and match the first list, but they cite the tribes differently.

In Genesis 49 we have the 12 sons of Jacob (or Israel, as God later calls him). As we go down Ezekiel's list, we get to where Levi should be, but he adds Manasseh instead—one of the sons of Joseph. When he gets to Joseph, he puts in Ephraim, the other son. By leaving out Levi and Joseph, he can add the two half tribes of Manasseh and Ephraim and still get 12 tribes. In Revelation we have Levi back in the list. Dan drops out, and Manasseh takes his place. Ephraim is not there, and Joseph is back. What's going on?

Before we can answer that, we must look at some other problems. If 144,000 is a literal number of people, how is it that an even 12,000 of a big tribe and an even 12,000 of a small one end up saved? Does God choose who is going to be saved regardless of what they think or what they believe? How is it that exactly 12,000 get redeemed from each of the tribes?

There's a third problem: they are all said to be male virgins. If 144,000 represents a literal number of specific individuals, they are men who never married or had sexual relations.

To take the number and the tribes as literal means missing what Revelation 1 says: "The Revelation of Jesus Christ, which God gave Him to show His servants—things which must shortly take place. And He sent and signified it by His angel to His servant John, who bore witness to the word of God, and to the testimony of Jesus Christ, to all things that he saw" (Revelation 1:1, 2).

Revelation has a lot of symbols in it. Think of the beast with seven heads comprised of different kinds of animals and 10 horns. I do not believe that we will actually see that literal beast walk out of the water somewhere. It is all the symbols of Daniel 7 merged into one.

Since we know that we have symbols in Revelation, when we start running into problems with a literal interpretation of a passage, we can rightly conclude, "This might be one of those symbols."

I believe that the 144,000 are symbolic, if nothing else because of the many problems that we run into with a literal interpretation. The people are all virgin males, each tribe has an even 12,000, and the names of the tribes here don't match other lists in the Bible. To figure it out, I go to the rest of the New Testament to find out what it teaches on the topic.

The Israel of Faith

In Galatians 3:7-9 Paul writes: "Therefore know that only those who are of faith are sons of Abraham. And the Scripture, foreseeing that God would justify the nations by faith, preached the gospel to Abraham beforehand, saying, 'In you all the nations shall be blessed.' So then those who are of faith are blessed with believing Abraham."

All who are of faith are sons of Abraham, including Gentiles by faith! Abraham is the true father of the faithful—the true father of Israel, so to speak.

Paul then adds, "You are all sons of God through faith in Christ Jesus. For as many of you as were baptized into Christ have put on Christ. There is neither Jew nor Greek, there is neither slave nor free, there is neither male nor female; for you are all one in Christ Jesus. And if you are Christ's, then you are Abraham's seed, and heirs according to the promise" (verses 26-29).

Paul asserts that in God's eyes there exists neither Jew nor Greek (Gentile). We have just run into a problem with many contemporary books on prophecy, because some of them say that, spiritually speaking, there is a split between Gentile and Jew—that they are not the same and never can be. That's what Hal Lindsey taught in his book *The Late, Great Planet Earth*.

Several others have presented similar concepts. But here is a Bible verse that declares there is neither Jew nor Greek, neither slave nor free, neither male nor female—no difference, because we are all one in Christ Jesus.

So we are all one in Christ. That makes sense. He does not care what nation we came from—Israel or otherwise. If we have accepted Him, we are His people!

But what about Hal Lindsey and others arguing that we have to have Israel on one side, the church on the other, and there is no mixing the two? Yet Galatians 3 sounds as if it is saying that God's people, His true Israel, are a mix of Jew and gentile ("gentile" as in non-Jewish).

Paul clarifies this in Romans 9:6-8: "It is not that the word of God has taken no effect. For they are not all Israel who are of Israel, nor are they all children because they are the seed of Abraham; but, 'In Isaac your seed shall be called.' That is, those who are the children of the flesh, these are not the children of God; but the children of the promise are counted as the seed."

In other words, it's not whether you are an Israelite genetically that matters. According to Paul, what is vital is whether you are spiritually—by faith—an Israelite.

Faith or Genes?

What implication does this have for the book of Revelation and prophecy? To understand God's end-time plan, we must take into account that it does not matter if a person is genetically related, but rather spiritually related. God says that He focuses His attention on those with faith, those who follow His Word.

Think back to the Old Testament. Did you have to be born an Israelite to be one? Not necessarily. Rahab, the prostitute who lived in Jericho, said she wanted to be on God's side. She ended up in the genealogy of Jesus. That makes her a pretty good Israelite. While she was not genetically an Israelite, she had faith. By faith she came in! Another woman, Ruth, was from Moab, but she had faith too. She is also in the lineage of Jesus. For a long time God has been letting people into Israel by faith. It is not a new idea.

"What shall we say then? That Gentiles, who did not pursue righteousness, have attained to righteousness, even the righteousness of faith; but Israel, pursuing the law of righteousness, has not attained to the law of righteousness. Why? Because they did not seek it by faith, but as it were, by the works of the law. For they stumbled at that stumbling stone" (Romans 9:30-32).

We're never going to make it by our own works, and if we want to push it so far as to reduce it all to genetics, that truly makes salvation "works of the flesh."

Many prophecy teachers claim a spiritual distinction between Jew and Greek (or gentile), but whenever I am studying any kind of prophetic theory and I find a scripture saying something different, I disregard the theory and follow the Bible. That is a simple plan I hope you follow also.

In Romans 11 Paul uses the illustration of an olive tree. "I say then, have they [the Jews] stumbled that they should fall? Certainly not! But through their fall, to provoke them to jealousy, salvation has come to the Gentiles. Now if their [the Jews'] fall is riches for the world, and their failure riches for the Gentiles, how much more their fullness! For I speak to you Gentiles; inasmuch as I am an apostle to the Gentiles, I magnify my ministry, if by any means I may provoke to jealousy those who are my flesh and save some of them" (verses 11-13).

How many genetic Israelites was Paul hoping to save? "Some of them." He did not say "all of them." Keep that in mind, because we are going to find Paul saying "all Israel" before we are out of this chapter. As a result, we need to determine what "all Israel" means. Is it genetic Israelites?

Now to the olive tree in verses 16-26: "For if the first fruit is holy, the lump is also holy; and if the root is holy, so are the branches. And if some of the branches were broken off, and you [Gentiles], being a wild olive tree, were grafted in among them, and with them became a partaker of the root and fatness of the olive tree, do not boast against the branches [genetic Israelites]. But if you boast, re-member that you do not support the root, but the root supports you. You will say then, 'Branches were broken off that I might be grafted in.' Well said. Because of unbelief they were broken off, and you stand by faith. Do not be haughty, but fear. For if God did not spare the natural branches, He may not spare you either" (verses 16-21).

The actions of the Israelite leaders during the time of Jesus' ministry tell the sto-ry. They refused to stay attached to the root anymore. When they hardened their hearts and rejected Jesus, they were cut off.

"Therefore consider the goodness and severity of God: on those who fell, sever-ity; but toward you, goodness, if you continue in His goodness. Otherwise you also will be cut off. And they also, if they do not continue in unbelief, will be grafted in, for God is able to graft them in again" (verses 22, 23).

Now, did Paul mean that the genetic Israelites were cut off without hope? Had they blown their chance forever? No, he does not state that.

"For if you [Gentiles] were cut out of the olive tree which is wild by nature, and were grafted contrary to nature into a cultivated olive tree, how much more will these [genetic Israelites], who are the natural branches, be grafted into their own olive tree? For I do not desire, brethren, that you should be ignorant of this mystery, lest you should be wise in your own opinion, that hardening in part has happened to Israel until the fullness of the Gentiles has come in. And so all Israel will be saved, as it is written: 'The Deliverer will come out of Zion, and He will turn away ungodliness from Jacob'" (verses 24-26).

Let me explain. Imagine an olive tree, rooted into the ground. It represents His Israel, and the branches are the people. When Jesus came along, did everyone in the nation have faith in the Messiah? No! Many of the Jewish branches were bro-ken off from the olive tree at that time because they did not have faith in Jesus. Those with faith in Jesus were still connected to the olive tree.

Then some Gentiles believed in Jesus. They are the branches from the wild olive tree. God grafted them into the first olive tree. So here we find a Gentile branch and a Jewish branch on the same tree. Over time, many Gentile branches are grafted in.

Some of the Israelites reconsidered and accepted Jesus as Lord and Savior, and then God picked them up and reunited them with the olive tree of Israel. They graft back in easily, according to the illustration. But do all the genetic Israelites get put back? No! You have a tree with some "wild" olive branches and some "tame" olive branches, and they are all now on the same tree. But they are all God's people, His Israel.

Paul looked at the olive tree and said, "And so all Israel will be saved." Was he talking about the broken-off branches on the ground—the genetic Israelites? No, rather he said that "all Israel" includes those grafted into the tree, both Jew and Gentile.

Now, catch the meaning of that. Israel consists of both Jew and Gentile. What's the definition of the church? The same thing! In the Old Testament, Israel was God's people of faith. In the New Testament, God's people of faith are also Israel. They are one and the same from His viewpoint. Keep that definition of Israel in mind when you think about prophecy. It is not a human definition but a biblical one.

Paul said pointedly that it is not genetic Israel that anyone should be looking at now, but the Israel of faith. Unfortunately, most prophecy students today are still focused on genetic Israel, not the Israel of faith that the Bible points to. Thus "all Israel will be saved" means not that every Jewish Israelite will be saved, but rather that everyone who has accepted Jesus Christ will be. All Israel consists of those who are forgiven.

Somebody might protest, "That's replacement theology." No, it's not! God's true people have always been His people of faith—they just have different names. The early church was the continuation of Israel.

If you doubt that, go to Revelation 12 and read about the symbolic woman. She comes along before the time of Christ and gives birth to the child Jesus, and the dragon attempts to kill Him. Then He is taken to heaven to be with God after His death and resurrection. The woman goes and hides in the wilderness, because she is being persecuted.

It's the same symbol before and after the time of Jesus—the pure woman, God's faithful people. It is those who were true to Him in Israel before the birth of Jesus, all the way through to those who were true to Him after Jesus goes back to heaven, Jew and Gentile together.

God uses the same symbols through time. He employs the imagery of a bride for Old Testament Israel (Ezekiel 16:8-14) as well as for New Testament Israel (Ephesians 5:23, 25). The symbol of a harlot in the Old Testament represents His people when they were not true to Him (Ezekiel 16:15, 32), and He uses a harlot for the New Testament believers when they are not faithful to Him (Revelation 12:14—starts out pure and becomes a harlot in Revelation 17:1-6).

In the Old Testament God employs the symbol of a "remnant" for those who remained faithful when the rest fell away (Micah 2:12). He uses the remnant imagery again in the New Testament for those who stay true to Him when the majority falls away (Revelation 12:11). From God's point of view, each symbol represents the same group throughout human history, not two separate groups in the Old and New Testaments.

Heard and Then Seen

Going back to Revelation 7, can we say that the 144,000 is a literal group of genetic Israelites? Or is it a symbolic one made up of God's people from all over the world? The book of Revelation demonstrates that it is a symbolic group, comprising people from every nation, tribe, and language. Here is how it works.

John announces, "I heard the number of those who were sealed" (verse 4), followed by the list of tribes, and then John adds, "After these things I looked, and behold, a great multitude which no one could number, of all nations, tribes, peoples, and tongues, standing before the throne and before the Lamb, clothed with white robes, with palm branches in their hands" (verse 9).

John is in vision, and he hears something. He does not see anything at this point, but he hears someone proclaim the list of tribes and the 144,000. And then he turns and observes a huge group of people from every nation, tribe, and people. I believe the list of the 144,000 that John hears and the vast group of people he sees are one and the same.

How do we know these two groups are identical? Revelation 7:13: "Then one of the elders answered, saying to me, 'Who are these arrayed in white robes?'" The elder is asking about the great multitude from every nation, tongue, and people.

(Notice they wear white robes. They are pure, spotless, clothed with the righteousness of Jesus Christ. All who believe, according to Paul, have the righteousness of Christ and are His Israel.) "Where did the multitude come from?" the elder inquires.

"And I said to him, 'Sir, you know.' " In other words, John says, "You tell me." "So he said to me, 'These are the ones who come out of the great tribulation, and washed their robes and made them white in the blood of the Lamb' " (verse 14).

That matches what Paul says about the Israel of faith. The vast group of people is following the Lamb. "Therefore they are before the throne of God, and serve Him day and night in His temple. And He who sits on the throne will dwell among them.

"They shall neither hunger anymore nor thirst anymore; the sun shall not strike them, nor any heat; for the Lamb who is in the midst of the throne will shepherd them and lead them to living fountains of waters. And God will wipe away every tear from their eyes" (verses 15-17).

Revelation 14:3 declares that "no one could learn that song [that they sang before the throne of God] except the hundred and forty-four thousand who were redeemed from the earth. These are the ones who were not defiled with women, for they are virgins."

The group from every nation, tribe, and people are wearing white robes. That matches the "not defiled, purity, virgin" language, doesn't it? But that's not all. The great multitude is following the Lamb wherever He goes. It's the same group.

So I am sure that the 144,000 are actually a great multitude from every nation, people, and tongue—Jew and Gentile—who have accepted Jesus Christ, and they are God's true Israel.

You may be thinking, I'm not so sure about this. I understand why, because many prophecy "experts" have said that God's Old Testament prophecies to Israel, such as the grand restoration described in Ezekiel, are history written in advance.

Therefore, since some of those prophecies have not yet come to pass, they will be brought about for geopolitical Israel in the future. But the "history written in advance" idea, in which every detail of prophecy for the nation of Israel will be fulfilled no matter what, is actually contrary to Old Testament teaching. Let me show you how.

Prophecy Says "If"

God set conditions on the nation of Israel concerning whether or not they would receive the blessings He promised. Deuteronomy 28:1, 2, 15 declares: "Now it shall come to pass, if you diligently obey the voice of the Lord your God, to observe carefully all His commandments which I command you today, that the Lord your God will set you high above all nations of the earth.

"And all these blessings shall come upon you and overtake you, because you obey the voice of the Lord your God. But it shall come to pass, if you do not obey the voice of the Lord your God, to observe carefully all His commandments and His statutes which I command you today, that all these curses will come upon you and overtake you" (verse 15).

God did not say that no matter what Israel did, He was going to fulfill the promises. Many so-called experts argue that no matter what happens, God will bring to pass His prophecies about the nation of Israel. But God Himself said that was not true—that the nation had a choice about its destiny. The people could either follow Him and receive the blessings or disobey and get the curses.

That is why the nation of Israel went into captivity in Babylon. They came under the curses because they rebelled against Him. And that is why pagan Rome destroyed Jerusalem in A.D. 70—because the nation of Israel did not follow God! So there was no fulfillment of the blessings for them.

That is not the only time in Old Testament prophecy when history was not written and set in advance. Jeremiah 18:6-10 states: "'O house of Israel, can I not do with you as this potter?' says the Lord. 'Look, as the clay is in the potter's hand, so are you in My hand, O house of Israel! The instant I speak concerning a nation and concerning a kingdom, to pluck up, to pull down, and to destroy it, if that nation against whom I have spoken turns from its evil, I will relent of the disaster that I thought to bring upon it.'"

Think about Jonah. He did not want to go to Nineveh and preach, because if he told the people that in 40 days they would be destroyed by fire, they might ask God to forgive them, and the Lord would.

Jonah wanted Nineveh to be destroyed. Jonah did not like the Ninevites. So God had to get Jonah's attention. Three days in the belly of the fish would certainly capture my attention! It spit him out on the shore, and he got up and walked many miles to Nineveh. Finally he reached the city and began announcing, "Forty days and you're toast!" "Thirty-nine days and you're toast!"

And the Ninevites responded, "Lord, forgive us." On the fortieth day Jonah left the city and waited for the fire from heaven. Did it come? No. Because the people had repented.

God's prophecies are not unchangeable history written in advance. They are conditional on obedience or disobedience. If the conditions are met, then the prophecy does become history written in advance. But if they are not met, the promised event does not happen. It's that simple.

God told Jeremiah, "The instant I speak concerning a nation and concerning a kingdom, to build and to plant it, if it does evil in My sight so that it does not obey My voice, then I will relent concerning the good with which I said I would benefit it" (Jeremiah 18:9, 10).

Remember that God started by saying, "Can't I do with you, Israel, like the potter does? Israel, if you don't do what I say, you're not going to get the blessing that I promised." According to God Himself, His promises to Israel are not unchangeable history presented in advance.

What about Daniel 9? Remember the 70-week prophecy we went over in the first chapter, spanning from the decree to rebuild Jerusalem in 457 B.C. down to the time of Christ? It declared that the children of Israel had 490 years either to accept or reject the Messiah. Do you think there were any prophetic implications for their ultimate decision? Oh, yes, some big ones.

Let us consider an incident during Jesus' life on earth. "Then Peter came to Him and said, 'Lord, how often shall my brother sin against me, and I forgive him? Up to seven times?' Jesus said to him, 'I do not say to you, up to seven times, but up to seventy times seven'" (Matthew 18:21, 22).

Where might Jesus have gotten that number of 70 times seven? From Daniel 9! In that chapter the prophet was concerned about his people, and God said, "I'm giving them some extra time to accept Me. I'm willing to forgive. I'm willing to give them another chance even after Babylon."

According to Jesus, if you can forgive your fellow human beings for 490 years, you're doing well. Since you're not going to live that long, it means, in essence, that you can't stop forgiving during your lifetime. But there was an end to the forgiveness of Israel: the end of the 490 years in A.D. 34. That was when the branches of unfaithful Jewish Israelites were broken off and the Gentiles grafted in.

Jesus lived His ministry based on Daniel 9. In Mark 1:15, after His baptism Jesus said, "The time is fulfilled." The time fulfilled was the end of the 69th week and the beginning of the last seven-year section of the prophecy. In Matthew 26:18, when He entered Jerusalem, He said, "My time is at hand." Think for a moment about His triumphal entry into Jerusalem. Everybody was saying to Him, "Jesus, we want to make You king! Hosanna to the son of David. We're going to make You king."

He replied, "I've come here to die." How did He know that? Three and a half years into His ministry, He realized that according to Daniel 9 He was going to be "cut off." In spite of the fact that the crowds were proclaiming that they wanted to make Him king, He said, "No, I'm going to Jerusalem to die."

When Jesus had visited Jerusalem earlier, His disciples feared that He would be killed there, but He said to them that His time was not yet (John 11:7-16). How did He know that? He had not reached the middle of the seven-year time period.

Jesus knew when He was going to die based on His knowledge of Daniel 9. He knew He would not be killed any earlier.

When Jesus left the earth, two angels told His disciples, "Go first to Jerusalem, then Judea, then Samaria, then to the uttermost parts of the world" (see Acts 1:8). They still had three and a half years to work in Jerusalem and Judea to see if the leadership there would accept Jesus as their Messiah.

How well did it work? Large numbers of converts came into the faith, but after a few years the Sanhedrin met and had Stephen put to death. Such an official act of the Sanhedrin was, in essence, a statement from the leadership of the nation of Israel, declaring, "We reject Jesus Christ and those who follow Him."

The Israelite leaders followed this up by sending Saul out to the world to persecute believers. On the road to Damascus, God knocked him down, transformed Saul into Paul, and commissioned him as an apostle to the Gentiles.

That marked the end of the "seventy times seven" for the nation of Israel, and it was time to start grafting the Gentiles into the true Israel of faith.

The Temple of God

As we noticed before, most contemporary prophecy teachers say that Israel and the church are spiritually separate. But in God's Word they are one and the same.

Consider how Acts 13 views it. "And when the Jews went out of the synagogue, the Gentiles begged that these words might be preached to them the next Sabbath. Now when the congregation had broken up, many of the Jews and devout proselytes followed Paul and Barnabas, who, speaking to them, persuaded them to continue in the grace of God. And the next Sabbath almost the whole city [Jew and Gentile] came together to hear the word of God.

"But when the Jews saw the multitudes, they were filled with envy; and contradicting and blaspheming, they opposed the things spoken by Paul. Then Paul and Barnabas grew bold and said, 'It was necessary that the word of God should be spoken to you [the Jews] first; but since you reject it, and judge yourselves unworthy of everlasting life, behold, we turn to the Gentiles'" (verses 42-46).

The incident clearly illustrates Paul's imagery of some branches being cut off and some new ones grafted in. The olive tree model of Israel as a mix of those Jews and Gentiles who accept Christ thus appears all the way through the New Testament. It is a concept that actually begins in the Old Testament. For example, consider what God says about the status of some of those outside ethnic Israel: "Do not let the son of the foreigner who has joined himself to the Lord speak, saying, 'The Lord has utterly separated me from His people'; nor let the eunuch say, 'Here I am, a dry tree.'

"For thus says the Lord: 'To the eunuchs who keep My Sabbaths, and choose what pleases Me, and hold fast My covenant, even to them I will give in My house and within My walls a place and a name better than that of sons and daughters; I will give them an everlasting name that shall not be cut off'" (Isa. 56:3-5).

That is significant in light of the olive tree illustration. God said that if any will trust in Jesus Christ, whether Jew or Gentile, foreigner or eunuch, as long as they do so, they will become a part of true Israel. It is not just Paul's idea in the New Testament.

"'Also the sons of the foreigner who join themselves to the Lord, to serve Him, and to love the name of the Lord, to be His servants— everyone who keeps from defiling the Sabbath, and holds fast My covenant—even them I will bring to My holy mountain, and make them joyful in My house of prayer. Their burnt offerings and their sacrifices will be accepted on My altar; for My house shall be called a house of prayer for all nations.' The Lord God, who gathers the outcasts of Israel, says, 'Yet I will gather to him others besides those who are gathered to him'" (verses 6-8).

The multitude of people John saw in Revelation came from every nation, tribe, and people. It is important that we not limit God's desire to save just to the physical, genetic Israelites. He has a lot more people in mind. Jesus shed light on this by what He said about the house of God: "Then Jesus went into the temple of

God and drove out all those who bought and sold in the temple, and overturned the tables of the money changers and the seats of those who sold doves. And He said to them, 'It is written, "My house shall be called a house of prayer," but you have made it a "den of thieves."'

"Then the blind and the lame came to Him in the temple, and He healed them. But when the chief priests and scribes saw the wonderful things that He did, and the children crying out in the temple and saying, 'Hosanna to the Son of David!' they were indignant" (Matthew 21:12-15).

Upset at the people getting healed and praising the Lord, the religious leaders were clearly mentally sick! But notice that Jesus, standing in the house of the Lord, calls it His house, and He is referring to Isaiah 56:3-8, which describes it as "a house of prayer for all people."

Later in Matthew 21 Jesus tells a story about Himself. "There was a certain landowner who planted a vineyard and set a hedge around it, dug a winepress in it and built a tower. And he leased it to vinedressers and went into a far country. Now when vintage-time drew near, he sent his servants to the vine-dressers, that they might receive its fruit. And the vine-dressers took his servants, beat one, killed one, and stoned another.

"Again he sent other servants, more than the first, and they did likewise to them. Then last of all he sent his son to them, saying, 'They will respect my son.' But when the vine-dressers saw the son, they said among themselves, 'This is the heir. Come, let us kill him and seize his inheritance.' And they caught him, and cast him out of the vineyard, and killed him. Therefore, when the owner of the vineyard comes, what will he do to those vine-dressers" (verses 33-40)?

The leaders should have stopped and carefully thought through how they replied, but it seemed such an easy question that they answered it off the cuff, and in so doing they passed their own sentence on themselves.

"They said to Him, 'He will destroy those wicked men miserably, and lease his vineyard to other vine-dressers who will render to him the fruits in their seasons'" (verse 41). Since the men were already planning to kill Jesus, they should have been more cautious in their response.

"Jesus said to them, 'Did you never read in the Scriptures: "The stone which the builders rejected has become the chief cornerstone. This was the Lord's doing, and it is marvelous in our eyes"'" (verse 42)? They were preparing to reject Jesus, but He is the Chief Cornerstone. "'Therefore I say to you, the kingdom of God will be taken from you and given to a nation bearing the fruits of it. And whoever falls on this stone will be broken; but on whomever it falls, it will grind him to powder'" (verse 43).

When you fall on Jesus and ask for forgiveness, you are broken, but you are also saved. Remember that Jesus is the Stone cut out in Daniel 2. When He comes, He grinds to powder everyone who does not follow Him.

The imagery is clear. Those who are of faith will be saved. But those who are not of faith will be destroyed.

So which Israel is important to God—the one of faith, or the one involving genetics? The one of faith is far more vital. While the geopolitical nation or land of Israel still has some significance, the people who are the Israel of faith are the primary matter in God's eyes.

A few days later Jesus spoke about the Temple again. He said, "'O Jerusalem, Jerusalem, the one who kills the prophets and stones those who are sent to her! How often I wanted to gather your children together, as a hen gathers her chicks under her wings, but you were not willing! See! Your house is left to you desolate" (Matthew 23:37, 38).

Earlier He had spoken of it as "My house," but now the Temple is "Your house," and it is "desolate." It is empty without Him. "'For I say to you, you shall see Me no more till you say, "Blessed is He who comes in the name of the Lord"'" (verse 39)! It was His house, and then it was not. Without Jesus, Jewish Israel was desolate, but Jews and gentiles with faith in Jesus are his true house of Israel.

Paul's writings also address the house of the Lord. In Ephesians 2:11-13 he declares, "Therefore remember that you, once Gentiles in the flesh—who are called Uncircumcision by what is called the Circumcision made in the flesh by hands— that at that time you were without Christ, being aliens from the commonwealth of Israel and strangers from the covenants of promise, having no hope and without God in the world. But now in Christ Jesus you who once were far off have been made near by the blood of Christ."

He states that we were "once strangers to the commonwealth of Israel," implying that we are now Israel in Jesus Christ.

"Now, therefore, you are no longer strangers and foreigners, but fellow citizens with the saints and members of the household of God, having been built on the foundation of the apostles and prophets, Jesus Christ Himself being the chief cornerstone, in whom the whole building, being joined together, grows into a holy temple in the Lord" (verses 19-21).

According to this verse, all believers, both Jew and Gentile, are the citizens of Israel! What is the temple now? The people of faith are God's new temple. We call it the church.

When Jesus talks about knowing that we are the temple of God and that we should take care of our bodies (1 Corinthians 6:19, 20), He means that we ourselves are His temple. Together, as believers, we comprise His temple. He is not focused on a literal Temple in Jerusalem. Rather, the New Testament temple is all who believe in Him.

Bigger and Better

I said before that the promises to the nation of Israel were not history written in advance, but rather were conditional on the people's obedience. But God now does something really awesome. "If the nation of Israel doesn't agree with Me or believe in Me or keep My commandments," He in essence announces, "then I will make the promises and prophecies bigger and better for the true people of Israel, the Israel of faith."

That is, for those who believe in Him and keep His

Promises to Israel and the Church		
O.T.		N.T.
Canaan	Land	Heaven
Jerusalem	City	New Jerusalem
Temple	Temple	Heavenly Temple
		Believer and Church
Believers in Christ are the N.T. people of Israel		

commandments. Note the comparisons in the table above. Old Testament Israel received the Promised Land of Canaan.

The New Testament believers have the promise of heaven and a wholly restored earth. Old Testament Israel had Jerusalem for a city. The New Testament promises us the New Jerusalem, first in heaven, then on earth. That's a lot better, isn't it?

Old Testament Israel had a temple building in Jerusalem, but the temple in the New Testament is a heavenly temple (Hebrews 9:11-28), the believer's own body (1 Corinthians 6:19), and also the church (Ephesians 2:11-22). Everything gets bigger and better for the New Testament believer. If the Old Testament believer did not accept what God was giving, and God was not able to fulfill the promise, He made it bigger and better and reapplied it in the New Testament for the believer in Christ—Jew or Gentile.

Some of the popular books on prophecy claim that in the Old Testament people were saved by works, and that in the New Testament people are saved by faith. But the Bible tells me that it is never "of works, lest anyone should boast" (Ephesians 2:8).

In Hebrews 11, the faith chapter, the faithful people listed there are all Old Testament individuals who were saved by faith. We are all saved by faith, both in the Old Testament and the New Testament. No one is ever saved by works. So the idea that there is a difference between Old Testament Israel and the New Testament church does not hold up either. The Bible declares that the redeemed have always been saved by faith.

The New Covenant

Revelation 7:1-4 speaks of "those who were sealed." In Deuteronomy 11:18 the people had the "seal of God" in their forehead. "Therefore you shall lay up these words of mine in your heart and in your soul," God said to the Israelites, "and bind them as a sign on your hand, and they shall be as frontlets between your eyes."

Today God is still waiting for His people to store up His Word and live by it before He lets the end-time events begin. That is what those four angels are waiting for. God wants His people to put His Word into their minds and into their hearts, not to be saved by works, but because of love for God.

Do you know where you find the new covenant? In the Old Testament—in Jeremiah 31:31-33: "Behold, the days are coming, says the Lord, when I will make a new covenant with the house of Israel and with the house of Judah—not according to the covenant that I made with their fathers in the day that I took them by the hand to lead them out of the land of Egypt, My covenant which they broke, though I was a husband to them, says the Lord.

"But this is the covenant that I will make with the house of Israel after those days, says the Lord: I will put My law in their minds, and write it on their hearts; and I will be their God, and they shall be My people."

Who is the "partner" in the new covenant? The house of Israel! This is why the New Testament calls even gentile followers of Christ, Israel, or family of Abraham. Where does God write it? On their minds and in their hearts. Because of their love for Jesus, they follow what they know of God's law. That is the new covenant. He inscribes it in our lives.

In the same terms, John says in Revelation that we hear God's message and do it (Revelation 1:3) because we love Jesus. While He was on earth Jesus said, "If you love Me, keep My commandments" (John 14:15). God's last-day people from all nations are trusting Christ and obeying Him, a reality echoed in Revelation 12:17, which speaks of those "who keep the commandments of God and have the testimony of Jesus Christ."

Again, Revelation 14 is the chapter where we began with the 144,000, and verse 12 states: "Here is the patience of the saints; here are those who keep the commandments of God and the faith of Jesus."

Do you see how that keeps playing out? We are getting God's Word directly in our minds. No one is saved by works, but only by faith in Jesus. And if you have faith in Him, you do what He says. If you claim to have faith in Him and don't do what He says, you are not His.

The Israel of Our Time

In the Old Testament the concept of Israel had more of a geopolitical definition. But in the New Testament it acquires a more spiritual definition—the people of faith, both Jew and Gentile. This matches what happened to the king of the North, which went from more politically defined as pagan Rome to more religious as papal Rome. Jesus' death on the cross changed everything for Israel.

Daniel 11 talks about "the Glorious Land," which is geographical. But notice that it does not speak about the people—only about the land. In Daniel 11 the geopolitical depicts real events, and after we go past the time of the cross, the localized struggles represent a worldwide spiritual/religious conflict as well.

Events will still happen in Jerusalem or the land of Israel, but God's people (the citizens of Israel in Ephesians 2) are those who are the true Israelites by faith. Everyone from around the world can choose to be a part of God's true Israel. As Jesus taught in Matthew 21, the vineyard is the same but the people have changed.

Notice this intriguing trend in the history and prophecy of Daniel 11. Whenever the king of the North (papacy) controls literal Israel, it also controls spiritual/religious Israel, the church. During the Crusades, the first conflict between the papacy and Islam, the papacy controlled literal Israel and also the church. During the second conflict with Islam (Ottoman Empire), the papacy never controlled literal Israel, and because of the Reformation it lost control of the church, spiritual/religious Israel.

At the time of the end, Daniel 11:40-45, the papacy once again controls Jerusalem, and Revelation 13:3 says that "all the world ... followed the beast," indicating that the papacy will once again have control over the worldwide church. The literal is a parallel to the spiritual/religious. It is not an either/or—it is both literal and spiritual/religious in Daniel 11:40-45.

Another intriguing trend is this. Just as the land of Israel suffered in the middle between the Papal king of the North and the Islamic king of the South, so God's new covenant believers have suffered persecution from both.

"Blessed is he who reads and those who hear the words of this prophecy, and keep those things which are written in it; for the time is near" (Revelation 1:3). It is time to listen and do it! You can't just hear God's Word and walk away. You have to put what you learn into practice, or it doesn't do you any good at all. If you don't practice what you learn, it makes you worse off, because now you know what you are missing and you are in rebellion. And so, when you hear these things, live them out in your life.

Chapter 7

ISLAM, THE KING OF THE SOUTH

Two Bold Powers

In Daniel 11, the Glorious Land is geographical Israel, but religiously or spiritually speaking, Israel is God's people. All who accept Jesus Christ and thus become heirs of Abraham, whether Jew or gentile, are God's true Israel worldwide.

The king of the North goes from being primarily geopolitical in nature during the eras of Greece and Rome to a geopolitical and religious power as the papacy.

Likewise, the Glorious Land evolves from being primarily geopolitical to being both geopolitical and religious, leading to a worldwide religious struggle. The geographical locations identified in Daniel 11 are a general guideline of where the conflict will take place.

The same principles hold true for the king of the South. That power, too, goes through a transition from being geopolitical to both geopolitical and religious.

The geopolitical phase is a model of the religious phase of a worldwide struggle, consistent in all three powers (king of the North, king of the South, and the Glorious Land) of Daniel 11. In prophetic interpretation we need to see consistency.

The two powers in Revelation 13 are the beast, which we identified as the papal system, and the power with lamblike horns that comes up in Revelation 13:11—the United States. Both are striving for world control.

In his book about Pope John Paul II, *The Keys of This Blood*, Malachi Martin observes: "He would endow his [John Paul's] papacy with an international profile and, as pope, move around among world leaders and nations, vindicating a position for himself as a special leader among leaders, because in that competition he plans to emerge as the victor."[1]

When John Paul II started his reign, three superpowers held sway in the world: the United States, the Soviet Union, and the papacy. By the time of his death only two remained. The Catholic Church and the United States worked on eliminating the third one, which they pushed to the side.

Here's evidence of American intentions at that time: "In a broad new policy statement that is in its final drafting stage, the Defense Department asserts that America's political and military mission in the post-cold war era will be to ensure that no rival superpower is allowed to emerge in Western Europe, Asia, or the territory of the former Soviet Union."[2]

Remember the peace dividend that everyone talked about at the end of the cold war era? People speculated about how much money the United States could save that it no longer had to spend on military capability. But it's hard not to notice how many wars the United States has had since the Cold War ended. Why so many conflicts? Because the U.S. is serious about making sure that nobody else gains power.

In our time, both the papacy and the United States strive to be number one. The book of Revelation depicts those two powers ultimately working side by side. The world may have witnessed this on a smaller scale in the alliance between President Ronald Reagan and the pope.

"Reagan and the pope agreed to undertake a clandestine campaign to hasten the dissolution of the Communist empire. Declares Richard Allen, Reagan's first National Security adviser: 'This was one of the great secret alliances of all time.' ... "Step by reluctant step, the Soviets and the Communist government of Poland bowed to the moral, economic, and political pressure imposed by the pope and the president."[3]

The two men supported the labor unions within Poland, building up their power. While the United States continued its arms race that was bankrupting the Soviet Union, the Catholic Church spread through Poland a moral message that sought

---

1   *Malachi Martin,* The Keys of This Blood *(New York: Touchstone, 1990), p. 480.*
2   *Patrick E. Tyler, "U.S. Strategy Plan Calls for Insuring No Rivals Develop,"* New York Times, *Mar. 8, 1992. Available online at http://query.nytimes.com/gst/fullpage .html?res=9E0CE5D61E38F93BA35750C0A964958260.*
3   *Carl Bernstein, "The Holy Alliance: Ronald Reagan and John Paul II,"* Time, *Feb. 24, 1992. Available online at www.time.com/time/magazine/article/0,9171,974931-1,00 .html.*

to undermine Communism. At a time of great social and technological change, and the combination of the Catholic Church's support of the labor unions and the military might of the United States, Reagan and the pope possibly transformed the course of history.

As we have seen, Revelation 13 tells us the United States will end up being the military might to help bring people in line with the papacy. The two powers have already taken advantage of times of change by working together to alter history. It would not be a surprise to see them cooperate again.

A Threat from the South

Where does Islam fit into the picture? To begin to answer that question, consider the view of the late Charles Malik, a prominent Lebanese politician and educator. Malik was Greek Orthodox, served as Lebanon's minister of education and arts, and lectured at several American universities, including Harvard and Dartmouth. He was even president of the United Nations General Assembly for one session.

A lifelong supporter of the Christian cause, Malik had this to say in 1979 about the future role of Islam and how the Christian West and the Christian East should handle Islam: "The only hope for the Western world lies in an alliance between the Roman Catholic Church, which is the most commonly influential, controlling, unifying element in Europe, and the Eastern Orthodox Church. Rome must unite with Eastern Orthodoxy, because the Eastern Orthodox Church controls the western Middle East, the east end of the Mediterranean.

"And if they don't solidify that control, Islam will march across Europe. Islam is political. The only hope of the Western world lies in a united Europe under the control of the pope."[4]

Malik was an Eastern Orthodox Christian, and he urged that Eastern Christianity should reunite with the papacy. The reason that he wanted to see a unified Christian world under the papacy was to meet the threat from Islam. I don't believe that Malik was studying prophecy, but being from the Middle East, he knew well the potential dangers.

Take a look at Daniel 11:40 again: "At the time of the end the king of the South shall attack him [the king of the North]; and the king of the North shall come

---

4   *This quote appears on many websites, but the best documentation is at www. atuio-ra/Resources/Sermons/27-08_The-Rise-and-Fall-of-the-World-Part2, where John MacArthur claims to have heard it in person. However, MacArthur gives a summary, not a direct quote.*

against him like a whirlwind, with chariots, horsemen, and with many ships; and he shall enter the countries, overwhelm them, and pass through."

During the Crusades, the king of the North was papal-dominated Western Christianity, and Islam was the king of the South. Islam was the powerhouse that came from the south of Jerusalem (see Daniel 11:23-28).

Daniel 2, 7, and 8 do not suggest another change in the series of kings from the north until the return of Jesus Christ, nor do we find any indication for a new identity of the king of the South. The king of the North should still be papal-led Christianity until the end of time, and the king of the South will continue to be Islam.

Charles Malik's statement sounds almost prophetic. I believe that we are looking at something that is in the process of fulfillment now. The conflict between Islam and Christianity is already taking on aspects of a holy war. If I am right, it places us at the beginning of the last showdown between Islam and Christianity. Things could go quickly from here.

Continuing with verses 41-43: "He [the king of the North] shall also enter the Glorious Land." This suggests that something will somehow compromise the sovereignty of the geopolitical nation of Israel.

"And many countries shall be overthrown; but these shall escape from his hand: Edom, Moab, and the prominent people of Ammon. He shall stretch out his hand against the countries, and the land of Egypt shall not escape. He shall have power over the treasures of gold and silver, and over all the precious things of Egypt; also the Libyans and Ethiopians shall follow at his heels."

In chapter 1 we saw that Daniel 11:24-39 covers the time period of the papacy's 1,260-year rule, which included both the Crusades against Islam and the Reformation. The king of the South during that period was Islam, and I believe it still is. The king of the South power changed from the political Ptolemaic kingdom, which was its beginning form, to the geopolitical and religious power of Islam.

Islam initially attacked Israel in 634 A.D., when four armies came up from Medina. Three of the armies traveled to the east of Jerusalem while one traveled to the west on their way north to Syria. The next year they came back down from the north and besieged Jerusalem.

You may think this attack on Jerusalem from the north would make them the king of the North. However, the Byzantine defenders of Jerusalem would only surrender to Omar the Caliph who, as leader of Islam politically and religiously, would be the king of the South. Omar was to the south in Medina. So the Muslim armies originally invaded Jerusalem from the south and Jerusalem surrendered when the Caliph or king of the South came from south.[5]

Looking at the globe, we note that the shaded area represents the nations predominantly controlled by Islam. Israel is the tiny country in the middle. After 14 centuries of conflict, Islam is still predominantly in the south.

In Daniel 11 there are three conflicts, or holy wars, between Islam and Christianity. The first is described in verses 25-28. "He shall stir up his power and his courage against the king of the South with a great army." This was fulfilled when Pope Urban II called for war against Muslims in the Holy Land, and Christian nations of Europe responded by starting the crusades because of the threat of Islam.

The second is mentioned in verse 29, which says: "At the appointed time he shall return and go toward the south; but it shall not be like the former or the latter. For ships from Cyprus shall come against him." This was fulfilled when Pope Pius V organized the "Holy League" to fight against the spread of Ottoman Islam. Once again the Christian nations followed because of the threat of Islam.

Verse 30 talks about how ships from Cyprus shall come against him, thus blocking him from going to Cyprus and on to the south. The historical fulfillment of

5   *Al-Tel, Othman Ismael.* First Islamic Conquest of Aelia (Islamic Jerusalem) : A Critical Analytical Study of the Early Islamic Historical Narratives and Sources. *Dundee, GBR: Al-Maktoum Institute Academic Press, 2003. ProQuest ebrary. May 3, 2016.*

this second movement of the king of the North towards the South is in the fourth Venetian/Ottoman war of 1570-1573. The fleet of the Holy league sailed towards Cyprus intending to drive the Muslims off the island.

The fleet never got there, however. The Ottoman fleet had sailed from Constanti-nople/Istanbul to Cyprus with 250-300 ships. At Cyprus they put ashore an inva-sion force of more than 30,000 men. The Ottoman fleet then sailed to its western outpost at Lapanto to block the fleet of the Holy League.

In the battle, the Ottoman fleet was destroyed, but was able to block the Holy League from sailing on to Cyprus. As result, the Ottomans were able to take and hold Cyprus. Within a year the Ottomans had rebuilt their fleet.

So the Islamic ships from Cyprus did stop the king of the North from regaining territory to the south. As the Grand Vizier argued, "You [Christians] come to see how we bear our misfortune. But I would have you know the difference between your loss and ours. In wresting Cyprus from you, we deprived you of an arm; in defeating our fleet, you have only shaved our beard. An arm when cut off cannot grow again; but a shorn beard will grow all the better for the razor."[6]

Similar and Opposite

In 2002 I received an email about Islam and the papacy. The writer believed that at the time of the end, Islam and the papacy would unite into one power, an idea he partially based on Martin Luther calling both Islam and the papacy the anti-christ. Martin Luther identified one leg of the Daniel 2 statue as the papacy and the other leg as Islam.

As I read the e-mail message from my friend, I thought, They are much alike, yet they are opposites, like polar north and south. When that thought went through my mind, I thought, Daniel 11! I opened my Bible and read it, and suddenly Dan-iel 11 made sense for the first time in my life.

If the papacy was the beast and was in the north, then the other power should have a point/counterpoint relationship to it. Let's go through the opposites and the correlatives to see if this works.

    1. The papacy emerged from within Rome. Islam spread through the southern territory of the Roman Empire, and papal Rome dominated the northern part.

---

6   A Military History of the Western World, *Major General J.F.C. Fuller. Funk and Wag-nalls Company, New York, 1954, Vol 1, pp. 559-579.*

101

2. Daniel said that the little horn, the papacy, would uproot three horns, and it did—the Heruli, the Vandals, and the Ostrogoths. Islam conquered three regions: North Africa, the Middle East, and Turkey.

3. Both powers have a "man at the head"—one the pope, the other Muhammad, and later a Caliph. Ask a member of the Roman Catholic Church, "Who's the man at the head of your church?" They'll say, "The pope." Then ask a Muslim, "Who's the man at the head of your movement?" and they will reply, "Muhammad." Following Muhammad, Islam has often had a Caliph, the leader of a Caliphate. There was an Arab Caliphate up to the time of the Crusades, then the Ottoman Caliphate or Turks, and now the Islamic State Caliphate.

4. The two powers would be "diverse," or different, from previous powers. They both shift from being a political to a religious power. Pagan Rome was political while papal Rome was political and religious. Egypt under the Ptolemies was political. But Islam is both strongly political and religious. The ancient world did not separate governments into religious and political spheres. The leader would often be the chief priest of the national religion. But papal Rome and Islam emphasized the religious aspects much more than ancient governments did. They focused primarily on religious conquest.

5. They are characterized as "speaking great words," or blasphemy. Even the term antichrist applies. The Greek term translated as "antichrist" means either "in place of Christ" or "against Christ." The papacy claims to be ruling in the place of Christ. Islam denies the divinity of Christ.

6. They would "persecute the saints." During the Crusades and the Inquisition the papacy killed Muslims, Jews, and Christians alike who did not believe as it does. Islam killed Christians, Jews, and Muslims who did not believe the same as they did, although at times both could be quite tolerant (as especially happened in Islamic Spain).

7. They would "receive the dragon's seat," or the capital of the Roman Empire. The Roman Empire had two capitals. Emperor Constantine moved the capital from the city of Rome to Constantinople. After he left, the city of Rome became the center of papal power. Constantinople later became Istanbul, capital of the Islamic Ottoman or Turkish Caliphate for many centuries. The papacy got one capital of the Roman Empire and Islam the other.

Some have seen allusions to Islam in Revelation 9:1-12: "Then the fifth angel sounded: And I saw a star fallen from heaven to the earth. To him was given the key to the bottomless pit." Two interpretations here might make sense. One is that the star was Muhammad, beginning as a true prophet of God and then wandering away. The other approach is the one that I lean more toward: the angel that fell from heaven is Satan.

Both the beast we find in Revelation and the power that some believe to be Islam come from the "bottomless pit." The bottomless pit is defined as a lifeless place, a desolate, abysmal area. The Bible commentators who believe that Muhammad has a role in Revelation 9 view the bottomless pit as the Arabian Peninsula, which seemed lifeless.

But Satan is the one who brings destruction from either beast. Verse 2 says: "He opened the bottomless pit, and smoke arose out of the pit like the smoke of a great furnace."

Smoke often represents the judgments of God, and I think that's what it is here, because by the time we get to verses 20 and 21, the smoke is indeed demonstrating that it was divine judgment: "And the sun and the air were darkened because of the smoke of the pit. Then out of the smoke locusts came upon the earth. And to them was given power, as the scorpions of the earth have power. They were commanded not to harm the grass of the earth, or any green thing, or any tree, but only those men who do not have the seal of God on their foreheads" (verses 2-4).

When we talked about the "seal of God," we found that it meant getting God's Word into our mind after we made the decision to follow Him, a concept that goes back at least as far as Deuteronomy 11:18. The new covenant in Jeremiah 31:31-33 described the same thing.

Don't think that the seal of God pertains only to end-time people. It has applied to His people for a long, long time. Throughout history individuals have accepted God and made a decision to follow Him. At the end of time, the same seal of God is in people's foreheads, and He protects them from the plagues to come.

Two Have Passed, One Is Yet to Come

What we just described was the first of three "woes" depicted in Revelation 9. "One woe is past. Behold, still two more woes are coming after these things" (verse 12). Some have interpreted the three woes as three historical phases.[7] The first woe was the Arab phase, the time when Muhammad conquered the Arabian Peninsula. As Islam continued to expand, it seized Egypt, Palestine, North Africa

---

7   *See the June 1944 Ministry magazine article listing views of many Bible commentaries from 1100 to the 1930s in appendix.*

and parts of Turkey. Although the Islamic armies tried to take Constantinople, they could not. So in the first 150 years of conflict, that's all Islam was able to conquer.

"And they were not given authority to kill them, but to torment them for five months." Those who hold this position regard the five months of prophetic days as 150 years.

Here's another aspect of the first woe. Revelation 9:3 talks about locusts. The desert locusts come out of the Saudi Arabian desert and spread across North Africa when the wind blows from east to west—or, if the wind goes from southwest to northeast, it sends the locusts that way. A map of the range of the desert locust shows that it is the same basic area as covered by the Arab phase of Islam.

In verses 13-17 comes the second woe. "Then the sixth angel sounded: And I heard a voice from the four horns of the golden altar which is before God, saying to the sixth angel who had the trumpet, 'Release the four angels who are bound at the great river Euphrates.' So the four angels, who had been prepared for the hour and day and month and year, were released to kill a third of mankind. Now the number of the army of the horsemen was two hundred million, and I heard the number of them. And thus I saw the horses in the vision: those who sat on them had breastplates of fiery red, hyacinth blue, and sulfur yellow; and the heads of the horses were like the heads of lions; and out of their mouths came fire, smoke, and brimstone."

Many old commentaries regard this group as representing the Turks.[8] The Turks came out of what is now Russia, advanced down through Persia, accepted Islam, spread along the area of the Tigris and Euphrates rivers, broke through the region's mountain passes, and reached the area now called Turkey, and as they did they brought in a brand-new phase of Islamic conquest. Capturing Constantinople, they pushed all the way up into Europe. By then they had put a lot of pressure on Western Christianity.

The Ottoman push ultimately enabled the Reformation to take root, because much of Christendom was preoccupied with trying to hold the line against the Islamic Turks. During that time period Martin Luther and other Reformers began to proclaim "the Bible and the Bible only," and the papacy could not immediately deal with them because of the threat from the Turks. Why would God allow the Islamic invasions? I believe that He used Islam to revitalize Christianity. It gave an opportunity for the Reformation to develop and spread.

---

8   *Ibid.*

Notice something interesting in verse 20: "But the rest of mankind, who were not killed by these plagues, did not repent of the works of their hands, that they should not worship demons, and idols of gold, silver, brass, stone, and wood, which can neither see nor hear nor walk." Both Western and Eastern Christianity increasingly used images and statues in their churches and worship, a practice that upset Muhammad and his followers.

During the earlier Arab phase, Muhammad and his people had left those Christians who were serious about following the Bible alone, but of those who seemed to worship statues, Muhammad's father-in-law, Abu Bakr, said they should "cleave their skulls."[9]

Some see this as God using Islam to attempt to bring Christianity back to truth, but it would not. Verse 21: "And they did not repent of their murders or their sorceries or their sexual immorality or their thefts." What did God use as the symbol of their spiritual falling away? He called them a harlot, a prostitute, just as He did with Old Testament Israel. As with Christianity, when Old Testament Israel worshipped idols, God sent in the children of the East (Abrahamic "cousins," descendants of Ishmael, Esau, and Lot) to punish Israel.

As Daniel 11 has three conflicts, so in Revelation there are three woes. Again, I suggest that God was using Islam as a wake-up call to bring His New Testament Israel, Christians, back to His Word. I believe the same pattern will occur in the end-time—Islam will be a tool in the hand of God to confront the world with His Word.

---

9   *Edward Gibbon*, The Decline and Fall of the Roman Empire *(New York: Random House, 1932), vol. 5, p. 286.*

Chapter 8

THE TIME-OF-THE-END HOLY WAR

The Three Conflicts

Daniel 11:29 states: "At the appointed time he shall return and go toward the south; but it shall not be like the former or the latter." This verse describes the second major conflict between Christianity and Islam. The king of the North has headed south for a second round, but it will not be like the "former," nor like the "latter."

From this statement we can conclude that three general periods of conflict take place between the kings of the South and North in Daniel 11:23-45. In Daniel 11:40 the first two conflicts have passed, and the third one begins. This leads me to conclude that we will see a third and final conflict between Islam and Christianity.

Furthermore, it suggests still another similarity between the kings of the North and South. A deadly wound would be healed, according to Revelation 13:3. The

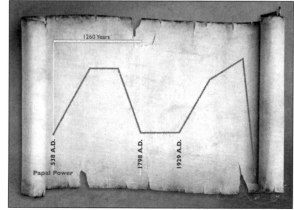

papacy was wounded in 1798, but eventually regained its power. What about Islam? Did it go through a period when it had great strength, lost it, and got it back again?

One day I decided to graph the power curve of the papacy. It rose to prominence in A.D. 538, increased in influence for centuries, reached a zenith, and then, after 1,260 years of strength, saw its power ended in 1798. In 1929 the papacy began to rise again and, according to the Bible, will expand in strength until Jesus destroys it at the very end.

Then I thought that I would find out what happens if I plot the power curve of Islam over that of the papacy. Here's what I got.

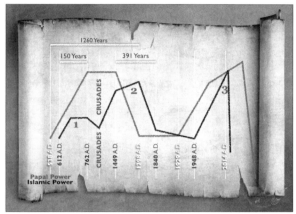

Wow! It's almost identical. If we regard Revelation 9 as portraying the role of Islam and interpret a day for a year (as suggested previously), then 150 years extends from A.D. 612 (about the period His followers believe that Muhammad began receiving revelations) to 762.

Starting in 1449 A.D., we have the 391 years of the second woe as the period of the Turkish Empire, and that brings us to 1840 and the change in the Ottoman Empire. From the mid-1800s to the mid-1900s Islam did not have much power at all.

It wasn't until about 1948, when Islamic countries acquired a common enemy, Israel, that these countries started drawing back together. That common enemy rallied Islamic nations, and instead of fighting each other as much, they would now turn on Israel.

At about the same time, many of those countries started earning petroleum dollars, so now they had funding for their fight. In the 1960s, the new tool of terrorism appeared. Radical Islam or Islamists had begun to grow in power.

Here in the graph is the early (with the Crusades), the middle (with the Ottoman Empire), and the latter struggles in Daniel 11. The third one is the one "at the time of the end"—the period we live in.

In the first edition of this book I said that I believed that a third holy war between Islam and Christianity could be expected. Five years later, the third and final "holy war" has begun. Let's look at the Daniel 11:40-43 description of this third and final conflict.

A Hard, Fast War

"At the time of the end the king of the South [Islam] shall attack him [the papacy and its alliance]; and the king of the North [the papacy] shall come against him [Islam] like a whirlwind, with chariots, horsemen, and with many ships; and he [the papacy] shall enter the countries, overwhelm them, and pass through. He [the papacy] shall also enter the Glorious Land, and many countries shall be overthrown; but these shall escape from his [the papacy] hand: Edom, Moab, and the prominent people of Ammon.

"He [the papacy] shall stretch out his hand against the countries, and the land of Egypt shall not escape. He [the papacy] shall have power over the treasures of gold and silver, and over all the precious things of Egypt; also the Libyans and Ethiopians shall follow at his [the papacy's] heels."

In Daniel's description of rapid destruction, the forces will "overwhelm them, and pass through. He [the king of the North, the papal alliance] shall also enter the Glorious Land, and many countries shall be overthrown."

Notice that these forces enter Israel. As I mentioned in chapter 6, that means the Israeli nation's sovereignty is compromised either by the Christian powers or, more likely, the Christian powers are "saving" Israel from radical Islam. Many countries will be overthrown—not just a couple of them, but many. The whole of the Middle East will be in turmoil.

The overwhelming attack from the north causes a three-way breakup of Islam:
1. Those who escape the king of the North
2. Those who are overthrown by the king of the North
3. Those who follow after the king of the North

We will first look at items 2 and 3, saving item 1 for last because it is the good news.

Egypt and Many Countries Overthrown

In this third and final "time of the end" conflict, the Bible says that Egypt and many countries will be overthrown. Remember that the king of the North, the king of the South, and Israel are geopolitical and religious. To be consistent, we should expect that Egypt will be geopolitical and religious as well. This means that I expect that the geopolitical nation of Egypt will radicalize and be overthrown.

Additionally, I also expect that the religious application will be the overthrow or destruction of radical Islam and end-time caliphate supporters around the world.

Libya and Ethiopia will follow the king of the North. Again, this should be geo-political and religious. I expect that the countries or areas of ancient Libya and Ethiopia will choose to follow papal-led Christianity rather than to face destruction. At the same time I expect that moderate or secular Islam will follow papal-led Christianity, basically saying "Don't kill us—we don't like radical Islam either."

It is no longer a question of whether this final holy war could happen or not. I believe it has already begun.

The Final Holy War Begins

For the first time since the Ottoman Empire, we now have a functioning caliphate, and for the first time since the Ottoman empire, the papacy has called for military action against the caliphate. Since the Ottoman conflict was the second conflict between Islam and Christianity in Daniel 11, the resumption of hostilities would be the beginning of the third and final conflict between Islam and Christianity.

Here is when and how the final conflict began. On June 29, 2014 the Islamic State Caliphate was declared. Here is how the London Telegraph reported it. "Abu Bakr al-Baghdadi, the self-proclaimed leader of the 'Islamic State' stretching across Iraq and Syria, has vowed to lead the conquest of Rome as he called on Muslims to immigrate to his new land to fight under its banner around the globe."[1]

Note that on day one of the Islamic State Caliphate's existence they said they would attack Rome and conquer the world. Daniel 11 said the king of the South would attack the king of the North. This matches perfectly!

During the next five weeks the Islamic State rapidly conquered a huge area of Syria and Iraq, killing thousands of Christians, Yazidis, and Muslims who did not join with them.

On August 7, 2014 the pope called for action. "Pope Francis appealed to world leaders on Thursday to help end the crisis in northern Iraq after a sweeping advance by radical Islamic state militants forced thousands of residents of Iraq's

---

1   *The Telegraph, July 1, 2014.*

biggest Christian town to flee their homes. His Holiness addresses an urgent appeal to the international community to take action to end the humanitarian tragedy now underway."[2]

Over the next few days, it became clear from papal diplomats' statements that this was a call for military action. "Referring to military action, Archbishop Giorgio Lingua, the Vatican's nuncio to Iraq, told Vatican Radio, 'This is something that had to be done, otherwise [the Islamic State] could not be stopped.

Such a call is virtually unprecedented for a papal envoy in modern times, but our age is an extraordinary one and the Islamic State has no interest in a bargaining table. Instead, the Islamic State is bent on genocide and barbarism, ruthlessly exterminating anyone who opposes them.'"[3]

Statement of the papal envoy to the United Nations , "The Holy See's ambassador to the United Nations, Silvano Tomasi, this weekend supported U.S. air strikes aimed at halting the advance of Sunni Islamic State (IS) militants, calling for "intervention now, before it is too late. Military action might be necessary," he said.

While the Vatican vocally disapproved of the U.S.-led campaign in Iraq in 2003 and the 2013 plan for air strikes on Syria, fearing that both might make the situations worse for Christians on the ground, fears of ethnic cleansing by Islamists has forced a policy change."[4]

Note that there is no question that the pope was calling for military action. Remember that in Daniel 11, the king of the South (Islam) attacks the North (papal-led Christianity) and the king of the North retaliates with military action. This is exactly the order of events we saw in 2014.

Not only was there a call for action, there was action. Just over a day after the pope called for military action the US began to bomb the Islamic State Caliphate. Earlier in this book, I stated that the U.S. would become the military enforcer for the papacy. Even the Islamic State now recognizes this to be true following the papal call for action.

---

2   Reuters, "Francis calls for action as Iraqi Christians forced to flee," August 7, 2014.
3   Catholic Online, "Chaldean Patriarch calls for Armed Response to defend Christians from Genocide," August 11, 2014.
4   Breitbart News, "Vatican's Approval of Iraq Strikes a Rare Exception to Peace Policy," August 13, 2014.

"Jihadi John said: 'To Obama, the dog of Rome. Today we are slaughtering the soldiers of Bashar and tomorrow we will be slaughtering your soldiers and with Allah's permission we will break this final and last crusade and the Islamic State will soon, like your puppet David Cameron said, begin to slaughter your people on your streets.'"[5]

So the Islamic State calls the U.S. the dog of Rome. This makes sense. The papacy said to attack, and just like a guard dog, the U.S. attacked.

Two weeks after the pope's call for military action, the Islamic State began to film the beheading of hostages and post the footage on YouTube. All of this was a part of the Islamic State's plan to anger the world in order to induce them to attack the Islamic State.

After the territory of the Islamic State came under attack, it slowed its expansion and began to lose territory. Internationally, however, they began to spread, with many radical Islamist groups swearing allegiance to the Islamic State. These groups included Nigeria's Boko Haram, Al Shabaab from East Africa, and many other Islamist groups.

With the Islamic State under military siege, the caliph called for terror attacks around the world. "Abu Bakr al-Baghdadi, the leader of extremist group ISIS, called on his supporters to 'erupt volcanoes of jihad' in an apparent new audio message."[6]

Since then, Islamic State followers have unleashed terrorism around the world. We have had major, well-publicized terrorist attacks in France, Belgium, and the U.S. There have also been far greater attacks in Africa, Asia, and the Middle East that the Western press has largely ignored.

During all of this activity, the papacy has been growing in power. It was because of anger at violent Islam that the Christian world followed the papal call for military action at the time of the crusades. It was because of the anger at violent Islam that it followed the papacy again at the time of the Ottoman Empire.

The following news quotes will show that the same is happening today. "Former Israeli President Shimon Peres has said that Pope Francis is more powerful than

---

5   London Telegraph, "US Army Veteran Peter Kassig 'Murdered by Isil,'" November 17, 2014.

6   NBC News, "ISIS Leader al-Baghdadi: 'Erupt Volcanoes of Jihad,'" November 13, 2014.

the United Nations when it comes to advocating peace. While visiting the Vatican earlier today, Mr. Peres asked Pope Francis to head a parallel United Nations called the "United Religions" to counter religious extremism in the world today.

Peres said the United Nations and its peacekeepers do not have the force or the effectiveness of any one of the pope's homilies, which can draw half a million people in St. Peter's Square alone. "So given that the United Nations has run its course, what we need is an organization of United Religions," Mr. Peres said, as "the best way to counteract these terrorists who kill in the name of their faith. What we need is an unquestionable moral authority who says out loud, 'No. God doesn't want this and doesn't allow it,'" he added.[7]

The problem is that historically, papal-led Christianity has been responsible for the deaths of millions of Christians, Jews, and Muslims who disagreed with their teachings. This is asking the fox to guard the henhouse. The papal power continues to grow.

"But shrewdly, methodically and with a showman's flair, the soft-spoken, 78-year-old Argentinian Jesuit priest named—Pope Francis—showed Thursday that he is running to become president of the planet ... "[8]

Prophetically, we are now in the early stages of Daniel 11's "whirlwind." Even the news stories give the feel of a whirlwind, such as this one from the New York Post. "These are unprecedented developments, veering so far from the norm and happening so fast that consequences are piling up faster than they can be comprehended. Alliances built over decades are shattered in a relative flash, inviting aggression and endless conflict. The toxic brew of Islamic fanaticism and nuclear proliferation could ignite a world conflagration."[9]

This is just what Islamists want. "The Caliphate seeks to unite dozens of factions of the Pakistani and Afghan Taliban into a single army of terror. It includes a never-before-seen history of the Islamic State, details chilling future battle plans, urges al-Qaeda to join the group and says the Islamic State's leader should be recognized as the sole ruler of the world's 1 billion Muslims under a religious empire called a *caliphate.*

---

7   *Catholic Herald, "Shimon Peres: Francis is More Powerful Peace Advocate than UN,"* September 4, 2014.

8   *Huffington Post, "Pope Francis Wants to be President of the World," September 24,* 2015.

9   *New York Post, "Obama's Race to Chaos," March 28, 2015.*

"'Accept the fact that this caliphate will survive and prosper until it takes over the entire world and beheads every last person that rebels against Allah,' proclaims an Islamic State recruitment document. 'This is the bitter truth, swallow it.'"[10]

Many Christian prophecy teachers have said that Russia is the king of the North. However, Russia did not attack Israel from the north since the breakup of Rome, so it cannot be the Daniel 11 king of the North.

Instead, Russia is a part of the papal-led Christianity king of the North. Russia would be a part of all the world that follows the Beast of papal-led Christianity. This is now becoming clear.

For years, Russia has had its own challenges with radical Islamic terrorism. Putin, the leader of Russia, has considered himself the protector of Orthodox Christianity in the Middle East. Now consider these facts that show Russia is fighting radical Islam in cooperation with the papacy.

"In an unusually blunt endorsement of military action, the Vatican's top diplomat at the United Nations in Geneva has called for a coordinated international force to stop the 'so-called Islamic State' in Syria and Iraq. He said the joint statement originated with Russia, which traditionally sees itself as a protector of Orthodox Christians in the Middle East."[11]

When Russia entered the war in Syria against radical Islam, FrontPage Mag posted a story entitled "Russia Declares 'Holy War' on Islamic State While Obama Sides With Christian Murdering 'Freedom Fighter.'"

It read, "The head of External Church Relations, Metropolitan Illarion ... asked Putin to make the protection of Christians one of the foreign policy directions in future. 'This is how it will be, have no doubt,' Putin answered."[12] So Russia is now a part of the papal-led Christianity, king of the North alliance.

There are several ways that Islamists could trigger papal-led Christianity into a even more intense holy war. The first would be to instigate more frequent and/or larger terrorist attacks in the Western world. The second would be to use a nuclear device of some type in a terror attack. The U.S. called an international

10   USA Today, "Islamic State Recruitment Document Seeks to Provoke 'End of the World,'" July 28, 2015.
11   Crux Now, "Vatican Backs Military Force to Stop ISIS 'Genocide,'" March 13, 2015.
12   FRONTPAGE MAG, "Russia Declares 'Holy War' on Islamic State While Obama Sides with Christian Murdering 'Freedom Fighters,'" October 7, 2015.

summit to deal with just this risk. Forbes said, "Front and center were potential nuclear terrorist threats, not surprising given last week's Brussels attack and the terrorist's surveillance of nuclear scientists and facilities."[13] The third way that Islamists could push the world into full-scale holy war would be to assassinate the pope, and they hope to do so. "What has been declared by the self-declared Islamic State is clear—they want to kill the Pope. The threats against the Pope are credible …

"The Pope had made himself a target by speaking out against the human rights abuses committed against Christians in Syria and Iraq, as well as by his approval of attempts by the US to try to roll back Isil."[14] This threat was also alluded to by Donald Trump in the U.S. presidential campaign: "If and when the Vatican is attacked by ISIS, which as everyone knows is ISIS' ultimate trophy … "[15]

While the threat of terror is causing fear and anger, Islamic immigration into the West is also causing additional fear and anger. "I don't think this wave can stop," said Sonja Licht of the International Center for Democratic Transition. "The global north must be prepared that the global south is on the move, the entire global south. This is not just a problem for Europe but for the whole world."[16]

This combined threat of terror and mass immigration is causing a rapid rise in power of the far right and in anti-Islam sentiment in the Christian world. Although I have focused on the threat of the Sunni Islamic State, the Shia Islamists of Iran could also attack the Western world and lead into a holy war.

Shia Islamists continue to threaten military expansion and the development of nuclear weapons, all the while threatening to wipe Israel off the map. The worst-case scenario would be for Sunni and Shia Islamists to join together to fight against Israel and papal-led Christianity.

At the time of this revision, I see the "time of the end," or third and final conflict between Islam and Christianity, already in its early stages. I am expecting it to intensify and to truly become a holy war from both sides. Radical Islam will be defeated, moderate Islam will follow papal-led Christianity, and there will be a group of Muslims that joins with a group of true Christians to share the final

---

13   Forbes, "Fallout from the Nuclear Security Summit," April 3, 2016.
14   London Telegraph, "ISIL Want to Assassinate the Pope, Says Iraq's Ambassador to Vatican," September 16, 2014.
15   New York Times, "Donald Trump Calls the Pope's Criticism Disgraceful," February 18, 2016..
16   New York Times, "A Mass Migration Crisis, and it May Get Worse," October 31, 2015.

warning message with the world in the greatest evangelistic opportunity of all time.

The Good News!

Now let's look at the good news. Edom, Moab, and Ammon escape from the king of the North in the third conflict as recorded in Daniel 11:40-43. The Hebrew word translated as *escape* is also in Daniel 12:1, but is translated as *delivered*. Those who are delivered in Daniel 12:1 will be followers of Christ who are written in the book.

Revelation 17:8 reports that "all the world follows the beast, except those whose names are written in the Lamb's book of life." Since Edom, Moab, and Ammon do not follow the king of the North, then they must be followers of Christ. Additional proof comes from Hebrews 2:3, 4: "How shall we escape if we neglect so great a salvation, which at the first began to be spoken by the Lord, and was confirmed to us by those who heard Him … ?"

Concerning the time of Christ's return, we find the following in 1 Thessalonians 5:2, 3: "For you yourselves know perfectly that the day of the Lord so comes as a thief in the night. For when they say, 'Peace and safety!' then sudden destruction comes upon them, as labor pains upon a pregnant woman. And they shall not escape."

Repeatedly the Bible says that those who survive the coming of Christ are those who trust in Jesus, and so I interpret "escape" in Daniel 11:41 as referring to those who trust in Jesus. The groups listed as "escaping" this third holy war—Edom, Moab, and the prominent people of Ammon—were called the "people of the East" in Bible times (Isaiah 11:14). They were related to Abraham through Lot, Esau, and Ishmael. Could any of them be people of the Book, or Bible-believing Christians?

Before the time of David, God used the people of the East to chastise Israel for its idolatry and disobedience. During the reign of David, their territory formed part of the Davidic kingdom. In a similar way, after using Islam to chastise modern Israel (Christians), God rescues those Muslims who refuse

to follow the papacy and accept Jesus instead, and He includes them as a part of Jesus' restored "Davidic" kingdom.

While Scripture focuses on the blessing given Isaac, we must not forget that God also blessed Ishmael (Genesis 21:13, 18). If Gentiles can be sons of Abraham by being grafted in, why can't a Muslim person become a "son of Abraham" through faith in Jesus also?

Within Islam today is a growing movement of people who accept Jesus Christ as their Savior. They believe in Him as their judge and believe that He is coming back to rescue them. In fact, they are willing to die for Him and trust Him with their lives. I believe that among Muslims, this group that believes in Jesus is the "Edom, Moab, and the sons of Ammon" in Daniel 11.

Many of these have had dreams or visions of Issa (Jesus), and He tells them to trust in Him for their salvation and to follow The Book (Bible). In Joel 2:28-32 it says, "And it shall come to pass afterward that I will pour out My Spirit on all flesh; your sons and your daughters shall prophesy, your old men shall dream dreams, your young men shall see visions … before the coming of the great and awesome day of the Lord. And it shall come to pass that whoever calls on the name of the Lord shall be saved. For in Mount Zion and in Jerusalem there shall be deliverance."

In a similar way Revelation depicts a group of people who come out of the king of the North/papal-led Christianity who truly follow Jesus and the Bible. Revelation 18:4 says, "And I heard another voice from heaven saying, 'Come out of her (Babylon or papal-led Christianity), my people, lest you share in her sins, and lest you receive of her plagues.'"

Consider one more thing about those who escape. Daniel 12:1 tells us: "At that time your people shall be delivered, every one who is found written in the book." According to Revelation 17:8: "Those who dwell on the earth will marvel, whose names are not written in the Book of Life … when they see the beast." All the world follows the beast except those who are included in the book of life.

We just learned that when the beast power, the king of the North, wipes out Islam with its counterattack, a group from within Islam will escape. In Revelation, we either follow the Lamb or follow the beast. The ones who escape the beast must be following the Lamb.

That applies to Muslims as much as anyone else. Christians should not look down their noses at Islamic people. We should share Jesus with them—should love them, not hate them. If we did that on both sides, we could really do some good and might lead many to become our brothers and sisters in Christ.

The big problem is that Satan, the power from the bottomless pit, has stirred up the majorities on both sides, and he is causing havoc in the world. God's people get caught in the middle between the kings of the North and the South. His people always find themselves in that position and often get hit from both sides in the worldwide spiritual battle.

While the Smoke Rises

The papacy and its allies (possibly NATO) eventually overthrow Islam, and that leaves the papacy and the United States in control.

My understanding of Islam is that God will use it as a counterweight against the problems of Christianity. The showdown between the various powers will bring people within Islam to a decision point. Will they go with the radicals? Will they choose the example of secular Islam and support the papacy? Or will they accept Jesus Christ and truly follow Him?

Likewise, those within the Christian world will have to decide whether they will join those who follow the papacy or will obey God's Word in the Bible. At that time, a core group of people will gather from both Christianity and Islam, one that holds true to Jesus Christ. Stuck between north and south, they will suffer abuse from both sides at the time of the end.

This will be the time of the greatest evangelistic opportunity of all time! Radical Islam is gone and moderate Islam is following the king of the North (pretending to be Christian) while papal-led Christianity is trying to consolidate. For a short time there will be no one to stop true believers from both sides who choose to follow Jesus and His Word the Bible.

And I heard another voice from heaven saying, "Come out of her, my people, lest you share in her sins, and lest you receive of her plagues." Are you ready to stand for Jesus when everyone else is following a counterfeit?

In the next chapter we will examine the aftermath of this third and final holy war.

Chapter 9

TIDINGS FROM THE EAST AND THE MARK OF THE BEAST

News From the East

Daniel 11:44, 45 describes the final moments of the beast power, the little horn—the king of the North. What does it do in the last little bit of time? When armies are about to lose, typically their commanders throw everything they have into one last-ditch effort. That is what Satan and his followers try.

"News from the east and the north shall trouble him; therefore he shall go out with great fury to destroy and annihilate many. And he shall plant the tents of his palace between the seas and the glorious holy mountain; yet he shall come to his end, and no one will help him" (Daniel 11:44, 45).

What is the news from the east? The Bible spells out the news from the east. First we go to Ezekiel 43:1-9 and a voice from heaven: "Afterward he brought me to the gate, the gate that faces toward the east. And behold, the glory of the God of Israel came from the way of the east. His voice was like the sound of many waters; and the earth shone with His glory" (verses 1-4).

So far, the news from the east is the glory of God and His very loud voice. "The Spirit lifted me up and brought me into the inner court; and behold, the glory of the Lord filled the temple. Then I heard Him speaking to me from the temple, while a man stood beside me. And He said to me, 'Son of man, this is the place of My throne and the place of the soles of My feet, where I will dwell in the midst of the children of Israel forever.

"No more shall the house of Israel defile My holy name, they nor their kings, by their harlotry or with the carcasses of their kings on their high places. When they set their threshold by My threshold, and their doorpost by My doorpost, with a wall between them and Me, they defiled My holy name by the abominations which they committed; therefore I have consumed them in My anger. Now let them put their harlotry and the carcasses of their kings far away from Me, and I will dwell in their midst forever'" (verses 5-9).

The news is that God is coming and has had enough of the sins of His people. He wants to get rid of the abominations so he can come without destroying His people.

Consider in Revelation 7:2, 3 that the sealing arrives from the east. God's messages keep coming from the east. "Then I saw another angel ascending from the east, having the seal of the living God. And he cried with a loud voice to the four angels to whom it was granted to harm the earth and the sea, saying, 'Do not harm the earth, the sea, or the trees till we have sealed the servants of our God on their foreheads.'"

Right before the end of time, the angel will finish his sealing ministry. Those who are sealed have made their decision to follow God and His Word—the Bible—in all that they do. That means getting rid of the abominations, the sins of rebellion and disobedience. And the message comes from the east. It matches the call to clean up the abominations that we found in Ezekiel.

How about the direction of Jesus' return? Matthew 24:27 reports: "For as the lightning comes from the east and flashes to the west, so also will the coming of the Son of Man be." Jesus' return to earth is seen coming from the east. What could be better tidings from the east than a message to "clear up your abominations, get right with God, because Jesus is coming"? This is great news for a Christian!

Revelation 18:1-8 is John's account of that message from the east, and it is a repeat of Revelation 14. It is the last warning to the world to get ready for the appearance of Jesus. The powerful message fills the earth with light and glory. But it is not a new message. God has presented it often over time. However, this time heaven repeats it with great power, signified by the whole earth being illuminated by the glory of the angel.

Get Rid of Abominations

"After these things I saw another angel coming down from heaven, having great authority, and the earth was illuminated with his glory. And he cried mightily with a loud voice, saying, 'Babylon the great is fallen, is fallen, and has become a dwelling place of demons, a prison for every foul spirit, and a cage for every unclean and hated bird! For all the nations have drunk of the wine of the wrath of her fornication, the kings of the earth have committed fornication with her, and the merchants of the earth have become rich through the abundance of her luxury.'

"And I heard another voice from heaven saying, 'Come out of her, my people, lest you share in her sins, and lest you receive of her plagues'" (Revelation 18:4).

The plagues strike just before the very end, so this message also occurs just before the Second Coming. The plagues attack the king of the North/ little horn (the beast, the antichrist power) and destroy it. So in the chronology of Daniel 11 these tidings from the east happen shortly before the plagues but after the third battle with Islam. God wants His followers to flee the beast power and get away from it.

"For her sins have reached to heaven, and God has remembered her iniquities. Render to her just as she rendered to you, and repay her double according to her works; in the cup which she has mixed, mix for her double. In the measure that she glorified herself and lived luxuriously, in the same measure give her torment and sorrow; for she says in her heart, 'I sit as queen, and am no widow, and will not see sorrow.'

"Therefore her plagues will come in one day—death and mourning and famine. And she will be utterly burned with fire, for strong is the Lord God who judges her" (verses 5-8).

Just before the destruction of the king of the North, or the beast and its allies, God sends His final warning message: Get rid of abominations and separate from them. Right before the plagues, the message declares, "Come out of Babylon, the false church, and don't have anything to do with her."

I have said before that I believe countless people within the Catholic Church (or any entity supporting it) are true Christians. According to this verse, that is not where God desires for them to stay. He actually wants them to get out in the open and follow His Word.

The Lord wants you and me to be serious about honoring His Word and being a true Christian. Those who do not do so will end up following the beast right into the plagues—and that would be fatal. But those who trust God are sealed and will spend eternity with Jesus. And that will be wonderful!

News from the North

In Ezekiel 44:4-6 we find a warning and judgment against abomination. It echoes the loud cry we read about in Revelation 18, which was a repeat of Revelation 14.

"Then He brought me by way of the north gate to the front of the temple; so I looked, and behold, the glory of the Lord filled the house of the Lord; and I fell on my face. And the Lord said to me, 'Son of man, mark well, see with your eyes and hear with your ears, all that I say to you concerning all the ordinances of the house of the Lord and all its laws. Mark well who may enter the house and all who go out from the sanctuary.

"'Now say to the rebellious, to the house of Israel, "Thus says the Lord God: 'O house of Israel, let us have no more of all your abominations'"''" (verses 4-6).

This doesn't apply just to Old Testament Israel. Remember that the New Testament calls anyone who follows Jesus Christ an Israelite.

God is saying to Israel—New Testament Israel—"I am tired of your abominations. Get rid of them, or you're in trouble."

Eliminate the false teachings and follow the Bible and the Bible only. Satan is a usurper, because God is the true king of the North. The north was always His cosmic direction.

Look at what Isaiah 14 says: "How you are fallen from heaven, O Lucifer, son of the morning! How you are cut down to the ground, you who weakened the nations!

"For you have said in your heart: 'I will ascend into heaven, I will exalt my throne above the stars of God; I will also sit on the mount of the congregation on the farthest sides of the north; I will ascend above the heights of the clouds, I will be like the Most High.' Yet you shall be brought down to Sheol, to the lowest depths of the Pit'" (verses 12-15).

The news from the east (the direction of Jesus' coming) is all the messages that say to get rid of abominations, or sins. The tidings from the north, from the real king of the North, is the message that Jesus is right, that Satan is wrong, and that it is time to get rid of anything that comes between us and God.

A Furious Fight

The news brings the dark truth about the devil and the beast powers into the open. What do you think is Satan's response? We've already read in Daniel 11:44, 45 that he seeks to annihilate all that he can.

As Revelation 12:12 puts it: "For the devil has come down to you, having great wrath, because he knows that he has a short time." When Satan realizes that he has at last run out of time, his side will make their last-ditch effort, their final stand. They will fight furiously to eradicate God's people.

Revelation 13:11-17 describes the devastation committed by that second beast that we found to be the United States. "Then I saw another beast coming up out of the earth, and he had two horns like a lamb and spoke like a dragon. And he exercises all the authority of the first beast in his presence, and causes the earth and those who dwell in it to worship the first beast, whose deadly wound was healed.

"He performs great signs, so that he even makes fire come down from heaven on the earth in the sight of men. And he deceives those who dwell on the earth by those signs which he was granted to do in the sight of the beast, telling those who dwell on the earth to make an image to the beast who was wounded by the sword and lived.

"He was granted power to give breath to the image of the beast, that the image of the beast should both speak and cause as many as would not worship the image of the beast to be killed. And he causes all, both small and great, rich and poor, free and slave, to receive a mark on their right hand or on their foreheads, and that no one may buy or sell except one who has the mark or the name of the beast, or the number of his name."

Daniel 11 depicts the king of the North as authorizing the destruction. The book of Revelation shows how that power gets its authority from the beast and denies people the opportunity to buy or sell. If you are not allowed to buy or sell, that destroys you financially.

Daniel's beast destroys or annihilates or kills, and the Revelation beast does not allow buying and selling and kills if you do not go along with it. So the seal or mark of the beast is put on those who follow it. Both Daniel and Revelation present the same idea from slightly different perspectives.

Here is the choice all people face at that time. In the short term, you can go along with the beast and acknowledge its authority, so that you avoid persecution, but you end up lost forever. The other option is that you accept God's seal, and while you might be persecuted or die in the short term, you're going to end up living forever. Everyone is going to be in difficulty one way or another. But you have to choose.

Would you rather be in trouble with human beings or with God? I have made my decision, and I hope I stay true to that decision. I would rather face the wrath of fallen humanity than God. Why? Because He gives some extreme warnings about following the beast power.

A Warning about the Mark

"And another angel followed, saying, 'Babylon is fallen, is fallen, that great city, because she has made all nations drink of the wine of the wrath of her fornication.' Then a third angel followed them, saying with a loud voice, 'If anyone worships the beast and his image, and receives his mark on his forehead or on his hand, he himself shall also drink of the wine of the wrath of God, which is poured out full strength into the cup of His indignation.

"And he shall be tormented with fire and brimstone in the presence of the holy angels and in the presence of the Lamb. And the smoke of their torment ascends forever and ever; and they have no rest day or night, who worship the beast and his image, and whoever receives the mark of his name'" (Revelation 14:8-11).

The book of Revelation speaks of a seal and a mark. You want God's sign—the seal—not the beast's sign, the mark. Would any sane person want to receive the mark? God is pretty emphatic with that warning.

The people with the seal are following Jesus, because they love Him. "Here are those who keep the commandments of God and the faith of Jesus," says verse 12.

The pressure builds in Revelation 18:1-5. "After these things I saw another angel coming down from heaven, having great authority, and the earth was illuminated with his glory. And he cried mightily with a loud voice, saying, 'Babylon the great is fallen, is fallen, and has become a habitation of demons, a prison for every foul spirit, and a cage for every unclean and hated bird! For all the nations have drunk of the wine of the wrath of her fornication, the kings of the earth have committed fornication with her, and the merchants of the earth have become rich through the abundance of her luxury.'

"And I heard another voice from heaven saying, 'Come out of her, my people, lest you share in her sins, and lest you receive of her plagues. For her sins have reached to heaven, and God has remembered her iniquities.'"

The book of Revelation follows more of a cyclic rather than chronological pattern, and so we find the plagues described earlier in Revelation 16:2: "The first [angel] went and poured out his bowl upon the earth, and a foul and loathsome sore came upon the men who had the mark of the beast and those who worshiped his image."

The ones targeted by the plague are those who have the mark of the beast. The mark is a lot more than a number. It shows which power you are worshipping. Are you ultimately worshipping God, or are you worshipping human traditions and thus in effect worshipping Satan?

The Sign of Worship

In the chapter on Israel in Bible prophecy, we concluded that worship of the true God is the seal that shows that the Israel of faith—those who trust in Jesus Christ—are heirs of Abraham. We find that group of people described in Revelation 7:1-3 and 9.

"After these things I saw four angels standing at the four corners of the earth, holding the four winds of the earth, that the wind should not blow on the earth, on the sea, or on any tree. Then I saw another angel ascending from the east, having the seal of the living God. And he cried with a loud voice to the four angels to whom it was granted to harm the earth and the sea, saying, 'Do not harm the earth, the sea, or the trees till we have sealed the servants of our God on their foreheads'" (verses 1-3).

"After these things I looked, and behold, a great multitude which no one could number, of all nations, tribes, peoples, and tongues, standing before the throne and before the Lamb, clothed with white robes" (verse 9).

·Here we see God's people, His true Israel, at the end of time. They are the ones who survive the great tribulation. But they are not pure by their own works. Rather, they are forgiven because Jesus died to save them from their sins. As a result, they are saved by being washed by the blood of Jesus.

In Deuteronomy 11:18, God urges His people to bring His words into their minds as though they were a frontlet on their foreheads. Some of the Jews actually hung a little piece of Scripture in a leather box on their forehead between the eyes, but that is not what God meant. He was talking about having us put His Word into our mind and live by it. At the end of time, God's people are keeping all His commandments with their mind and heart and are following the faith of Jesus.

Likewise, the new covenant that we found in Jeremiah 31:31-33 was God's law being written in our hearts and our minds. Remember that the new covenant comes in the Old Testament, and it is about worship. We worship the Creator God who is the judge of all, or we worship the beast and ultimately Satan, who is behind the beast. So the seal of God or the mark of the beast ultimately indicates which one you are worshipping.

Shortly after the third conflict with radical Islam and its destruction, we will see a showdown over how serious we are about God's Word. On God's side are those who worship Him who made heaven and earth, worship in spirit and in truth, keep the commandments of God and have the faith of Jesus, have the seal on their forehead, and have the Father's name in their forehead.

On the beast's side are those who worship the beast and the beast's images, ascribe to the commandments and traditions of men, follow the teachings of Babylon, and have the mark of the beast and the beast's name in their forehead. In this showdown, everyone chooses a side.

The new covenant in Jeremiah 31 and Revelation thus speak of the same thing: God's people observing His commandments and having the faith of Jesus. Similarly, 1 John 5:3 declares: "This is the love of God, that we keep His commandments. And His commandments are not burdensome." That is not an Old Testament text but a New Testament one.

The Sign of the Sabbath

Ezekiel 20:12 identifies the sign that we are God's and that He is ours. "I also gave them My Sabbaths, to be a sign between them and Me, that they might know that I am the Lord who sanctifies them." He said that His sign or mark is the Sabbath.

We saw earlier that the king of the North shifted the day of the Sabbath from Saturday to Sunday, and that the king of the South established his primary day of public assembly and sermon on Friday. Satan is counterfeiting the Sabbath on both sides. Notice the words God announces in Exodus 31:13: "Surely My

Sabbaths you shall keep, for it is a sign between Me and you throughout your generations, that you may know that I am the Lord who sanctifies you."

Some claim that by observing the Sabbath we try to make ourselves holy, but exactly the opposite is true. God said that keeping the Sabbath is a reminder that it is He who renders us holy. It's interesting how human beings get that twisted around.

In ancient times, one form of a seal was an inscribed signet ring. The signer of an agreement would press the ring into wax or clay to authenticate a document. The seal of a king would show the name of the person, his title, and his territory. If you look through God's law—the Ten Commandments— you find that only one commandment has the seal of God in it.

Read it in Exodus 20:8-11: "Remember the Sabbath day, to keep it holy. Six days you shall labor and do all your work, but the seventh day is the Sabbath of the Lord your God." This identifies who God is.

"In it you shall do no work: you, nor your son, nor your daughter, nor your man-servant, nor your maidservant, nor your cattle, nor your stranger who is within your gates. For in six days the Lord made the heavens and the earth, the sea, and all that is in them, and rested the seventh day. Therefore the Lord blessed the Sabbath day and hallowed it." What is God's territory? He is the Creator of all and has "Lord God" as His title. And the Lord blessed the Sabbath day and hallowed it. There you have His seal in the fourth commandment.

Only one of the commandments starts out with the word "remember." If you had children and were giving them directions, and you wanted them to follow them carefully and were concerned lest they forget one of them, you would put the word "remember" in front of the one you thought that they might forget. Isn't it interesting that the one commandment God said to remember is, in fact, the commandment that most of the world has forgotten.

Revelation 12:17: "The dragon was enraged with the woman, and he went to make war with the rest of her offspring, who keep the commandments of God and have the testimony of Jesus Christ."

What does Satan especially target at the end? The seventh-day Sabbath. It is the one commandment that God said was His sign. It is His seal placed within the totality of the commandments.

God's people of faith get caught in the middle just like the land of Israel gets caught in the middle. The king of the north changed the Sabbath from Saturday to Sunday, the king of the south changed it to Friday, and God's people—His true  Israel—as they honor His Word, find themselves worshipping on the Saturday Sabbath, between the two days. Once again God's people get caught in the middle. "Here is the patience of the saints; here are those who keep the commandments of God and the faith of Jesus" (Revelation 14:12).

The people of God have to be patient while they are caught in the middle. They have to hang on to Jesus even though the going gets tough for a while.

When Revelation 14 warns about not receiving the mark of the beast, it declares that Satan's people do receive the mark while God's followers keep the commandments. It also says: "Fear God and give glory to Him, for the hour of His judgment has come; and worship Him who made heaven and earth, the sea and springs of water" (verse 7).

Does that last sentence sound familiar? It is a quote from Exodus 20, the fourth commandment! Here is God's seal once again. When the apostle John cites the Old Testament, he always does it for a reason, and he does it a lot.

He intends for you to realize: "Oh! The fourth commandment is an issue. God's people keep His commandments, and the fourth commandment, the seal of God, is a sticking point."

The Status of the Sabbath

In the beginning, God created the earth and then rested on the seventh day, and He blessed and sanctified that day (see Genesis 2:2, 3). When He brought Israel out of Egypt, He caused manna to fall six days a week, but on the seventh day, the Sabbath, it did not come. God put His approval on the seventh-day Sabbath at the beginning of the world, and He has never changed it.

People ask me, "If the Sabbath is God's seal, didn't He change it to Sunday in the New Testament?" Remember, a number of catechisms claim that the Roman Catholic Church had the authority to change the day of worship. But that is not what the New Testament presents.

For example: "And when the Jews went out of the synagogue, the Gentiles begged that these words might be preached to them the next Sabbath" (Acts

13:42). Many years after Jesus died and went back to heaven, the apostle Paul met with Jews and Gentiles on which day of the week? The seventh-day, Saturday, Sabbath. If the Sabbath had shifted to Sunday after Jesus died, then the New Testament church would have known about it. But they met on the seventh-day Sabbath.

What happened the next week? "When the congregation had broken up, many of the Jews and devout proselytes followed Paul and Barnabas, who, speaking to them, persuaded them to continue in the grace of God. And on the next Sabbath almost the whole city came together to hear the word of God" (verses 43, 44).

Paul and Barnabas did not say to the Gentiles, "Come back on Sunday. We will meet with the Jews next Saturday, and we'll meet with Gentile Christians on Sunday." No, they all gathered again on the seventh-day Sabbath.

This was not an isolated occurrence. "He reasoned in the synagogue every Sabbath, and persuaded both Jews and Greeks" (Acts 18:4). Paul met with the people "every Sabbath."

Seven verses later verse 11 comments: "He continued there a year and six months, teaching the word of God among them." Meeting every Sabbath for a year and a half indicates Paul's normal practice with Jew and Gentile. We find no alteration of Sabbath in the New Testament.

The most important clue to the status of the Sabbath comes from the example of Christ Himself while He lived on earth. All we have to do is go back to the practice of Jesus to decide if Sabbath is still the seventh day of the week or not. It is really pretty easy. He worshipped every week on the Sabbath (see Luke 4:16), so He put His seal of approval on the seventh day in His time.

Some of the confusion about the Sabbath comes from the days around Jesus' death. At the time of His death, the Jewish council member Joseph of Arimathea "went to Pilate and asked for the body of Jesus. Then he took it down, wrapped it in linen, and laid it in a tomb that was hewn out of the rock, where no one had ever lain before" (Luke 23:52, 53). He removed the body because Jesus had just died on the cross on a Friday.

"That day was the Preparation [day], and the Sabbath drew near. And the women who had come with Him from Galilee followed after, and they observed the tomb and how His body was laid. Then they returned and prepared spices and fragrant oils. And they rested on the Sabbath according to the commandment.

"Now on the first day of the week, very early in the morning, they, and certain other women with them, came to the tomb bringing the spices which they had prepared. But they found the stone rolled away from the tomb" (Luke 23:54-24:2). The stone no longer sealed the tomb because Jesus was not in it anymore. He had been resurrected.

Luke was not a Jew by birth. He was a Gentile physician, an educated man. If Jesus had changed the day of rest to Sunday, here would have been a wonderful chance for the Gospel writer to point out that the seventh-day Sabbath was the day that the Jews kept holy but that Christians would not be doing that anymore. But Luke does not say any such thing, and neither do the other New Testament writers. Instead, Luke announces that Jesus died on the preparation day, the day most people today call Good Friday. Then the Sabbath came.

The word is *Sábado* in Spanish. How did Spanish get the name "Sábado" for the seventh day? More than 100 different languages have a form of the term "Sabbath" for the name of the seventh day of the week. Is that an accident? I don't think so.

Jesus was resurrected on the first day of the week, today commonly called Easter Sunday. Luke does not say anything about a change of the Sabbath to that day. Actually his account proves that the Sabbath is the day between Good Friday and Resurrection Sunday, or the Saturday Sabbath!

The Jews have not lost track of the seventh day of the week, and they still say it is Saturday. Nor has God made any decree since the time of Jesus to transfer the holy day of God. We can be certain that Saturday is the biblical seventh day, which is the sign that we are God's and He is ours and that He sanctifies us.

As mentioned before, some people argue that if you honor the seventh-day Sabbath, you are trying to get to heaven by works. But the Bible says it is a sign of sanctification—that it is God that actually makes you holy. "He [God] has spoken in a certain place of the seventh day in this way: 'And God rested on the seventh day from all His works'" (Hebrews 4:4).

"There remains therefore a rest for the people of God. For he who has entered His rest has himself also ceased from his works as God did from His" (verses 9, 10). Sabbath-keeping is a sign that we stop our own works and trust in God's works.

At Creation, God made the world and then rested on the seventh day. When Jesus came to save us and to remake us, He died on the sixth day, rested in the tomb on the Sabbath, and then started working for us again on the first day of the week. So on both the Sabbath at Creation and the Sabbath at our redemption, He rested. The rest is now a symbol of the completed sacrifice of Jesus Christ. We don't do it on our own! He does it for us.

The Sabbath is not a sign of works, but rather of righteousness by faith and resting in His works. Some people have probably tried to work their way to heaven by observing Sabbath, but they have twisted what the Bible says. The Bible says that the Sabbath is a representation of trusting God for our salvation.

False Claims

The conflict raging on earth has only two sides. God's side worships Him who made heaven and earth. Serious about all of God's commandments, including the fourth, they follow the faith of Jesus, have the seal of God in their forehead, and have been forgiven and cleansed by God.

Then there is the beast's side of the conflict. As described in Daniel 11, the king of the North "attacks God's covenant" or law. In Daniel 7:25, the little horn intended to change times and laws, an act that ultimately becomes the mark of the beast and its claim of authority over Scripture. Repeatedly the papacy has offered this as the symbol of its religious power and sovereignty.

"The Pope is of so great authority and power that he is able to modify, declare, or interpret even divine laws. The Pope can modify divine law, since his power is not of man but of God, and he acts as vicegerent of God upon earth with most ample power of binding and losing his sheep."[1]

"What is the Third Commandment? Remember that thou keep holy the Sabbath day. Which is the Sabbath day? Saturday is the Sabbath day. Why do we observe Sunday instead of Saturday? We observe Sunday instead of Saturday because the Catholic Church transferred the solemnity from Saturday to Sunday."[2]

The church claims that it did that at the council of Laodicea in A.D. 360. That sure wasn't the time of Jesus, was it? Notice the following quote from a Roman Catholic church newsletter.

---

1   Translated from the Latin in F. Lucius Ferraris, "Papa, Articulus II," Prompta Bibliotheca: Canonica, Juridica, Moralis, Theologica, Ascetica, Polemica, Rubristica, Historica (Paris: J. P. Migne, 1858), vol. 5, pp. 25-29. Retrieved from www.aloha.net/~mikesch/ prompta.htm.
2   See Peter Geiermann, The Convert's Catechism of Catholic Doctrine (St. Louis: Herder Book Co., 1946), p. 50.

"Perhaps the boldest thing, the most revolutionary change the Church ever did, happened in the first century. The holy day, the Sabbath, was changed from Saturday to Sunday. 'The Day of the Lord' (*dies Dominica*) was chosen, not from any directions noted in the Scriptures, but from the Church's sense of its own power. The day of the resurrection, the day of Pentecost, 50 days later, came on the first day of the week. So this would be the new Sabbath. People who think that the Scriptures should be the sole authority should logically become Seventh-day Adventists and keep Saturday holy."[3]

Here, a Roman Catholic priest is saying that if you want to follow the Bible only, you should keep the Saturday Sabbath. I completely agree with the author. Again and again the Catholic Church has made such statements. They don't hide from it. The church claims to have the right to change God's Word. I should add that there are many Sabbath-keeping Christian groups besides Seventh-day Adventists.

The Catholic Record states bluntly: "The Church is above the Bible; and this transference of Sabbath observance from Saturday to Sunday is proof of that fact."[4]

In the late 1930s John O'Brien wrote a book called *The Faith of Millions*. In it he observed: "But since Saturday, not Sunday, is specified in the Bible, isn't it curious that non-Catholics who profess to take their religion directly from the Bible and not from the Church, observe Sunday instead of Saturday?

"Yes, of course, it is inconsistent; but this change was made about 15 centuries before Protestantism was born … They have continued the custom, even though it rests upon the authority of the Catholic Church and not upon an explicit text in the Bible. That observance remains as a reminder of the Mother Church from which non-Catholic sects broke away—like a boy running away from home but still carrying in his pocket a picture of his mother or a lock of her hair."[5]

When radical Islam attacks the papacy in Daniel 11:40 and the papacy and its allies conquer or overturn Islam, the papacy and its allies are in control. I'm suggesting that Sunday worship will be the sign of allegiance to the papal brand of Christianity.

---

3   *St. Catherines Catholic Church Sentinel, May 21, 1995, p. 1.*
4   *The Catholic Record, Sept. 1, 1923.*
5   *John A. O'Brien,* The Faith of Millions *(Huntington, Ind.: Our Sunday Visitor, 1974), pp. 400, 401.*

What better sign of their new allegiance to the papacy and the papal alliance than for moderate Muslims to show it by changing their day of worship from Friday to Sunday?

Some have pointed out to me that Islam really does not observe Friday as a holy day. That is true. However, Friday is, in practice, the special time for sermon and prayers. Muslims don't keep the whole day as holy.

But then neither do most Christians fully honor Sunday, either. They go to worship for an hour and then afterward do whatever they want. There's not much difference between Christian and Muslim worship times—it is just observing an hour or two as holy, not a day.

Keeping the first day of the week holy would be a good sign of allegiance to the beast power. God's people will honor Him by keeping the full Sabbath day holy, 24 hours from sundown Friday to sundown Saturday night.

Will the papal alliance try to enforce Sunday observance on the world? Yes, it will. The most recent Catholic catechism was written during the time of Pope John Paul II.

The person in charge of putting it together was Joseph Cardinal Ratzinger. Cardinal Ratzinger became Pope Benedict, so this catechism has authority in the Catholic Church. Here's what it says: "In respecting religious liberty and the common good of all, Christians should seek recognition of Sundays and the Church's holy days as legal holidays."[6]

The church would like to have civil laws to enforce its rules. I do not believe I am stretching things when I say I expect it to be a worldwide showdown between God's day and the one that the church says it wants laws to enforce. In the European Union religious leaders are already working to get their wish. Sunday laws are being urged there.

Jesus said in the Bible, "In vain they worship Me, teaching as doctrines the commandments of men" (Matthew 15:9; Mark 7:7). So if you are following human teachings, how good is your worship? It is in vain.

Ultimately, if you are following after the beast, you find you are following the dragon, Satan. You may not be worshipping quite the one you thought you were.

---

6   Catechism of the Catholic Church, *2nd ed. (Doubleday, 1995), p. 585.*

Not a Seventh-day Adventist Doctrine

Is the seventh-day Sabbath just a Seventh-day Adventist thing? No, we find many statements by others about the Sunday Sabbath being the mark of the beast. The concept did not originate with Seventh-day Adventists.

The furthest back I can find Sunday-keeping explained as the mark of the beast is more than 200 years before any Seventh-day Adventists existed.

In 1657 Thomas Tillam, a Protestant, wrote a book entitled *The Seventh-Day Sabbath Sought out and celebrated. Or, The Saints last Design upon the man of sin, with their advance of Gods first institution to its primitive perfection, being a clear discovery of that black character in the head of the little Horn, Dan. 7.25. The Change of Times & Laws. With the Christians glorious Conquest over that mark of the Beast, and recovery of the long-slighted seventh day, to its antient [sic] glory, wherein Mr. Aspinwal, may receive full answer to his late piece against the SABBATH.*

Right on the title page, Tillam describes the little horn in Daniel 7 and the change of times and laws. The papacy's claim is thus not a new discovery. It is a claim that the papacy has been making for a long time.

With the Christian's glorious conquest over the mark of the beast outlined right on the cover of the book, Tillam identified Sunday-keeping as the mark of the beast in 1657. (You can find it on my website, www.islamandchristianity.org.)

Remember that I said I would go back to the Reformers a lot? This is another example. What did the Reformers get for printing messages like this? Many of them suffered death for what they said.

People could get killed either by Islam or the papacy (it didn't much matter), but you actually had a better chance of survival with Islam than you had with the papacy if you preached these ideas. The coin from the Vatican pictured here shows a woman holding a cup. Coming out of the cup is a sunburst.

The Catholic Church says that it took as a new day of worship one that the pagan world regarded as the day of the sun. Church artists put halos around the heads of the saints, which is the solar-disk imagery familiar to those who worshipped the sun. Christians employed the trappings of the cult of Mithras, a religion that included elements of sun worship.[7]

Remember Constantine's coin when he made the league between Christianity and the pagan Roman Empire? It had an image of the sun god and the sun to which he added a cross symbolizing the league between the two. Yet Scripture regarded sun worship as an abomination (see Ezekiel 8:15-18).

What did Revelation 18 say? To get rid of the abominations and separate from them, lest you partake of the plagues. It is an important message to remember in light of Ezekiel 20:12: "I also gave them My Sabbaths, to be a sign between them and Me, that they might know that I am the Lord who sanctifies them."

The Real Spirit

God's law is a test of love and loyalty. Jesus said, "If you love Me, keep My commandments" (John 14:15). He did not say to observe the commandments so you can be good enough to go to heaven, but rather, "If you love Me, keep My commandments."

He went on: "I will pray the Father, and He will give you another Helper, that He may abide with you forever" (verse 16). The prerequisite for getting the real Holy Spirit was loving Jesus and honoring His commandments.

"The Spirit of truth, whom the world cannot receive, because it neither sees Him nor knows Him; but you know Him, for He dwells with you and will be in you" (verse 17).

Notice that the beast had a counterfeit of the Holy Spirit: the fire from heaven that worked signs and miracles and deceived the whole world. Scripture calls the second beast in Revelation 13 the false prophet, because it has the wrong spirit.

---

7   *The cult of Mithras appeared in the century before Jesus was born and remained strong in Roman society, especially among the civil service and military, into the fourth century A.D. The god Mithra was the sun, and the emperor his representative on earth. Franz Cumont, in The Mysteries of Mithras (1903), wrote: "They [worshippers of Mithras] also held Sunday sacred, and celebrated the birth of the Sun on the 25th of December" (p. 119). And: "Sunday, over which the Sun presided, was especially holy" (p. 105). The History of Christianity in the Light of Modern Knowledge (1903), notes: "It had so much acceptance that it was able to impose on the Christian world its own Sun-Day in place of the Sabbath, its Sun's birthday, 25th December, as the birthday of Jesus, its Magi and its Shepherds hailing the divine star, and various of its Easter celebrations" (pp. 73, 74).*

That power has its own traditions—human laws. If you follow them, you get the counterfeit spirit. But if you obey God's law because you love Him, you receive the real Spirit. Both the Sabbath and the Spirit are linked in Scripture as the seal of God.

What about people who unknowingly worship on the wrong day? "Truly, these times of ignorance God overlooked, but now commands all men everywhere to repent, because He has appointed a day on which He will judge the world in righteousness by the Man whom He has ordained. He has given assurance of this to all by raising Him from the dead" (Acts 17:30, 31).

Jesus, the one raised from the dead, is the judge. God takes into account ignorance (the King James Version says that He winks at it), so those people who do not understand, He forgives.

The context of Acts 17 is that God was overlooking the Gentiles' worship of idols when they did not understand that it was the wrong thing to do even though it was breaking one of His commandments.

The Bible explains that if you break one, you have violated them all (James 2:10-12). So which commandment we break does not matter. But when we disobey the commandment out of ignorance, God understands why.

If we love Him, and we are following Him according to what we know, He will accept that—but He does not want to leave us ignorant. He wants us to come to Him and to understand the truth before the judgment—before the end.

"The lawless one will be revealed, whom the Lord will consume with the breath of His mouth and destroy with the brightness of His coming. The coming of the lawless one is according to the working of Satan, with all power, signs, and lying wonders, and with all unrighteous deception among those who perish, because they did not receive the love of the truth, that they might be saved.

"And for this reason God will send them strong delusion, that they should believe the lie, that they all may be condemned who did not believe the truth but had pleasure in unrighteousness" (2 Thessalonians 2:8-12).

What is God saying here? At the end, each one of us will be following His Word because we love it—or if we don't, we are on the way to destruction. If we decide to be willingly ignorant, we have chosen to be led into deception and condemnation. Scripture gives a strong warning— a life-and-death warning.

The simple question is, Whom do we choose to follow: God or human traditions? Sometimes people tell me God won't care if I don't keep the Sabbath commandment. Look at what Jesus says, however, right after saying "If you love Me, keep My commandments." In verse 24 He says, "He who does not love Me does not keep My words."

Our actions show whether we are really loving and following Him. If we know what the Bible says and don't do it, that shows we value someone or something more than God.

Revelation 18:4, 5 tells us where we really need to be: "And I heard another voice from heaven saying, 'Come out of her, my people, lest you share in her sins, and lest you receive of her plagues. For her sins have reached to heaven, and God has remembered her iniquities?'"

Before the final destruction, I encourage you to separate from anything that is not biblical.

Surrounded by Support

As you get closer to Jesus return, you need a supportive fellowship or church family to keep you true to God's Word. "Let us consider one another in order to stir up love and good works, not forsaking the assembling of ourselves together, as is the manner of some, but exhorting one another, and so much the more as you see the Day approaching" (Hebrews 10:24, 25).

Do you want to belong to a fellowship that downplays biblical teaching and instead emphasizes human tradition? Beware of that! You need to surround yourself with those who will encourage you to follow all of God's Word and not just part of it. And do not continue in known, willful sin. "For if we sin willfully after we have received the knowledge of the truth, there no longer remains a sacrifice for sins" (verse 26).

In the third and final conflict, Islam will be divided three ways. Radical Islam will be destroyed, moderate Islam will follow papal-led Christianity, and a group of Muslims will take their stand with Christians that are truly following the God and the Bible, not human traditions.

Together, they will participate in the greatest evangelistic opportunity of all time. This is known as the tidings from the east and the north in Daniel 11 and as the loud cry in Revelation 18. Since Satan will be attacking God's people who keep the commandments, the Sabbath will be the sign that these people are really following God, not the papal system that claimed to have changed the day of worship to Sunday.

Just as before, this also fits on the map. The Christians that stand firm are bringing the message from the north and Edom, while Moab and Ammon, the Muslims who support Jesus and the Bible, are to the east of Jerusalem.

Humanity will divide into those loyal to God, and those who align themselves with fallen humanity. Those who follow the dragon, and those who follow Jesus Christ. Which side do you choose?

Your actions speak louder than your words. Such love for God—to obey His commandments—is not burdensome. Choose well, because it is right after this that the king of the North—the little horn, the man of sin, the beast—is destroyed. You don't want to perish with it. I encourage you to follow God. Follow His Word—all of it.

Chapter 10

WHEN MICHAEL STANDS UP

The Rescue Begins

We have seen how Satan has been working in the world and how God's people found themselves caught between the kings of the North and South. At the end of Daniel 11, the king of the South comes to its end.

The king of North—the papal beast power—claims all authority, and when his power is challenged, he will destroy and annihilate many. The mark of the beast—a criterion that allows people to buy or sell—comes into play, and people face death unless they have the mark.

Finally, God annihilates the beast power—the king of the North. As we get past the last moments of the king of the North-beast power, we begin to see in Daniel 12 the rescue and reward of God's people. I know the relief and joy to be rescued. I and my group of eight were once rescued by a park ranger after being stranded in flood waters at near freezing temperatures.

However, this is nothing compared to seeing Jesus when He comes to rescue His people from earth. Daniel 12 gives the picture of how it will happen: "At that time Michael shall stand up" (Daniel 12:1). Daniel 10, 11, and 12 repeatedly mention Michael, the prince of the covenant, the great prince.

Martin Luther and the Reformers, as well as the early church, taught that Michael is Jesus Christ, and I agree with them. Dr. Frances N. Lee, Professor Emeritus of systematic theology and church history at Queensland Presbyterian Theological Seminary, says: "The dominant Pre-Mediaeval view was that [Jesus] the Second Person of the Triune God Himself is 'The Angel of the Lord.'[Michael] This mainline traditional view of the Early Church was rediscovered by the Protestant

Reformation and stressed also by Calvin, and later by Matthew Henry, Haevernick, Keil, etc."[1] How do we know this is true?

The name Michael means "one who is like God," but does that mean Michael is God? Scripture also calls Michael the archangel (Jude 9), but "archangel" does not require that someone be a created being. Rather, He is commander of the angels.

When Joshua was outside the Israelite camp, he met someone who said He was the commander of the Lord's host (see Joshua 5). Joshua fell down and worshipped Him, and the Being accepted his worship. Earlier, the Angel of the Lord met Moses at the burning bush. Moses asked, "Who are you?" and God said from the bush, "I AM" (see Exodus 3).

Read these passages carefully. In both Hebrew and Greek, the word translated "angel" has a dual meaning—and here it does not mean a created being, but rather God's message or messenger.

Note how Hosea 12:1 equates the Angel of the Lord with God. "And in his strength he (Jacob) struggled with God. Yes, he struggled with the Angel and prevailed…. That is, the Lord God of hosts. The Lord is His memorable name."

We know that it was God who made the covenant with the nation of Israel, but Judges 2:1 says that it was the Angel of the Lord who made the covenant with Israel. John Calvin, in the notes on Daniel 12:1 in the Geneva Bible, said that Michael is Jesus Christ. Martin Luther was clear in his belief that Jesus was, in this instance, called an angel, and I agree with Luther.

Michael the Archangel is Jesus Christ, the Son of God, the second person of the Trinity, the one who has always been God. If we understand Michael the Archangel, the great prince, to be Jesus Christ, then we see Jesus in Daniel 11 and 12. As usual it was the papacy that changed the teachings of the early church. Pope Gregory the Great, who died in A.D. 604, first brought into the church the teaching that Michael was not Jesus.[2]

"And there shall be a time of trouble, such as never was since there was a nation, even to that time. And at that time your people shall be delivered, every one who is found written in the book" (Daniel 12:1). God sent 10 plagues when He delivered ancient Israel from Egypt. That was a time of great trouble—but because of

---

1   See www.dr-fnlee.org/docs/witaotl/witaotl.pdf.
2   Ibid.

the plagues, God's people were delivered. The book of Revelation describes the time of trouble, or tribulation, near the end of the world, and it likewise involves plagues.

Verse 2: "Many of those who sleep in the dust of the earth shall awake, some to everlasting life, some to shame and everlasting contempt." Jesus comes to earth, and He resurrects those who died trusting in Him. "Those who are wise shall shine like the brightness of the firmament, and those who turn many to righteousness like the stars forever and ever" (verse 3). After their rescue, God's people live and reign with Him forever!

"But you, Daniel, shut up the words, and seal the book until the time of the end; many shall run to and fro, and knowledge shall increase" (verse 4). We have seen that the last showdown is between the kings of the North and South. This, however, was a prophecy that would be grasped only at the time of the end. In our day, everything should be fitting together, and we can begin to interpret the prophecy.

When verses 40 and following happen (and they have been unfolding during the past several years), understanding comes. Have you ever tried to explain two things occurring at the same time? Since you can really only explain one at a time, eventually you find yourself having to say, "This one happens, but then this other thing happens at the same time."

I have previously shown how Daniel 11:1–12:3 is sequential, but we find an exception in the last verse of chapter 11 and the first verse of Daniel 12. As I studied them, I came to the conclusion that Daniel 12:1 overlaps with Daniel 11:45. That is why Daniel starts out chapter 12 by saying, "At that time." The last segment was verse 45, which is the period after the third Islam-versus-Christianity conflict. At that same time, God starts to deliver His people, and the deliverance begins with Michael standing up.

As you can see in the table below, at the time of the tidings from the east, the king of the North goes out to annihilate as many as possible, and then he himself is destroyed in verses 44 and 45. Immediately after Michael stands up, we experience the time of trouble—the tribulation and the plagues.

Revelation 16 ties the destruction of the beast power (the little horn, the king of the North) to the events right at the end of the plagues. In Daniel 11:45 the king of the North reaches its end. Revelation tells us this is at the conclusion of the plagues, so Michael's standing up occurs just before the king of the North ceases to exist in verse 45. I have said all along that the Daniel 11 prophecy is sequential, and it is, except for those events that happen simultaneously and are pointed out as such by Daniel himself.

Why Michael Stands Up

Why does Daniel 12:1 say that Michael "stands up"? Think back over the prophecies. Did Jesus ever sit down at some previous time? If He sat down before, then we know when He started something. Now, when He stands up, we know that whatever He started to do when He sat down has been completed.

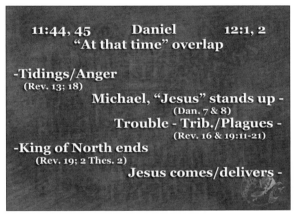

11:44, 45   **Daniel**   12:1, 2
"At that time" overlap

-Tidings/Anger
(Rev. 13; 18)

     Michael, "Jesus" stands up -
     (Dan. 7 & 8)

     Trouble - Trib./Plagues -
     (Rev. 16 & 19:11-21)

-King of North ends
(Rev. 19; 2 Thes. 2)

     Jesus comes/delivers -

Consider some reasons you might stand up. You would stand up when you are done with eating a meal, or you could stand up if you were upset about something. In this case I believe Jesus is done with something and He is upset.

At the end of Daniel 11 God's people face annihilation by the king of the North. Jesus stands up to put an end to it and rescue His people. Jesus apparently did something similar at the stoning of Stephen in Acts 7:56,[3] which was the end of the 70 weeks for the nation of Israel. At the end of the time of judgment, Jesus stands up for His people.

Now we turn to Daniel 7, which helps us to see what has been happening since Jesus went back to heaven. The beast power is on the earth, doing what the prophecy predicted.

"After this I saw in the night visions, and behold, a fourth beast, dreadful and terrible, exceedingly strong. It had huge iron teeth; it was devouring, breaking in pieces, and trampling the residue with its feet. It was different from all the beasts that were before it, and it had ten horns" (verse 7).

Rome's pagan aspect was about to metamorphose into a religious form, the papacy. Verses 8 and 9: "I was considering the horns, and there was another horn,

---

3   *Stephen said: "Look! I see the heavens opened and the Son of Man standing at the right hand of God" (Acts 7:56)!*

a little one, coming up among them, before whom three of the first horns were plucked out by the roots. And there, in this horn, were eyes like the eyes of a man, and a mouth speaking pompous words."

We have heard before about the little horn and the pompous words. While he is uttering his blasphemous words and thinking he's really something when he's not, we read verses 9 and 10: "I watched till thrones were put in place, and the Ancient of Days was seated." The little horn beast thinks he is someone really special, but while he's thinking that, something is going on in heaven, and it does not bode well for the little horn beast. Somebody is being seated. But who is it?

The Ancient of Days is God the Father. "His garment was white as snow, and the hair of His head was like pure wool. His throne was a fiery flame, its wheels a burning fire; a fiery stream issued and came forth from before Him. A thousand thousands ministered to Him; ten thousand times ten thousand stood before Him. The court was seated, and the books were opened" (Daniel 7:9, 10). The little horn is about to be judged.

"The books were opened" refers to the kind of judgment book mentioned in Daniel 12:1, which speaks about those inscribed in the book. Likewise, in Revelation it is the Lamb's book that God will consult to make judgment.

Notice that while this is going on in heaven, the beast power is still on earth doing its evil deeds. "I watched then because of the sound of the pompous words which the horn was speaking" (verse 11). It does not know that its days are numbered. The beast power is being judged and found wanting, just like the king of Babylon at the end of the Babylonian Empire. Then "I watched till the beast was slain, and its body destroyed and given to the burning flame" (verse 11). That is the same description as we find at the end of Daniel 11.

"As for the rest of the beasts, they had their dominion taken away, yet their lives were prolonged for a season and a time" (verse 12). Every one of the previous beasts, when its power ended, continued on in some form. We still have Greece today, Babylon in the form of Iraq, and Persia as Iran. They still existed in some form after the end of their prophetic kingdoms. But when the little horn beast power ends, it will completely cease to exist. For the little horn, when it's over, it's completely over.

Verses 13 and 14: "I was watching in the night visions, and behold, One like the Son of Man, coming with the clouds of heaven! He came to the Ancient of Days, and they brought Him near before Him." Jesus enters the judgment chamber to meet the Father, and He arrives on clouds. This tells me the heavenly courtroom is huge! Millions of angels stand in it. The courtroom is set up, Jesus arrives, and He sits down on the judgment throne and joins the judicial session.

"Then to Him was given dominion and glory and a kingdom, that all peoples, nations, and languages should serve Him. His dominion is an everlasting dominion, which shall not pass away, and His kingdom the one which shall not be destroyed" (verse 14). Jesus, the King of kings, receives His kingdom in heaven before He comes to claim it on earth.

Daniel 7:26, 27 repeat the sequence for explanation and emphasis. "But the court shall be seated, and they shall take away his [little horn's] dominion, to consume and destroy it forever. Then the kingdom and dominion, and the greatness of the kingdoms under the whole heaven, shall be given to the people, the saints of the Most High. His kingdom is an everlasting kingdom, and all dominions shall serve and obey Him."

Here are the people whom Jesus delivers when He stands up. When Jesus comes, He presents the kingdom to His people. He has not given it yet, because not everybody on earth is serving and obeying God. In fact, most people are not.

At a particular time, then, a judgment was set up, or "seated," in heaven. Near the end of time it will take place in heaven while simultaneously the beast is causing havoc on earth. I'm suggesting that as Daniel 12:1 indicates, when the judgment concludes, Jesus stands up. He comes to rescue His people and bring them the dominion and power that He just received from His Father.

When that happens, it is all over for the little horn, because his destruction quickly follows. We do not know its exact time, but it accompanies the little horn's last stand (as we learn from Daniel 7 and from further details in Daniel 8).

Destruction of the Little Horn

Daniel 8 reveals the path and behavior of the little horn power from its inception to the final days of its destruction. This passage must match the Daniel 11 scenario. "And out of one of them came a little horn which grew exceedingly great toward the south, toward the east, and toward the Glorious Land" (Daniel 8:9).

Some people argue that one of the Seleucid kings, Antiochus Epiphanes IV, is the little horn power. However, Antiochus' kingdom shrank during his reign and did not grow as described in the verses, so he cannot be the little horn.

"And it [the little horn] grew up to the host of heaven; and it cast down some of the host and some of the stars to the ground, and trampled them. He even exalted himself as high as the Prince of the host" (verses 10, 11). The Prince of the host is Jesus, the commander of the host who accepted worship from Joshua (Joshua 5:14).

"And by him [the little horn] the daily sacrifices were taken away" (Daniel 8:11). The sacrifice of Jesus that is available to us every day was subverted by the teaching that a sinner must come to the Catholic Church to be forgiven. The papacy claims to control who is a saint in heaven—who makes it and who does not. It asserts that it has authority over the powers of heaven.

"He cast truth down to the ground. He did all this and prospered" (verse 12).

The End of the 2,300 Days

"Then I heard a holy one speaking; and another holy one said to that certain one who was speaking, 'How long will the vision be, concerning the daily sacrifices and the transgression of desolation, the giving of both the sanctuary and the host to be trampled underfoot?'

"And he said to me, 'For two thousand three hundred days [evenings and mornings in the Hebrew, meaning it is one of those symbolic situations, not one of the terms for normal days]; then the sanctuary shall be cleansed.'

"Now it happened, when I, Daniel, had seen the vision and was seeking the meaning, that suddenly there stood before me one having the appearance of a man. And I heard a man's voice between the banks of the Ulai, who called, and said, 'Gabriel, make this man understand the vision.' So he came near where I stood, and when he came I was afraid and fell on my face; but he said to me, 'Understand, son of man, that the vision refers to the time of the end'" (Daniel 8:13-17).

At the end of Daniel 8 the prophet has literally become sick because he does not understand what the 2,300 days means. He has heard a time prophecy without a beginning point, and he desperately seeks to find out what it means.

He is also thinking about another time prophecy, given when he was a young man, saying that the exiled Israelites would remain in Babylonian captivity for 70 years. At the end of the 70 years they would be able to go back to Jerusalem. Now Daniel is an old man, and he knows it is time to return. But he hears something about 2,300 days and then the sanctuary being cleansed. Does that mean it will be 2,300 days/years before the Israelites get their Temple back? That thought overwhelms him.

In Daniel 9:24 and following he receives an answer. "I've come to give you an understanding of the vision," an angel announces. He will reassure the prophet that the 70-year prophecy would be fulfilled as promised and provide Daniel with understanding of both the 70-week prophecy and the 2,300-day prophecy.

The angel begins to explain that 70 weeks, or 490 years, had been designated for the time after the 70 years in exile. The 70 weeks, or 490 years, are set for the Israelites, during which Christ makes an end of sin and brings in everlasting righteousness. The angel dates the 70 weeks, or 490 years, from the decree that would order the restoration of Jerusalem following the 70 years of exile.

Daniel has just received the key to both the 70-week and 2,300-day prophecies: They have the same starting date. The Daniel 9 prophecy was cut off from (meaning simultaneous with) the longer one of Daniel 8. The starting point for both is the decree to restore Jerusalem in 457 B.C. (see Ezra 7).

The prophecy declares that after 2,300 days, or years, the sanctuary will be cleansed. What does that mean? To understand the cleansing of the sanctuary, we must read about the Day of Atonement in Leviticus 16:30-33: "On that day the priest shall make atonement for you, to cleanse you, that you may be clean from all your sins before the Lord. It is a sabbath of solemn rest for you, and you shall afflict your souls. It is a statute forever.

"And the priest, who is anointed and consecrated to minister as priest in his father's place, shall make atonement, and put on the linen clothes, the holy garments; then he shall make atonement for the Holy Sanctuary, and he shall make atonement for the tabernacle of meeting and for the altar, and he shall make atonement for the priests and for all the people of the congregation."

In ancient Israel, the Day of Atonement was a time of judgment. It was a day on which all confessed sins were cleansed and erased from the record. The Day of Atonement was one day a year when the high priest made a cleansing atonement, not just for one person's sin, but for all the people and for the Temple, or sanctuary, itself. It was a symbol of how salvation works.

Although the priests offered animal sacrifices back then, the sacrifice really pointed to Jesus. The high priest is also Jesus. This shows how Jesus cleanses us from sin.

On any other day of the year, when an Israelite had sinned, they approached the door of the sanctuary with an animal sacrifice. They would place their hands on the animal and confess their sins, then the lamb or other animal representing Jesus died for the sin, and the person was forgiven through the blood of the sacrifice. The sacrifice symbolized Jesus Christ dying on the cross.

The blood of the sacrifice depicted sins being brought to God for Him to deal with in heaven, where Jesus is our high priest. To understand better how this works, read the book of Hebrews. The whole book is about Jesus acting as our high priest in the heavenly tabernacle. The earthly tabernacle was only a model of what God showed Moses of the heavenly one (see Exodus 25). Moses viewed the heavenly reality, and when he built the tabernacle, he was building a representation of the real thing in heaven.

The individual Israelite's record of sin had been placed on the sacrificial animal and transferred to the sanctuary. The guilt of the sin was taken on into the sanctuary and deposited in the holy place, where the smoke symbolizing the prayers went over into the Most Holy Place, thereby taking the record of sin—the guilt of sin—and storing it up for God to deal with. The Israelite at the entrance walked away free, because the sin was now God's problem, not his. By faith the Israelite was forgiven.

On the once-a-year Day of Atonement the high priest entered the holy place, the second room in the tabernacle. He took all of the sins of the year and symbolically placed them on a goat called the "scapegoat."

That act cleansed the tabernacle of sin and made it clean again. Someone took the scapegoat far away from the Israelite camp so that it could never return. This symbolized God's forgiveness for the sin and cleansing of the sin from the tabernacle. God held that sin, and all the others presented to Him, until Jesus Christ Himself deals with it as our sacrifice and high priest.

When Jesus died, rose again, and went back to heaven, He said He was going to sit down at the right hand of the Father. In the illustration of the sanctuary above, notice the table of shewbread: two stacks of bread, six pieces of bread per stack.

Model of the Heavenly Sanctuary
Exodus 25:9 and Hebrews 8:1, 2

I suggest that the table of shewbread represents the throne of God. After all, Jesus said, "If you've seen Me, you've seen the Father" (see John 14:9). There are two piles of bread, and they are seated side by side on the throne, a fitting symbol of the throne room in heaven. Revelation 4 pictures Jesus in a room in the sanctuary, and He is on the throne with the Father.

But which room is it? Before the throne is a seven-branched candlestick (verse 5). That tells us He is in the outer room of the sanctuary. Here are the Father and the Son, sitting together, and here is the Holy Spirit, depicted by the fire. On the day of atonement—the day of judgment—they move into the Most Holy Place, to the mercy seat or judgment seat. In Daniel 7 the Ancient of Days, the Father, sits down, showing that the Trinity has advanced to the next phase of salvation ministry. And Jesus joins Him.

The high priest entered the holy place only on the Day of Atonement, the day of cleansing. The prophecy given to Daniel said, "For two thousand three hundred days; then the sanctuary shall be cleansed" (Daniel 8:14). This indicates when the special time of cleansing begins in the heavenly sanctuary as the Father and Son sit down. And remember, this happens while the little horn is still active on earth.

The 70-week prophecy started in 457 B.C.: 457 (the date of the decree to rebuild Jerusalem in Ezra 7) + 70 weeks = A.D. 34, and 457 + 69 weeks = A.D. 27. The latter calculation brought us from the decree to rebuild Jerusalem in 457 B.C. to Jesus' baptism in A.D. 27. Jesus was cut off in the middle of the last week (A.D. 31). The end of the time period for the exclusivity of the Jewish nation was A.D. 34. That explains the 490 years given in the prophecy.[4]

What about the 2,300-day period we saw earlier that begins at the same time? If we add 2,300 days (years) to 457 B.C., it brings us to A.D. 1844.

What was supposed to happen in 1844? Would it be something taking place on

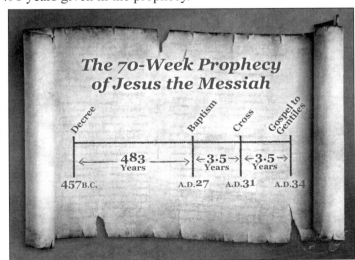

The 70-Week Prophecy of Jesus the Messiah

Decree · Baptism · Cross · Gospel to Gentiles

483 Years → ←3.5 Years→ ←3.5 Years→

457 B.C.   A.D. 27   A.D. 31   A.D. 34

---

4   *See chapter 1 of this book for a detailed description of the 70 weeks.*

earth that year? No, because the prophecy says that the cleansing takes place in the heavenly judgment room/Most Holy Place while the little horn is still active on earth. The little horn continues to run around exercising his power during the judgment, so the judgment is not taking place on earth.

You recall that when Jesus died, the veil of the earthly Temple that shielded the Most Holy Place was torn in two from top to bottom. Because of His death, the animal sacrifices on earth no longer applied—they were no longer needed.

From this we know that Daniel's prophecy of the 2,300 days indicates a heavenly sacrifice. Jesus died for us as the Lamb of God, and He is now serving in heaven as both priest and sacrifice. It is His blood that cleanses our sins, and He is ministering, or applying, it for us in the heavenly sanctuary.

When Jesus left this earth, He told the Jews: "See! Your house is left to you desolate" (Matthew 23:38). In Daniel 9:27 we are told the temple would be desolate even to the "consummation," and I believe that the consummation is the time that Jesus returns for His people. As far as God is concerned, there will be no more sacrifices that He will honor in an earthly temple.

For us to offer such sacrifices would be blasphemy, because it would mean denying that Jesus Christ was the sacrifice! It would be right up Satan's alley, though, to claim something false like that.

I do not know if there ever will be another Temple in Jerusalem, as some are expecting. But if it is built, it will never be God's temple, because He said He was going to leave it desolate until the consummation. While the Dome of the Rock and the Mosque of Omar occupy the site of the former Temple, it is desolate from the viewpoint of scripture.

According to Daniel 8:17, the prophecy that begins with the decree to rebuild Jerusalem after the Exile will extend to "the time of the end."

Look what happens when we graph the power of the papacy and the power of Islam together. I call it their political power curve.

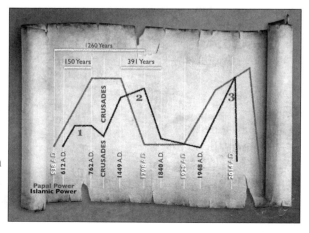

In Daniel 7 and 8, the little horn acts with power both before and during the judgment. On the political power curve chart, the judgment commences right in the valley between the second conflict and the third and final conflict, at or during the time of the end. The judgment starts, and the little-horn/king of the North power regains its power and causes havoc simultaneously with the judgment taking place in heaven.

When Jesus came to the Ancient of Days, it was not to this earth. He went to where the Father was—the next part of that heavenly sanctuary.

Just think of everything that sprang up on earth during this time period, however. This era saw the emergence of Communism, the theory of evolution, Mormonism, and countless other movements.

One in particular, called the Millerite movement, preached that Jesus would return to earth in 1844, the natural end of the 2,300-year prophecy. But they were not alone.

Sir Isaac Newton, a scientist fascinated with eschatology, believed that too! The Reformers also taught that something connected with the last days might happen during the mid-1800s.

How did the Millerites and others misunderstand the relationship of Daniel 8 and the second advent of Jesus? They saw, in Daniel 7:13, Jesus coming to the Ancient of Days with clouds, and they assumed that since Christ arrives with clouds when He returns to earth, that verse must indicate the Second Coming.

They missed the detail in Daniel 7 and 8 that He was going in to the Ancient of Days in the clouds, not to the earth. The little-horn power was still actively doing its activities on the earth.

And so the Millerites, and others before them, misinterpreted the prophecy's identification.

The Millerites were historicists, which means that they believed that prophecy is in a process of fulfillment from the time it was written to the final end of the age. They were following the methods of the Reformers.

Unfortunately, Protestants soon began looking for a different way of viewing prophecy, and they switched to futurism, which believes that all or most of prophecy represents an end-time fulfillment, with little applying now—and thus they ignored historicism.

You don't have to follow what the Millerites taught about the Second Coming in 1844, though, to be a historicist. You can believe that Jesus actually started the judgment in heaven at that time.

We can see, then, that according to Daniel 7 and 8, the judgment in heaven and the time of the end started in 1844, at the end of the 2,300 years, when the court was seated to judge the little-horn beast and to cleanse the sanctuary from sin. The judgment and the "time of the end" concludes when Jesus stands up in Daniel 12.

We have a beginning date of 1844 that inaugurates the time of the end, and we have an ending time, a date not known by anyone, when Jesus stands up and finally rescues His people by bringing the kingdom and power to them. That is exactly what Daniel 7 says the judgment is for.

Now we need to see if we can find the same thing in the New Testament. Is there any evidence there of a judgment taking place before Jesus' second coming?

Consider Revelation 14:6, 7: "Then I saw another angel flying in the midst of heaven, having the everlasting gospel to preach to those who dwell on the earth—to every nation, tribe, tongue, and people—saying with a loud voice, 'Fear God and give glory to Him, for the hour of His judgment has come; and worship Him who made heaven and earth, the sea and springs of water.'"

Clearly there is a time on earth when Jesus' judgment is already in process before He returns. "And another angel followed, saying, 'Babylon is fallen, is fallen, that great city, because she has made all nations drink of the wine of the wrath of her fornication'" (verse 8).

What is the result of the judgment in heaven? Just as in Daniel 7 and 8, it deals with the little horn/the beast/the papacy, here symbolized by Babylon.

"Then a third angel followed them, saying with a loud voice, 'If anyone worships the beast and his image, and receives his mark on his forehead or on his hand, he himself shall also drink of the wine of the wrath of God'" (verses 9, 10).

That's what the judgment involved—pronouncing and implementing the divine verdict against the beast and those who followed it. We see the same thing in the New Testament.

Who is the judge? Again in the New Testament, John 5:22, 27 says: "The Father judges no one, but has committed all judgment to the Son ... because He is the

Son of Man." Ultimately, the judge is Jesus. Entering the presence of the Ancient of Days, He joins the tribunal, and the Father lets Him do the judging.

Acts 17:30, 31 confirms it: "Truly, these times of ignorance God over-looked, but now commands all men everywhere to repent, because He has appointed a day on which He will judge the world in righteousness by the Man whom He has ordained."

Again, who is the judge? Jesus. And again it says that He has appointed a day on which He will judge the world. Daniel 8:14 designates when judgment will begin, which starts the "time of the end" scenario. After that time, both Islam and the papacy commence their climb back up from their loss of political power. They think they are doing really well, but the judgment announces that their days are numbered.

At the end of those days, as the judgment in heaven winds down, the last message from the east goes out: "Come out of her, my people" (Revelation 18:4)—get away from Babylon, flee from the beast/king of the North power. Satan knows his time is running out, and he tries to annihilate all that he can because he realizes that the judgment is almost finished.

If God is our judge in the heavenly investigation, then who seeks to prosecute us? Revelation 12:10 says: "Then I heard a loud voice saying in heaven, 'Now salvation, and strength, and the kingdom of our God, and the power of His Christ have come, for the accuser of our brethren [called the devil and Satan in verse 9], who accused them before our God day and night, has been cast down.'" Satan is the accuser. He tempts us to sin and then reminds God the wages of sin is death.

In every court case the defendant finds himself or herself standing before the judge, awaiting the verdict. But we have good news. It will either be us or Jesus as the defendant when our cases come up. We get to choose which one goes on trial.

"We must all appear before the judgment seat of Christ, that each one may receive the things done in the body, according to what he has done, whether good or bad" (2 Corinthians 5:10).

We are not saved by our works, but the verse tells us that we stand judged according to our deeds. If we have one sin on our record, the heavenly court may not be a good thing for us, unless … and here comes that good news again. Before we get to that, though, we need to focus on the reality that all of us will face judgment.

I have heard people say that if you are a believer in Christ, you are not under judgment. But that is not what the apostle Peter said. "The time has come for judgment to begin at the house of God" (1 Peter 4:17). God's house is His Israel, the Old and New Testament people of faith, so the judgment starts with believers. But that is a good thing if you really understand it.

Since the judgment "begins with us first, what will be the end of those who do not obey the gospel of God? Now 'if the righteous one is scarcely saved, where will the ungodly and the sinner appear?' Therefore let those who suffer according to the will of God commit their souls to Him in doing good, as to a faithful Creator" (verse 19). God will be faithful to get you through the judgment.

Romans 8:1: "There is therefore now no condemnation to those who are in Christ Jesus, who do not walk according to the flesh, but according to the Spirit." While God's people will undergo judgment first, they do not find themselves condemned. The phrase "in Christ" is very important. Remember the saved people in Revelation who are wearing a white robe? Jesus offers us His righteousness when we ask for forgiveness, and He cleanses us and gives us His righteousness. His life/record covers our life/record when we ask Him to take our place. It is no longer I but Christ living in me, as Paul puts it.

So here's the key. We ask Jesus to take control of our lives, and then it is no longer us but Christ living in us. When our case is called in the judgment, it is not our record but His that appears there. As long as we let Him take our case, we win! Now we can begin to see how the court is set up in our favor. That is really good news.

Finally, who is the defense attorney in the courtroom? "My little children, these things I write to you, that you may not sin. And if anyone sins, we have an Advocate with the Father, Jesus Christ the righteous" (1 John 2:1). An advocate is a defense attorney, and ours is Jesus Christ Himself.

Let's review the lineup in the celestial courtroom. The judge is Jesus, the accuser is Satan, the defendant is either me or Jesus, and the defense attorney is Jesus if I let Him take my case.

What kind of law operates in the divine court? The New Testament tells us that clearly it is the Ten Commandments. "For whoever shall keep the whole law, and yet stumble in one point, he is guilty of all. For He who said, 'Do not commit adultery,' also said, 'Do not murder.' Now if you do not commit adultery, but you do murder, you have become a transgressor of the law. So speak and so do as those who will be judged by the law of liberty" (James 2:10-12).

John 14:15-17 reminds us: "If you love Me, keep My commandments. And I will pray the Father, and He will give you another Helper, that He may abide with you forever, even the Spirit of truth." The commandments mentioned there are the Ten Commandments—do not kill, don't commit adultery. In other words, all of them. That is the foundation. So we know which law is being applied in the heavenly court.

Are the Ten Commandments really a law of liberty? Yes, they are. Imagine what life would be like if everyone followed the Ten Commandments. The fact that they don't means you are not at liberty to believe everything you are told. Nor are you at liberty to safely walk any street at any hour of the day or night. People do not follow God's law. If they did, you could safely go on any street at any time, believe everything that you're told, and not need a key or a lock. That would be heaven.

And you can be sure that God's laws will be practiced in heaven. His people will obey every one of them, including the Sabbath commandment. "And it shall come to pass that from one New Moon to another, and from one Sabbath to another, all flesh shall come to worship before Me, says the Lord" (Isaiah 66:23).

In the new heaven and the new earth, the Sabbath commandment still applies. If anyone was not following God's law in heaven you would still need locks and could not believe everything you hear.

Either reward or punishment is the result of the judgment. Jesus said: "Behold, I am coming quickly, and My reward is with Me, to give to every one according to his work" (Revelation 22:12).

There it is again! Make sure you are trusting in Christ so you can be rewarded for His works in place of yours!

Hebrews 10:26, 27 tells us that "if we sin willfully after we have received the knowledge of the truth, there no longer remains a sacrifice for sins, but a certain fearful expectation of judgment, and fiery indignation which will devour the adversaries."

Remember the Day of Atonement? If an Israelite had, earlier in the year, offered a sacrifice for a sin and afterward they no longer cared about God has His law, on the Day of Atonement their guilt went back on them. If you accept Jesus Christ as your Lord and Savior, but deliberately reject following God and part of God's law and continue to live in sin, your guilt is still with you.

Hebrews says that if I ask for forgiveness and then I later stubbornly persist in deliberate sin, I lose my forgiveness, the sacrifice for sins. Jesus will not cover willful sin. He will cover ignorant sin, as seen in the continuous sacrifice given for those who did not know they were sinning, but He cannot overlook deliberate continued sin in the judgment.

Each person will receive either reward or punishment: reward if they are trusting and obeying Jesus, punishment if they willfully refuse to trust and obey Him.

The reality is that when Jesus rewards His people, He is rewarding them for His (Jesus') perfect life in place of ours, and He is rewarding us for all the good that the Holy Spirit has done through us. The reward is the result of Jesus replacing our sinful record with His perfect record.

The Judgment Ends

Right now the judgment is still going on in heaven. According to the 2,300-day prophecy, the judgment in heaven began in 1844, and it does not end until just before the plagues. How do I know that it ends then? Daniel 12 tells us that immediately before the time of trouble, Michael stands up. The book of Revelation presents the same events. Look at Revelation 14:7; 22:11; 15:8; and 16.

"For the hour of his judgment has come" (Revelation 14:7). The judgment has been going on in heaven, and then Revelation 22:10, 11 describes how the process reaches an end.

"Do not seal the words of the prophecy of this book, for the time is at hand. He who is unjust, let him be unjust still; he who is filthy, let him be filthy still; he who is righteous, let him be righteous still; he who is holy, let him be holy still." A decree comes from heaven that the judgment is over. Everyone has made up his or her mind. With all people's final choice made, Jesus stands up.

When does that decision to end the judgment happen? It is not during the time of the tidings from the east, because the loud cry urges, "Come out of her, my people." During the period of the loud cry, God is still offering forgiveness and cleansing to any who want it, so the end of the judgment occurs after that point.

In Revelation 15:8 we find that "the temple was filled with smoke from the glory of God and from His power, and no one was able to enter the temple till the seven plagues of the seven angels were completed."

Right now our forgiveness is taking place in the heavenly sanctuary, the temple in heaven. At the beginning of the plagues we will no longer be able to come to Jesus to ask for salvation. Why not? Because Jesus has finished His work there. He has stood up because all the decisions have been made and His ministry is complete. It happens right before the plagues in Revelation 15:8.

We know that the judgment has closed in heaven just before the plagues because Revelation 16 says the plagues are poured out on those who have the mark of the beast, and no one changes his or her mind during the time of the plagues or after. Instead of confessing their sins, the wicked curse God. During the plagues both the righteous and the filthy remain as they were before.

Strange as it may seem, this fact is really good news for us. If I am a sinner, and I am, I'm a forgiven one. When my case goes to the court in heaven, Jesus is the judge. Satan makes an accusation against me.

At this point I have a choice. I can defend myself and my record, or I can say, "Jesus, how about putting Your record in place of mine?" It is no longer me but Christ in me. I say to Him, "Jesus, You're in charge." And now Christ's record is the one on trial. How many sins does Jesus have in His record? None! I am going to be OK!

But it gets even better. The defense attorney is Jesus. How would you feel about going into a courtroom if your defense attorney was also the judge? The deck is stacked in your favor. You are not going to get a hung jury here—there is no jury. The judge rules in this courtroom.

What happens if I decide to represent myself and present my own case? In that situation Jesus is still the judge. Satan accuses me, and he has a strong case against me.

I have to be the defense attorney and defend myself, because I have rejected Jesus Christ. The law is the Ten Commandments, and it says that I am guilty. And the wages of sin is death! The result for me is punishment.

The person who accepts Jesus Christ as His attorney and lets Him be the defendant comes out of the judgment sentenced to eternal life with Jesus. I love the judgment! It sets me free from Satan, and it frees me from the little-horn/king of the North/beast that thinks he is ruling the world right now. Since I believe I'm going to be sentenced to live with Jesus forever, I'm willing to accept that verdict!

Thus the judgment is not a bad thing. It is good news for everyone who is written in the Lamb's book of life. Everyone who continues to love and serve Jesus Christ and has allegiance to Him has their name included in the Lamb's book of life.

It's important to note that the judgment has a definite time period. Twice the New Testament tells us that a date was set for the judgment to begin, and the prophecy fixing the date appears in Daniel 8. The end of the 2,300 years from the decree to rebuild Jerusalem brings us to 1844, and that date inaugurates the time of the end.

According to that prediction, the judgment would go on until just before the plagues. That is when Jesus stands up. The smoke of God's presence fills the heavenly sanctuary, and the righteous and the wicked have made their final and permanent choice of what they will always be. Jesus has been waiting until the very last moment, hoping for a chance to cleanse your record and mine.

Then, when He stands up, He is not saying arbitrarily, "Time's up!" He has given every warning message He could, and He has let the world get into all kinds of trouble to allow people time to decide, and finally the last individuals have made their decision. Then He can declare, "That's it! There is no point in waiting anymore—it's done! I'm getting up, and I'm coming to rescue My people."

Chapter 11

THE WORST-EVER TIME OF TROUBLE

We saw in the previous chapter that a judgment convenes in heaven and that the court is in session. When Michael stands up just before the time of trouble, the judgment is over.

The heavenly temple is the place in which Jesus Christ has been working out our salvation, and when He is finished there, He declares, "Let the righteous be righteous still, and the filthy be filthy still" (see Revelation 22:11). It is done! We have all made our choices, one way or the other.

"After these things I looked, and behold, the temple of the tabernacle of the testimony in heaven was opened. And out of the temple came the seven angels having the seven plagues … Then one of the four living creatures gave to the seven angels seven golden bowls full of the wrath of God who lives forever and ever. The temple was filled with smoke from the glory of God and from His power, and no one was able to enter the temple till the seven plagues of the seven angels were completed" (Revelation 15:5-8).

The plagues begin to fall. When they do, no one changes sides. The wicked get only angrier at the God they refuse to follow and God's people dig in deeper and hang on to Him.

The time of the plagues is parallel to Daniel's time of trouble and will be worse than anything the world has ever experienced. Once it has passed, we will be able to look back and see that it was the most terrible period of earth's history.

Daniel 12:1 describes it as "a time of trouble such as never was," but it is followed by deliverance. It is part of God's process for rescuing His people. "At that time Michael shall stand up, the great prince who stands watch over the sons of your people; and there shall be a time of trouble, such as never was since there was a nation, even to that time. And at that time your people shall be delivered, every one who is found written in the book." I want to be deliberate about being found in God's book. Don't you?

The Bible talks about the time of trouble in a variety of places, and we will look at them in this chapter. We need to see how the Bible sheds light on this tumultuous period.

Exodus and Revelation both speak about plagues followed by deliverance. When God's people were in Egypt, 10 plagues befell the Egyptians, and then deliverance came. The book of Revelation presents a series of seven plagues and then deliverance.

In Exodus 5:5 Moses summons the Israelites to worship God and rest. Pharaoh protests: "You make them rest from their labor!" As slaves, they had been forced to work seven days a week. Pharaoh was not going to let them off work. When Moses assumed the leadership of Israel, he got them back into the "rest mode," back into a Sabbath cycle. In Revelation, God summons people to worship the Creator: "Worship Him who made heaven and earth, the sea and springs of water" (Revelation 14:7). That is a quote from the Sabbath commandment. So we have a call to worship and rest in both Exodus and Revelation.

God instructs Moses: "Go to Pharaoh and say to him, ' … Let My people go, that they may serve Me'" (Exodus 8:1). God called His people out of Egypt. In Revelation 14 and 18:4 He summons His people out of Babylon. "Come out of her, my people, lest you share in her sins, and lest you receive of her plagues" (Revelation 18:4). The call out of Babylon is just like the call out of Egypt. Do you see the similarities?

Here is another parallel. In Exodus 11:4-7 we find a "death warning" before the deliverance. Revelation 14:9-11 also has a "death warning" before deliverance. Both warnings were not for God's people, but rather for those who opposed them.

Exodus 11 says: "Then Moses said, 'Thus says the Lord: "About midnight I will go out into the midst of Egypt; and all the firstborn in the land of Egypt shall die … But against none of the children of Israel shall a dog move its tongue, against man or beast, that you may know that the Lord does make a difference between the Egyptians and Israel"'" (verses 4-7).

Similarly, we find a death warning right before deliverance in Revelation 14: "Then a third angel followed them, saying with a loud voice, 'If anyone worships the beast and his image, and receives his mark on his forehead or on his hand, he himself shall also drink of the wine of the wrath of God, which is poured out full strength into the cup of His indignation. And he shall be tormented with fire and brimstone in the presence of the holy angels and in the presence of the Lamb'" (verses 9, 10).

The firstborn sons in Egypt perished, and at the end of time anyone who has the mark of the beast likewise faces a death penalty, or worse—fire-and-brimstone punishment.

The last seven plagues in Egypt targeted particular people, and the seven plagues in Revelation focus on certain people also. While the first three Egyptian plagues may have affected both Israelites and Egyptians, during the last seven plagues, only Egyptians suffered, not the Israelites.

For example, Exodus 8:22 announces: "And in that day I will set apart the land of Goshen, in which My people dwell, that no swarms of flies shall be there." The differentiation was so that the Egyptians would recognize that the Lord was the God of Israel. When Moses pronounced a death penalty, it would hit only the Egyptians, so that they would understand that the Israelites were following the Lord God.

We find a similar parallel with Revelation's seven last plagues. Revelation 16:2 portrays the first plague: "So the first went and poured out his bowl upon the earth, and a foul and loathsome sore came upon the men who had the mark of the beast and those who worshiped his image."

It targeted those who had the mark of the beast. If you want to be delivered from the plagues, don't follow the beast and get his mark.

The psalmist David wrote about God's people going through this very difficult time in Psalm 91. He points out that we will see the result of what happens to the wicked, but the plagues will not afflict us.

"He who dwells in the secret place of the Most High shall abide under the shadow of the Almighty. I will say of the Lord, 'He is my refuge and my fortress; My God, in Him I will trust.' . . . A thousand may fall at your side, and ten thousand at your right hand; but it shall not come near you. Only with your eyes shall you look, and see the reward of the wicked. Because you have made the Lord, who is my refuge, even the Most High, your habitation, no evil shall befall you, nor shall any plague come near your dwelling; for He shall give His angels charge over you, to keep you in all your ways" (verses 1-11).

Many have taught that God would remove His people from the earth at this time, because surely they could not remain here lest they suffer the plagues. Hal Lindsey taught this in The Late, Great Planet Earth years ago.

The important question, though, is: Were God's people living in Egypt during the time of the plagues? Yes. Did they suffer the last seven of those plagues? No, because God has good aim! Likewise, at the end of time, in the book of Revelation, God has good aim. He targets only those who have the mark of the beast. Psalm 91 tells us that God's people, His Israel of faith, will see the results of the plagues, but the plagues will not come near them.

So what does this tell us? That God has perfect aim, and that He will not remove His people from this world before the plagues. After the model of the plagues in Egypt, the end-time plagues in the terrible time of trouble are part of the setup to deliver God's people. They are aspects of the deliverance process.

What about the conditions that God's people will endure as they go through this? It will not be easy for them. Jeremiah 30:7 talks about "Jacob's trouble." Remember, anyone who has faith in Jesus is an heir of Abraham and is thus part of the Israel of faith. If you belong to God's Israel, then you are a child of Jacob. Jeremiah 30:5-7 describes the experience that His people will go through.

"For thus says the Lord: 'We have heard a voice of trembling, of fear, and not of peace. Ask now, and see, whether a man is ever in labor with child? So why do I see every man with his hands on his loins like a woman in labor, and all faces turned pale? Alas! For that day is great, so that none is like it; and it is the time of Jacob's trouble, but he shall be saved out of it.'"

Jeremiah explains that after the period of trouble, God will save or deliver His people. Guess what happens right after the trouble in Daniel 11? God's people are delivered! Jeremiah 30 continues explaining.

"'For it shall come to pass in that day,' says the Lord of hosts, 'That I will break his yoke from your neck, and will burst your bonds; foreigners shall no more enslave them. But they shall serve the Lord their God, and David their king, whom I will raise up for them'" (verses 8, 9).

Who is "David their king" whom God raises up for us? Jesus Christ, the son of David. Why are the people of God living through such a terrible time of trouble? Two reasons: One, the king of the North is furious, and he seeks to destroy anyone who refuses to receive his mark. If people are trying to kill you, would it be just a little bit stressful for you? Satan's people are trying to annihilate God's

160

people. Just as Egypt was difficult for the Israelites, God's people experience a difficult time right before the deliverance.

A second reason that God's people go through the time of trouble is the questions that it raises. Once the plagues start being poured out, and you realize that everything has been settled in heaven, one of the first questions that will come to my mind (and I'll bet to yours too) is, "Have I made everything right with God?"

By then it is too late to change. It is crucial that we confess our sins now and trust Jesus for forgiveness now. We also need to practice placing our assurance in God and not in ourselves. God's people will then be relying completely on the Holy Spirit.

What's really interesting is that during this time, God's people are filled with the Spirit and living by His power, and they know that it is vital to do so. On the other hand, Satan's people have totally rejected the Spirit. The two groups have become polar opposites.

Notice that God's people are not on their own at this time. But instead of cleansing them from sin, Jesus is now keeping them clean from sin by the indwelling Spirit, because He has ended the judgment in heaven.

Revelation 16:1 declares: "Then I heard a loud voice from the temple saying to the seven angels, 'Go and pour out the bowls of the wrath of God on the earth.'" Let's take a look at the various plagues. Each one strikes at some different aspect of the beast power, or false worship.

The first plague is described in verse 2: "So the first went and poured out his bowl upon the earth, and a foul and loathsome sore came upon the men who had the mark of the beast and those who worshiped his image."

We have already gone past the time of the "tidings from the east and the north." The king of the North has already become infuriated and inflicted death and destruction upon those who are resisting.

Suddenly those following the beast are getting nasty, horrible sores all over them. We don't know at this point if it is a worldwide plague of sores, but toward the end of the plagues people still continue to suffer from them.

The second plague is as follows: "Then the second angel poured out his bowl on the sea, and it became blood as of a dead man; and every living creature in the sea died" (verse 3). Suppose when you were at the beach one day the waves turned from clear water into bloody water and began to stink as dead fish floated to the surface. That would get people's attention, wouldn't it?

Verse 4 describes the third plague: "Then the third angel poured out his bowl on the rivers and springs of water, and they became blood." Somebody opens the tap in the morning to get a drink of water, and they fill their glass with blood.

Notice verses 5-7: "And I heard the angel of the waters saying: 'You are righteous, O Lord, The One who is and who was and who is to be, because You have judged these things. For they have shed the blood of saints and prophets, and You have given them blood to drink. For it is their just due.' And I heard another from the altar saying, 'Even so, Lord God Almighty, true and righteous are Your judgments.'"

"You've been killing My people, shedding their blood!" God reminds them. In the past, the king of the North/beast power, the papacy, was a persecuting power for more than 1,000 years. At the end of time, the beast is a persecuting agency again.

God says, "You are bloodthirsty? OK, drink blood. Get what you want. You say you are out to get the blood of My people? Have some blood to drink." And the angels say, "God, that is fair."

Do the people with the mark of the beast change their minds once the plagues strike? No, not at all. Jesus has already announced, "Let the righteous be righteous still, and the filthy be filthy still" (see Revelation 22:11). Jesus has already stood up from the judgment seat, and everybody's case has already been decided.

The fourth plague is as follows: "Then the fourth angel poured out his bowl on the sun, and power was given to him to scorch men with fire. And men were scorched with great heat, and they blasphemed the name of God who has power over these plagues; and they did not repent and give Him glory" (verses 8, 9). This fourth plague causes the people of the beast to be burned by the sun.

Remember, the people of the beast are during this time enforcing a death penalty on anyone who does not worship on Sunday, the "day of the sun." God says, "You want the sun? OK, I'll turn up the heat. I'll give you a little more sun!"

The fifth plague: "Then the fifth angel poured out his bowl on the throne of the beast." Where's the throne of the beast? It could be the Vatican. Remember, though, that in Daniel 11, at the end, before the beast's destruction, he moves to the "Glorious Land" and sets up the tents of his headquarters there. So his throne could be situated in either Israel or the Vatican. I'm not sure which it will be.

"Then the fifth angel poured out his bowl on the throne of the beast, and his kingdom became full of darkness" (verse 10). The people have been complaining, "We're tired of the burning sun!" God says, "OK, no more sun." And this marks where the problem is. Spiritual darkness is what the papacy has given the world. God turns that location dark, wherever that headquarters is.

"And they gnawed their tongues because of the pain. And they blasphemed the God of heaven because of their pains and their sores, and did not repent of their deeds" (verse 11). They still have their sores here during the fifth plague.

I don't know how long the plagues take, but I don't want to be suffering the pain of sores during that time. I would rather be one of God's people during this period.

The sixth plague is described in verse 12: "Then the sixth angel poured out his bowl on the great river Euphrates, and its water was dried up, so that the way of the kings from the east might be prepared."

The United States military crossed the river Euphrates a few times during different battles in Iraq. Is the river Euphrates a major challenge for a modern-day military operation? No, not at all. I suggest that this is probably symbolic at the end of time, especially when you consider that Babylon sits on the Euphrates River, and Babylon in Revelation is a spiritual power.

There's historical background to the waters drying up in Babylon. Note the comparisons between the experiences of ancient Israel and spiritual Israel.

- The book of Jeremiah tells us that Babylon oppressed God's ancient people. In Revelation 17 Babylon also persecutes God's people.

- In Daniel 3 God's ancient people were forced to worship an image. In the end-time, God's people also find themselves being compelled to worship an image.

- In Daniel 4:30 Nebuchadnezzar refers to his empire of Babylon (the enemy of God's people) as "great." Revelation 17:5, at the end of time, calls the final enemy of God's people "Babylon the Great."

- In the Old Testament Babylon "sits on many waters" (Jerermiah 51:12, 13). In Revelation, at the end of time, Babylon "sits on many waters" (see Revelation 17:15 where it says the water represents people).

- In Isaiah 44 in the Old Testament God rescues His people by the drying up of the Euphrates River. Revelation 16:12 also tells us that God will rescue His people by the drying up of the river Euphrates.

- In Jeremiah 51 God summons His people out of Babylon. In Revelation 18:4 they are called to "come out of her" (Babylon) at the end of time.

- In the Old Testament Isaiah 45 calls Cyrus the anointed one when it predicted his rescue of ancient Israel. Daniel 9 refers to the coming New Testament divine rescuer as the Messiah, the anointed one. Jesus the Messiah is the rescuer who comes at the end as well.

- In Isaiah 45 both rescuers emerge from the east. Cyrus came from the east in the Old Testament. In the New Testament Jesus comes from the east for the final rescue.

Revelation 16 continues: "And its water was dried up, so that the way of the kings from the east might be prepared. And I saw three unclean spirits like frogs coming out of the mouth of the dragon" (verses 12, 13).

We have a lot of symbols running through this particular plague. The dragon is a symbol for Satan, the beast is the symbol of the papal system, and the false prophet, we discovered, is the United States in prophecy. "For they are spirits of demons, performing signs, which go out to the kings of the earth and of the whole world, to gather them to the battle of that great day of God Almighty" (verse 14).

Verse 15 announces something very significant: "Behold, I am coming as a thief. Blessed is he who watches, and keeps his garments, lest he walk naked and they see his shame." The reason I emphasize "coming as a thief" is that we are going to talk about the timing in that statement.

Many prophecy students today talk about Jesus coming "as a thief" before the time of tribulation and the plagues. But right there between the sixth and seventh plagues, Jesus says He is coming as a thief. That is not past tense. It means at the time of the sixth plague He is about to come as a thief. This is a very important distinction to make.

What happens next? Revelation 16:16 explains: "And they gathered them together to the place called in Hebrew, Armageddon." Satan's people—God's enemies—are starting to lose their cohesiveness, and Satan has to reassemble his forces because they are all suffering from those plagues. They are starting to get tired of listening to the beast and the dragon and enduring the plagues. Now they come together for a final battle at a place called Armageddon.

Have you heard the idea that the final battle will take place on the Plain of Megiddo? I have visited it. The place is rather small for a major worldwide battle. Revelation does not say the plain or valley of Megiddo; verse 16 says "Har Megeddon," which means the Mountain of Megiddo. That is not the Plain of Megiddo. But a mountain sits right alongside the Plain of Megiddo, and it is called Mount Carmel. That is where a showdown took place between the prophets of Baal and the prophet Elijah—and the God of heaven won.

What did we just see in Revelation 16? That Satan's forces have gathered for a showdown with God. At issue is: Who is the real God? Who is the real power? The struggle is for the divine throne. Satan says, "I am going to take God's place."

"For you [Satan] have said in your heart: 'I will ascend into heaven, I will exalt my throne above the stars of God; I will also sit on the mount of the congregation . . . I will be like the Most High'" (Isaiah 14:13, 14). It is Satan's last-ditch effort, because he is losing.

The plagues are not going well for his side. This is a battle for the throne just before Jesus comes, a struggle between the true Trinity and the false trinity. Go back to the fall of ancient Babylon for a moment. Babylon was located on the Euphrates River, and the river went right through the city with a moat around most of it.

THE CITY OF BABYLON

When the Medes and the Persians besieged the city of Babylon, the ruler of Babylon decided to show his contempt for them by hosting a feast.

During the feast, he had the sacred cups and bowls from God's Temple in Jerusalem brought out for his guests to drink wine from.

Suddenly a disembodied hand wrote this on the wall: "MENE, MENE, TEKEL, UPHARSIN" (Daniel 5:25). Nobody could read it. The ruler brought in the prophet Daniel, and Daniel interpreted the inscription: "You have been weighed in the balances and found wanting. This night your kingdom will be taken from you" (see verses 26-28).

As Daniel spoke, the armies of Cyrus the Persian, led by his general Gobryas, encircled the city. Now, Daniel was no dummy. He must have known that Isaiah had predicted that someone named Cyrus would attack Babylon and conquer it (see Isaiah 45). Just as Daniel knew the prophecies, we need to know the prophecies too, or we will be blindsided, as the people in Babylon were.

Daniel said to the king, "Your kingdom will be taken from you." Tradition tells us that Cyrus diverted the river through a canal he excavated. He then sent his army marching right under those gates that were over the river, and they got inside. That same night the Persian army marched into the palace and killed the ruler of Babylon.

The nation of Babylon fell because of the drying up of the river Euphrates. At the time of the end, spiritual Babylon falls because of a drying up of the river Euphrates. The people who had supported the false trinity now begin to abandon it. Satan has to reorganize everything and hype everything up again to get his people to gather for the final struggle with God.

Finally, we come to the seventh and last plague: "And the seventh angel poured out his vial into the air; and there came a great voice out of the temple of heaven, from the throne, saying, It is done. And there were voices, and thunders, and lightnings; and there was a great earthquake, such as was not since men were upon the earth, so mighty an earthquake, and so great.

"And the great city was divided into three parts, and the cities of the nations fell: and great Babylon came in remembrance before God, to give unto her the cup of the wine of the fierceness of his wrath. And every island fled away, and the mountains were not found.

"And there fell upon men a great hail out of heaven, every stone about the weight of a talent: and men blasphemed God because of the plague of the hail; for the plague thereof was exceeding great" (Revelation 16:17-21, KJV).

God's wrath is being poured out as hailstones weighing 75 pounds each. Such hailstones would come crashing through the roof, right through you, and right on down to crack the floor—if you happen to have the mark of the beast. But if you don't have the mark of the beast, they smash into something beside you and do not hit you. I do not want to have the mark of the beast in that kind of hailstorm.

I believe that the seventh plague is the beginning of Christ's return. You will find descriptions of His return in Revelation 6 and 19, and both of them reveal that Jesus Christ Himself finishes pouring out the wrath of God. What are the plagues? The wrath of God.

Revelation 6:14, describing God's response to the slain martyrs' plea for justice, tells us: "Then the sky receded as a scroll when it is rolled up, and every mountain and island was moved out of its place."

It is part of a description of the Second Coming (see verse 17). During the seventh plague in Revelation 16, the islands and mountains are also moving around as Jesus is about to make His grand appearance.

Chapter 12

THE FALSE PROPHET EXPOSED

Picture the armies of Satan massed together to fight against God. "The kings of the earth, the great men, the rich men, the commanders, the mighty men" (Revelation 6:15) have gathered to fight, and Jesus comes for the fight and rescues His people. He arrives to enforce God's plan.

The armies on the earth have all the military might of the world ready to fight against Jesus and His host of angels. Revelation 19:11 depicts Him riding a white horse. I can imagine NASA getting a signal that something unidentified is approaching earth through space—Jesus and His millions of angels.

I can picture the military leaders of the world planning the redirection of their nuclear weapons, no longer aimed at each other but at whatever this phenomenon in space is. If they did launch a nuclear weapon, the lead angel would just laugh. He would grab the little nuclear missile, turn it around, and throw it back.

According to the Bible, terror spreads among the wicked when they see Jesus coming closer. See what it is like for them: "The kings of the earth, the great men, the rich men, the commanders, the mighty men, every slave and every free man, hid themselves in the caves and in the rocks of the mountains, and said to the mountains and rocks, 'Fall on us and hide us from the face of Him who sits on the throne and from the wrath of the Lamb! For the great day of His wrath has come, and who is able to stand'" (Revelation 6:15-17)?

Remember what is happening during the seventh plague and while Jesus is coming? The mountains rise and collapse and islands shift out of their place. The people scream, "Let the rocks and mountains fall on us," and God says, "You get your wish." Revelation 19 says that all those mighty men and all the slaves and everyone else end up dead.

Jesus' coming is the worst thing that the wicked could face, and it is the best thing that God's people could hope for. It depends on whether you are 100 percent filled with the Holy Spirit or have nothing of Him.

People ask me, "Pastor, will Jesus' return happen before the time of tribulation [worst-ever time of trouble], or after the tribulation?" You may be thinking, "I didn't know there was a discussion on that topic."

Some people believe in Jesus' arrival before the time of trouble/tribulation, and some believe that He will appear after the trouble/tribulation. I get questions about this all the time. We are going to answer that now. Does Jesus make His appearance before, during, or after the plagues and the time of tribulation?

The members of the early Christian church believed that an antichrist would arise. Paul said it was already starting in his day. A time of tribulation and plagues would come, but it would be of an indefinite duration.

They did not have a time set for it, and they did not apply the last seven years of the 70-week prophecy to the tribulation, as some do today. During those early years, Christians believed that they would be present on earth during the plagues and the tribulation.

The time of trouble/tribulation will end with the second coming of Christ at the time of the seventh plague. That is when Jesus will return. His arrival will be visible to all, a resurrection of the saved will take place, and His coming will start the millennium, the 1,000 years for God's people to be with Him in heaven. A variety of early church teachers taught much of this during the first and second centuries.[1]

During the Protestant Reformation, the Reformers taught almost the same thing, but with one change: Calvin, Luther, Wesley, Wycliffe, and others not only preached about the antichrist, but also identified it as the papacy. They had no question that the antichrist, the little horn/beast power, was the Roman Catholic papal system.

Again, we must remember that it is not Catholic people, but the Roman Catholic papal structure that represents the little horn power. "In calling the pope the 'antichrist,' the early Lutherans stood in a tradition that reached back into the eleventh

---

1   *I recommend that you read George Eldon Ladd's* The Blessed Hope *(Grand Rapids: Eerdmans, 1990), which details the history of the teachings about Christ's return through the Christian Era.*

century. Not only dissidents and heretics but even saints had called the bishop of Rome the 'antichrist' when they wished to castigate his abuse of power."[2]

In other words, Martin Luther was teaching what the early church had presented in the past. It was during the time of ecumenical dialogue a couple decades ago that Pope John Paul II pulled Martin Luther out of hell, because an earlier pope had consigned him there—that is, if you believe the Roman Catholic Church has the power to put people in and out of hell. But I don't think Martin Luther was too worried about that. Here is what we have today.

At the top of the graphic, you can see the part I have labeled A. It is the historicists' viewpoint, and it shows what I have been sharing with you. It matches what the Reformers taught, and it is also what I find in Daniel 11—a sequential, step-by-step presentation.

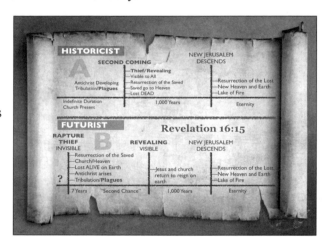

The Counter-Reformation occurred from A.D. 1560-1648, when the Roman Catholic Church instituted a series of reforms in response to the views and influence of the Reformers. During the Counter-Reformation, the Catholic Church introduced the view called futurism. If you go into a Christian bookstore, you will find that almost every book on prophecy is based on that concept. The futurist view as commonly presented today is labeled B in the graphic above.

I discovered, that what Futurists present and what the Bible teaches do not match. However, what the Reformers taught, historicism, does match what the Bible says.

Remember that Revelation 16:15 said that between the sixth and seventh plague Jesus was about to "come as a thief" (KJV)? The basic question, as we look at the table above, is: Which view, A or B, matches Revelation 16:15? Does this agree with what the Reformers taught or with what most futurists commonly teach to-

2   Joseph A. Burgess and Jeffrey Gros, eds., Building Unity: Ecumenical Dialogues With Roman Catholic Participation in the United States (Mahwah, N.J.: Paulist Press, 1989), p. 140.

170

day? Let's see which one of these has Jesus arriving as a thief, right after the 6th plague, matching the description of Revelation 16:15.

The historicists and the Reformers taught that the plagues will come first, and then Jesus. That is a match. But futurists teach that Jesus comes as a thief, and then they have the plagues at the end of the seven years.

Did the Bible get this wrong, or is it more likely that the people writing the popular prophecy books did? So far, I find that the historicist teaching (A) is right, and not the futurist teaching (B).

2 Thessalonians 2:1, 2 declares: "Now, brethren, concerning the coming of our Lord Jesus Christ and our gathering together to Him, we ask you, not to be soon shaken in mind or troubled, either by spirit or by word or by letter, as if from us, as though the day of Christ had come."

The word "come" used here is a translation of the Greek word *parousia*, which futurists call the "rapture," when Christ returns invisibly in the clouds at the beginning of a seven-year time of trouble/tribulation. At that time, futurists claim, the antichrist rises in power.

For three and a half years he is friendly to the Jews, but then he receives the "deadly wound," comes back to life, and emerges as an enemy against Israel for three and a half years. The plagues happen during those last three and a half years. But, the futurists say, the seven years started with the Parousia, the coming of Christ.

2 Thessalonians 2:3 says, "Let no one deceive you by any means; for that Day"— the Second Coming, the Parousia—"will not come unless the falling away comes first, and the man of sin is revealed, the son of perdition." The antichrist power will manifest itself before Jesus arrives in His parousia.

Look at the chart and find out which one, A or B, matches this verse. The A side has the emergence and unveiling of the antichrist, and then Jesus is revealed at His parousia.

But on the B side, the parousia occurs in what futurists call the secret rapture, and then the antichrist gains his ascendancy. Futurists have the order reversed.

This should set off all kinds of alarm bells in your head, because Satan is up to something. I'm going to show you part of his scheme. I don't think I understand it all, but I've got part of it.

171

Our next verse is 2 Thessalonians 2:8. "And then the lawless one will be revealed, whom the Lord will consume with the breath of His mouth and destroy with the brightness of His coming." Again, the word for coming is parousia, which the futurists want to say is the rapture or the invisible return of Christ, as well as the beginning of the seven years.

According to the text, the parousia should consume or destroy the antichrist power. Let's take a look at the chart. On the A side, according to the Reformation teachers, the antichrist would develop, and then when Jesus returns, He would destroy the antichrist. That's a match!

But the B side puts the parousia before the antichrist arises. In other words, according to what the futurists are teaching, the power vacuum created when Jesus snatches all the believers away will lead to the rise of the antichrist. Again the order is backwards. The Bible says that Jesus' parousia destroys the antichrist rather than setting him up in power. So, A matches the Bible verse and B does not.

Now let's consider 2 Peter 3:10: "But the day of the Lord will come as a thief in the night, in which the heavens will pass away with a great noise, and the elements will melt with fervent heat; both the earth and the works that are in it will be burned up."

If a metal chair you are sitting on burns and melts from under you, what would it be like? Would there be a survivor? No. I had a friend who worked in a steel mill, and one of his coworkers was discouraged and going through a hard time. This discouraged man took a running jump into a furnace. He was gone before he hit the molten steel.

When the heat is enough to melt metal elements, people don't survive. God said that He was going to destroy the antichrist/man of sin and those who follow him by the "brightness of His coming" (2 Thessalonians 2:8).

According to 2 Peter 3:10, when Jesus comes as a thief, the lost die. But when the futurists talk about Jesus' returning as a thief, they write a whole series of books that say the lost are wandering around on earth, saying, "Where did everyone go? What happened?" Did you notice that the futurists got almost everything wrong? Don't trust the novels and the films. Put your confidence in God's Word.

What about Matthew 24 and Luke 17? The Reformers taught that "coming as a thief" and "revealing" were different terms for the same event. The futurists say the "thief" and the "revealing" are separate terms for separate events. Let's allow the Bible to describe for itself whether it involves one event or two. We will put Matthew 24 and Luke 17 side by side.

Matthew 24:27: "For as the lightning comes from the east and flashes to the west, so also will the coming of the Son of Man be." Luke 17:24: "For as the lightning that flashes out of one part under heaven shines to the other part under heaven, so also the Son of Man will be in His day." It definitely seems as if they have the same event in mind.

Matthew 24:37-39: "But as the days of Noah were, so also will the coming of the Son of Man be. For as in the days before the flood, they were eating and drinking, marrying and giving in marriage, until the day that Noah entered the ark, and did not know until the flood came and took them all away, so also will the coming of the Son of Man be."

Luke 17:26: "And as it was in the days of Noah, so it will be also in the days of the Son of Man." Does it sound as if we are hearing the same sermon that Jesus is giving about the same event?

Matthew 24:40: "Then two men will be in the field: one will be taken and the other left." This verse is foundational for Tim LaHaye's understanding of prophecy in the Left Behind series—that one would be snatched into heaven and the other remain on earth.

Compare Luke 17:35, 36: "Two women will be grinding together: the one will be taken and the other left. Two men will be in the field: the one will be taken and the other left." The two verses parallel passages in Matthew and Luke and have basically the same order within the chapters. The problem for the futurist is that Matthew calls it the parousia (futurists say "rapture"), but Luke labels the same event as the "revealing" (see Luke 17:30).

Do these passages describe one event with two different names, or are we reading about two separate events? Clearly they are one event, with slightly different words used to present the same thing.

Does God use different explanations to describe the same thing in other parts of the Scriptures? What about the Lamb slain on the throne, and the Lion of Judah? They are the same person (Jesus) under different names. They are not two separate Saviors. "Lord of lords and King of kings" is another name for Him.

The Bible often employs two or more terms to refer to the same thing. Here we see that the Reformers were right again.

Another assertion of futurists is that the lost continue to wander around on the earth, wondering what happened. The historicists have said, "No, they are destroyed by the brightness of Jesus' coming at the very end."

The people killed by the Flood did not wonder where Noah went. They were dead! Matthew 24:38, 39: "For as in the days before the flood … [they] did not know until the flood came and took them all away, so also will the coming of the Son of Man be." How many kinds of people were there in Noah's day? Those who got on the ark and lived, and those who didn't and died.

Luke says the same thing, and he adds a reference to Sodom and Gomorrah. "On the day that Lot went out of Sodom it rained fire and brimstone from heaven and destroyed them all. Even so will it be in the day when the Son of Man is revealed" (Luke 17:29, 30).

Again, how many kinds of people were there in Sodom and Gomorrah? Those who got out when God said to, and they lived; and those who didn't, and they died.

Now look at Luke 17:35-37: "One will be taken and the other left. And they answered and said to Him, 'Where, Lord?' So He said to them, 'Wherever the body is, there the eagles will be gathered together.'" The eagles gather where the dead bodies lie. God's people who are rescued will not be dead at that time.

So who is dead here? The wicked! Those who refuse to trust Jesus! Are the wicked going to be left wandering around on the earth for seven years, puzzled at what happened to the rest? No! They are dead. Jesus was very clear. So side A in our diagram works again, and the B side does not.

What about New Testament Israel? The authors of the Left Behind series, *The Late, Great Planet Earth*, and other books believe that all Bible prophecies for ancient Israel will literally be fulfilled for the Jews, and they ignore the conditional aspect of the prophecies.

They say that God's New Testament people (the church) and His Old Testament people (Israel) are not the same, even though the New Testament declares that God's Old Testament and New Testament people are indeed the same and that there is no line of distinction between Jew and Gentile.

Anyone who has accepted Christ is an heir of Abraham and a part of the commonwealth of Israel. So which one is right, A or B? Side A matches on that one too.

What about the seven years? The futurists get it from Daniel 9. When we studied Daniel 9[3], we looked at the historicists' (or Reformers') viewpoint that 70 weeks equals 490 years. The last week, or the last seven years, started in A.D. 27 when the Messiah was anointed. Jesus was anointed at His baptism in A.D. 27.

In the middle of the week, after three and a half years, the Messiah would die. He would be "cut off" and bring an "end to sacrifices." When Jesus died, it did terminate the significance of animal sacrifices. You don't offer a lamb as a sacrifice whenever you sin now.

And then the gospel goes to the Gentiles in A.D. 34. So that seventh week—those seven years—were fulfilled in the first century. And Jesus is the center of those seven years!

But the futurist says, "Oh, no, it's not! We're going to disconnect the seven years from the rest of the prophecy, and we're going to move them about two thousand years into the future, and instead of it being about Jesus, we're going to have this long gap, and we're going to start the prophetic time clock again at rapture, when Jesus comes."

And they say nobody will see Him at that time, but that in the middle of the week, the antichrist will receive a deadly wound, and finally Jesus Himself will visibly show up at the end of the seven years. But in this scenario, who is the center of the prophecy after three and a half years? The antichrist.

Remember that Satan said he wanted to take the place of God? He does exactly that in the futurists' version of prophecy! Notice that the futurist view of prophecy repeatedly fails comparisons with Scripture. If it doesn't match Scripture, and it puts Satan in the center of the prophecy instead of Jesus, do you think there is a problem here? A huge one! Satan is deceiving people!

You recall that in the sixteenth century the Roman Catholic Jesuit priest Francisco Ribera employed futurism to take the heat off the papacy. The Reformers were studying the antichrist power, the beast, the little horn, and they concluded, "The antichrist is the papal system."

But Ribera said, "No, Daniel and Revelation and the antichrist are all in the future. The prophecy has nothing to do with the papacy." So he threw it out into the future, and now almost every Protestant has adopted futurism. This was prophesied, because Revelation says that all the world would end up following the beast.

---

3   *See chapter 1.*

Protestant futurism came by way of Samuel Maitland, who in the 1820s wrote that the descriptions of the antichrist do not fit the pope. Edward Irving, in the 1840s, began to be a futurist. Margaret McDonald, a woman in his congregation, had a "tongues" vision, and when she came out of the vision she said, "There are going to be two comings of Christ, separated by a time period, and that's when the antichrist will be active."

Until Margaret McDonald had her vision in the 1840s, the church had never had a concept of two comings of Christ, separating the "coming as a thief" from the coming as the "revealing." Up until then it was known as one event only. Remember that Revelation promised there would be signs, wonders, and miracles to deceive people, and this new idea came from a "tongues" vision. I believe in tongues, and I believe in visions, but I also believe there are counterfeits, because God's Word said counterfeits would surface to deceive people.

John Nelson Darby picked up futurism from there and created *dispensationalism* in 1848. By this time he was teaching that the Jews in the Old Testament were saved by works, contrary to Hebrews 11, which declares that they were all saved by faith.

Futurism went into the Scofield Reference Bible about 1909, and Hal Lindsey picked it up in the 1970s in his book *The Late, Great Planet Earth*. Then came religious films such as "Years of the Beast" and "A Thief in the Night." Once people have seen the film, they "know" what is going to happen, so why should they read the Bible? As a result, many Christians, especially in North America, believe in a seven-year tribulation, or worst-ever time of trouble.

Now you know how this belief came to be. It resulted not from careful Bible study, but rather from an attempt to take the focus off the papacy and from a vision. One commentator I read recently who believes in the seven-year tribulation admitted that you could not find the seven-year tribulation in Scripture if you didn't already know about it. And the only way anyone knew about it was through Margaret McDonald's vision.

Does it really matter what you believe on this topic? Yes! I have heard people say, "Well, if I miss the first coming of Jesus (when He arrives as a thief), I'll have to go through seven years of really troubled times, but I can be ready for when He returns at the 'revealing.'"

What if there were no second chance? Wouldn't Satan like for us to assume that we have an additional opportunity, and we can wait to make our decision for God? But the Lord says that now is the day to accept Him. Don't put it off.

What about preparation for the time of tribulation? Those who believe and follow God and are still alive during that time of trouble on earth, although they know they will be protected by God, realize that it is still going to be tough to get through and that they will have to hang on for however long it takes. They understand that they have got to be making spiritual preparation, which means being filled with the Holy Spirit. We can do that only by digging into God's Word and following what it says in every aspect of our lives.

Others, who believe they are going to get raptured out of this world and taken away at the beginning of the seven years, assume that they don't need to be ready for hard times. Do you remember the parable of the 10 virgins who wanted to get into the wedding? Five were prepared, and five were not. The first five made it through, while the latter five did not. That's important to keep in mind.

Those who believe they will be raptured also get blindsided by the antichrist. Here's the problem. Whom do many Christians accept as a worldwide leader of the Christian church? Both Protestants and Roman Catholics acknowledge the pope as a major figure in Christianity. The Bible says that all the world would follow after him. The greater the Islamic threat, the more people turn to the papacy for leadership. They are watching for the papacy, not as the antichrist, but rather as someone to oppose an Islamic antichrist.

When we talked about the United States in prophecy, we found that the country starts out as a beast with lamblike horns, and ends up being the false prophet. Do you know which region of the world most pushes prophetic futurism? The United States. (I'm talking about the seven-year tribulation, getting Israel back in charge of the Temple Mount, building the third temple, and all the rest of the package that is dispensationalism and futurism.)

God does not require that the Jerusalem Temple be rebuilt. If the Temple were rebuilt and sacrifices started again, that would be blasphemy. From God's perspective, sacrifices ended at the death of Jesus, for He was the true sacrifice, the Lamb of God. Also, Daniel 9:26, 27 announces that the Temple will be desolate until the confirmation. Jesus called it "desolate" when He left it for the last time. And it will remain that way until the return of Christ. If the Temple is rebuilt, it will be part of Satan's counterfeit.

I know that what I'm saying may not be the same as what you often find in many Christian bookstores. Revelation 18:4 says, "Come out of her, my people." It's important to know that you are following what the Bible says, and not what a majority of people are teaching. It is vital to surrender to Jesus Christ and to His Word.

Chapter 13

JESUS RESCUES HIS PEOPLE

We've gone over the overlap in Daniel 11:44, 45 and Daniel 12:1. The tidings, or final warning, have gone out, and then the anger of the king of the North/beast power dominates. Jesus finishes the judgment, and the time of trouble begins. The king of the North meets his end, and Jesus rescues God's people when He returns.

Now we will focus on Jesus delivering His people. In the Daniel 2 vision of the statue, Nebuchadnezzar sees the head of gold, Babylon, then Persia, Greece, Rome, and divided Europe. The dream ends with a rock cut out without hands that strikes the statue, destroys it completely, and takes over the world.

That rock is Jesus, the King of kings and Lord of lords.

One of my favorite promises about the coming of Jesus is John 14:1-3. "Let not your heart be troubled; you believe in God, believe also in Me. In My Father's house are many mansions; if it were not so, I would have told you. I go to prepare a place for you. And if I go and prepare a place for you, I will come again and receive you to Myself; that where I am, there you may be also."

Jesus promised that He is going to pick us up and take us to our "mansions" in heaven. A special place in heaven has your name on it. You don't want to miss out on that. What do we know about Christ's coming? Here are five facts.

Number 1: It will be literal. I know pastors who claim that the Second Advent is spiritual and that Christ will never physically return to earth. They say that Jesus comes back every time someone accepts Him into their heart, but that He will not appear in the clouds to bring an end to sin and suffering. How depressing is that! But they believe it.

In Acts 1:9-11 the Bible tells us: "Now when He had spoken these things, while they watched, He was taken up, and a cloud received Him out of their sight. And while they looked steadfastly toward heaven as He went up, behold, two men stood by them in white apparel, who also said, 'Men of Galilee, why do you stand gazing up into heaven? This same Jesus, who was taken up from you into heaven, will so come in like manner as you saw Him go into heaven.'"

Jesus was a tangible human being when He left. The disciple Thomas doubted the reality of the resurrected Savior, and Jesus said to him, "Come touch Me. Check Me out. Give Me something to eat and watch Me eat it. I'm real." When Jesus departed in a cloud, the disciples watched Him leave. If He was a physical being when He left earth, then when He comes back He will also be a physical being.

Number 2: Jesus at His coming will be visible to every living person on earth. Revelation 1:7 declares: "Behold, He is coming with clouds, and every eye will see Him, and they also who pierced Him. And all the tribes of the earth will mourn because of Him." Will only His followers be aware of Him? No! Every eye will witness His arrival. We will be able to see Him. The people who teach an invisible return of Christ cannot be correct. When Jesus appears at the Second Advent, He arrives in the clouds, and He is seen just as He was when He left.

Matthew makes it clear that if someone appears on earth and claims to be Jesus Christ, they are lying. "For false christs and false prophets will arise and show great signs and wonders, so as to deceive, if possible, even the elect. See, I have told you beforehand. Therefore if they say to you, 'Look, He is in the desert!' do not go out; or 'Look, He is in the inner rooms!' do not believe it" (Matt. 24:24-26).

If someone announces that they are the Messiah and walks around on the earth, and only a few people are seeing them, you know they are not Jesus Christ. When Jesus returns, every eye sees Him.

Number 3: His coming will be audible. "For the Lord Himself will descend from heaven with a shout, with the voice of an archangel, and with the trumpet of God" (1 Thessalonians 4:16). Not only will you see the coming of Jesus, but you will also hear it loud and clear.

Number 4: It will be glorious. "For the Son of Man will come in the glory of His Father with His angels, and then He will reward each according to his works" (Matthew 16:27).

When Jesus was resurrected, one angel showed up and gave a little burst of glory. What happened to the soldiers guarding the tomb? They fell down as dead men. Imagine what it will be like when Jesus arrives in His full glory. He comes with the Father's glory and with the radiance of millions of angels. Who is going to miss that?

In the last chapter we saw the rebellious calling for rocks and mountains to fall on them to hide them from the brightness. When Jesus returns, it will be the worst thing in the world for those who don't trust in Him, and it's the best thing for those who do.

How will the antichrist, the little horn beast (papal system), end? "And then the lawless one will be revealed, whom the Lord will consume with the breath of His mouth and destroy with the brightness of His coming" (2 Thessalonians 2:8). God's glory is a consuming fire to sin and wickedness.

"It is a righteous thing with God to repay with tribulation those who trouble you, and to give you who are troubled rest with us when the Lord Jesus is revealed from heaven with His mighty angels, in flaming fire taking vengeance on those who do not know God, and on those who do not obey the gospel of our Lord Jesus Christ. These shall be punished with everlasting destruction from the presence of the Lord and from the glory of His power" (2 Thessalonians 1:6-9).

The glory of God can be destructive. Remember that God told Moses that if he were to see Him in all His glory, the brightness of it would kill him? The Lord gave him just a little glimpse, and Moses literally glowed for days afterward.

The Israelites asked him to wear a veil because his appearance scared them. And that was the result of only an indirect view of God! So the appearing of Jesus will be glorious beyond comprehension.

Number 5: His appearing will be climactic. "For as the lightning comes from the east and flashes to the west, so also will the coming of the Son of Man be" (Matthew 24:27).

Those who have had lightning hit near them do not easily forget it. I've had lightning strike close enough for the electrical shock to make my muscles contract. It was behind me. Because I was headed for cover, I didn't look to see what got hit. Another time, I was driving down the road in a storm and I glanced at a transformer just in time to watch it blow apart. The pole stood there smoking—what was left of it. This kind of event is climactic. You are not going to miss it.

"Then the sky receded as a scroll when it is rolled up" (Revelation 6:14). No one will be unaware of the sky disappearing.

"And every mountain and island was moved out of its place. And the kings of the earth, the great men, the rich men, the commanders, the mighty men, every slave and every free man, hid themselves in the caves and in the rocks of the mountains, and said to the mountains and rocks, 'Fall on us and hide us from the face of Him who sits on the throne and from the wrath of the Lamb! For the great day of His wrath has come, and who is able to stand?'" (Revelation 6:14-17).

This is the wrap-up of earth's history. You can't miss it. You see it, you hear it, it's glorious, it's climactic, it's awesome!

The coming of Jesus Christ is a rescue mission. It will be the best time of our lives when we look up at Him and He smiles at us and says, "I'm on the way to save you."

Remember, if you've been living through the end-times, you've been on earth when the king of the North/beast power has been threatening to kill you. People were out to get you, but now they've got problems of their own to deal with. The rocks and the mountains are starting to collapse, and islands are disappearing.

Suppose you had been hiding out in the mountains and suddenly the mountain below you is disappearing. You're going to look up at Jesus and say, "Oh, wow, am I glad to see You!" And then He takes you up into the clouds to meet Him. I will be glad to be out of here.

Death and the Resurrection

On top of all that, not only are we rescued, but also the ones who died trusting in Jesus are resurrected to be taken to heaven with us. Every one of us has lost loved ones. Having already laid one of my children in the grave, I'm looking forward to meeting her again. It's going to be a party on that cloud as we greet each other.

Sadly, most people are not looking forward to that resurrection as they should be because of one of the papal systems deceptions inspired by Satan: what happens when we die.

To help you grasp how wonderful the resurrection is, and why all of God's Word is pointing forward to Jesus' coming and the resurrection as the climax of His salvation ministry, you need to understand what He teaches about death.

No Truth from the Dead

A lot of people think they can communicate with the dead. But here's the truth: The Bible says that you cannot. Then who are people contacting? The one who is a liar and a deceiver—Satan.

Isaiah 8:19, 20 warns: "When they say to you, 'Seek those who are mediums and wizards, who whisper and mutter,' should not a people seek their God? Should they seek the dead on behalf of the living?" Should you go to God's Word or to a fortuneteller to find out what's coming in the future? You definitely don't go out to cemeteries to find the truth.

"To the law and to the testimony! If they do not speak according to this word, it is because there is no light in them" (verse 20). Anybody who speaks contrary to God's Word has only darkness in them. I have many prophecy books in my collection that have no light in them because they are contrary to God's Word. So how do I find out what the truth is? I check with the Word. Jesus is the Word—the Bible is the Word.

Death is a Sleep

The Bible has a number of things to say about grief and death. Paul writes: "I do not want you to be ignorant, brethren, concerning those who have fallen asleep, lest you sorrow as others who have no hope" (1 Thessalonians 4:13). He calls death a sleep.

The apostle did not say that Christians would not have sorrow, but rather that Christians would not have hopeless sorrow. There is a huge difference. Having been a pastor for many years, I've been involved in many funerals, and I have watched people who had hopeless sorrow. Part of the good news is that we can have sorrow with hope. But we still have to say goodbye for a while.

"For if we believe that Jesus died and rose again, even so God will bring with Him those who sleep in Jesus. For this we say to you by the word of the Lord, that we who are alive and remain until the coming of the Lord will by no means precede those who are asleep. For the Lord Himself will descend from heaven with a shout, with the voice of an archangel, and with the trumpet of God. And the dead in Christ will rise first. Then we who are alive and remain shall be caught up together with them in the clouds to meet the Lord in the air. And thus we shall always be with the Lord. Therefore comfort one another with these words" (1 Thessalonians 4:14, 15).

He did not say to them, "I know you lost a loved one, but when you die, you get to meet them in heaven." Nor did he assure us that there would be a reunion in heaven immediately after death. Rather, he spoke of a reunion when Jesus comes in the clouds and resurrects us!

How many funerals have you attended in which something like the following is stated? "George has been met by his dad up in heaven. They had a wonderful meeting." That is not how Paul said we should have hope. Rather, he told us to have hope in the resurrection.

To make sense of this, look at what Daniel says about the resurrection. "And many of those who sleep in the dust of the earth shall awake, some to everlasting life, some to shame and everlasting contempt" (Daniel 12:2).

Again, the Bible calls death a sleep. When your loved one is sleeping in the dust of the earth, they are dead. They receive their everlasting life at the resurrection, when God wakes them up from their sleep.

God in essence told the prophet, "Daniel, you are not going to understand this, so relax. But go your way till the end, for you shall rest [sleep in death], and you will arise to your inheritance at the end of the day" (adapted from verse 12).

When was he going to be in heaven? At the end of days, at the end of the time of the end. We haven't finished that period yet. Daniel still has not arrived in heaven, according to his own book. He is resting in his dusty grave, waiting for the resurrection.

That is sadly not what the church has taught for most of its history. Early Christian apologists took the pagan idea that when people die, they go right on to heaven or hell, and they brought it into Christianity itself.

What did Jesus Himself say about death being a sleep? When one of His closest acquaintances died, He said to His disciples, "Our friend Lazarus sleeps, but I go that I may wake him up" (John 11:11).

When somebody was dead, He could wake them up. It was no big deal for Him. "Then His disciples said, 'Lord, if he sleeps he will get well.' However, Jesus spoke of his death, but they thought that He was speaking about taking rest in sleep. Then Jesus said to them plainly, 'Lazarus is dead'" (John 11:12-14).

Very clearly Jesus calls death a sleep.

The Dead Know Nothing

The Bible tells us the dead aren't aware of anything. "For the living know that they will die; but the dead know nothing, and they have no more reward, for the memory of them is forgotten. Also their love, their hatred, and their envy have now perished; nevermore will they have a share in anything done under the sun" (Ecclesiastes 9:5, 6).

Can a dead person come back and haunt you because they did not like you? No. The Bible says that the dead know nothing and that their hatred is forgotten. Can a dead person who loves you give you a warning from the other side? Again, no! They do not know anything. They have no consciousness at all.

Have you ever had a really good night's sleep? Exhausted, you went to sleep as soon as your head hit the pillow, and the next thing you knew it was morning. Jesus says death is like a good night's sleep. You're not aware of anything. Perhaps you have heard it said that someone who is sleeping is dead to the world. That's a Biblical way of describing the sleep of death.

What is a good way to shorten a long car trip, assuming you're not driving? Going to sleep. The next thing you know, you're there! Think about the beauty of the idea. When you drop off into sleep, you're unaware of everything else, and in death you don't know anything until Jesus wakes you up. So you lie down and sleep in death, and then next thing you realize is that Jesus is there. Not bad—not bad at all.

The Mortal Soul

People sometimes protest, "But, what about that immortal soul that I've been taught about for so many years?" Look up the word "immortal" in a concordance. See if you can find where the Bible says that we have an immortal soul. It is not in there.

But here's what the Bible does teach: "Behold, all souls are Mine; the soul of the father as well as the soul of the son is Mine; the soul who sins shall die" (Ezekiel 18:4).

If you have an immortal soul right now, can God say that it will die? No! So which will you believe: the traditions that are, unfortunately, taught within the Christian church, or God's own Word? Sadly, most Christians will persist in following traditions and not God's Word.

What about 1 Timothy 6:15, 16? "He who is the blessed and only Potentate, the King of kings and Lord of lords, who alone has immortality, dwelling in unapproachable light." If we have immortality, can the Bible be true if it says that only God possesses it? Would you rather that God be a liar—or that Christian tradition be wrong? Remember, He says that when you worship according to tradition, you worship in vain. It is pretty clear that tradition is not the path to follow.

Paul told the Corinthian believers what would happen at the moment the dead in Christ are resurrected. "Behold, I tell you a mystery: We shall not all sleep, but we shall all be changed—in a moment, in the twinkling of an eye, at the last trumpet. For the trumpet will sound, and the dead will be raised incorruptible, and we shall be changed. For this corruptible must put on incorruption, and this mortal must put on immortality" (1 Corinthians 15:51-53).

Human beings were mortal at Creation. We know this because Adam needed to eat from the tree of life to stay living. Still mortal, we will take on immortality as a gift from God only at the resurrection. If we already had immortality, then why would God have to endow us with it at the resurrection?

"So when this corruptible has put on incorruption, and this mortal has put on immortality, then shall be brought to pass the saying that is written: 'Death is swallowed up in victory'" (1 Corinthians 15:54).

Now you can see the importance of the resurrection. It is the time of the great reunion. Everything is on the line then. If there is no resurrection, salvation does not work!

A lot of Christians have blown by the resurrection because they thought, Well, I'm going to meet my family when I die, and since they've already died, and we're going to meet in heaven, that's how we get to heaven. No, we reach heaven by being resurrected by Jesus, and we go there together as a whole human family of the saved. And we have a celebration with Jesus on the way to heaven.

The Spirit in a Person

What about the spirit of a person returning to God? "Then the dust will return to the earth as it was, and the spirit will return to God who gave it" (Ecclesiastes 12:7). The spirit does go to God who gave it—I have no question about that. But does that mean we have an immortal soul, or that we live and know things in heaven after we die? No, we don't, and we know that because the Bible said the dead know nothing.

So, then, what is the spirit? It is the breath of life given in Genesis 2: "The Lord God formed man of the dust of the ground, and breathed into his nostrils the breath of life; and man became a living being" (verse 7). The gift of life—the breath of life—is the spirit. When we die, the gift that came from God goes back to Him. It does not mean we live as a spirit in heaven. The gift of life that He has presented to us He holds in Himself after we die, until He comes and wakes us at the resurrection and gives it back.

Genesis 2:7 says that "man became a living soul" (KJV). When an airplane goes down, we may hear in news reports that it had 55 souls on board, meaning 55 people who died. Those people started out as living beings, and they ended as dead bodies.

If the soul were something separate, how do we read verse 19? "Whatever Adam called each living creature, that was its name." The term "living creature" here is the same term the Bible uses in verse 7—a living being, a soul. The animals were living beings. Do they have an immortal soul? No. We are all the same in that way—we are living creatures.

According to the Genesis formula, then, body plus breath (or spirit) equals soul, which is now a living being. Soul (or living being) minus the breath equals death—a corpse, a pile of dirt. God took the body (the dirt) and gave it breath, and it became a living person. At death the breath went out from the living person, and he or she became a mound of dirt again. It is a pretty simple equation.

Here's another way of looking at it: Suppose a lightbulb represents the human body. How much light does the lightbulb give off by itself? It reflects a little bit of light from the outside, but has no light in itself. But if you connect the lightbulb to the electrical power grid—to God's power, His gift of life—what do you have? A light in the bulb.

What happens when you disconnect that gift of life? All you have is a lightbulb and no light. The light ceases to exist—vanishes. Where does the living being go when the spirit leaves? It too ceases to exist, and what was once a living person is no longer. We have the gift of life in God waiting for the resurrection and a dead body on earth. The living person no longer exists because "the dead know nothing."

Remember, in Genesis 3:4, the devil's first lie, "You will not surely die"? "Go ahead, Eve, eat this fruit and you'll become like God (and be immortal)." But only God is inherently immortal. Satan was saying that Eve would become like God, so from the very beginning he was promulgating a lie: follow me, and you'll be immortal. The truth is, if you sin you will die, not be immortal. Eve died, didn't she? So did Adam. So has everybody else since.

Who was right—God or Satan? God is the only immortal one. Why does the majority of the world accept Satan and his lie and believe that when you die you become immortal and thus like God? It is contrary to the Scriptures.

No Ghosts

You cannot be haunted by a dead person, nor can you be visited by any kind of dead individual. If that appears to happen, you are dealing with one of Satan's angels, a counterfeit of some dead person. Tell the apparition, "Get behind me, Satan." Have nothing to do with it.

I believe that we're going to encounter more and more of this kind of experience as Satan tries to deceive us and get us to follow something other than God's Word. Satan will tempt us to listen to all kinds of messages from the dead. Satan's lies about death and ghosts are already being told by the entertainment media on a regular basis.

The truth is that you cannot communicate with the dead. The Bible actually tells us in the Old Testament that anyone who tried to do so was to be be cut off from the nation of Israel, or killed. It was a serious offense. God did not like to have anyone trying to contact the dead, because they are really communicating with Satan. God does not want His people to listen to messages from Satan. Do you blame Him?

The False Christian Tradition

Revelation 17:1, 2 describes "the great harlot who sits on many waters, with whom the kings of the earth committed fornication, and the inhabitants of the earth were made drunk with the wine of her fornication."

The world becomes drunk from the stuff in her cup—the corrupted unbiblical teachings that changed into Christian traditions. The world has become intoxicated with it, and it likes spiritual alcohol better than truth. People like having their minds numbed by error, so they don't have to think of the truth.

"The woman was arrayed in purple and scarlet, and adorned with gold and precious stones and pearls, having in her hand a golden cup full of abominations and the filthiness of her fornication" (Revelation 17:4).

The fornications—the spiritual adultery—happened when the early church took human traditions and mixed them with God's Word and created a mix of human ideas (which really means the devil's ideas) and God's Word for the traditions and teachings of the church. It caused people to follow after supposed messages from the dead, to be looking the wrong direction for hope. That's not good, because there is hope only in God's truth.

The State of the Dead

Right before my daughter's death, she asked, "Dad, what's it like to die?" She said, "I'm not afraid of death, because I know it is just a sleep until Jesus comes. But I'm not so sure about dying."

My daughter was experiencing the uncertainty that we all feel as we approach death. What we do not have to be uncertain about is what happens after death.

The Christian tradition that a person goes to heaven at death has serious consequences. To see the results of this belief, let's take a fictional scenario of a young woman who died and left behind a couple of young children. We will let our story play out both in the form that Satan has taught us and the way that God has taught us—the false traditions versus God's truth. Let's present God's version first.

The young mother lies there in the coffin. She has left two little girls, and her husband is in great grief. Buried, she rests there until Christ comes again. The woman is not conscious of anything that happens while she is in that grave for however long she is dead, be it days or centuries. Because the dead know nothing, she is not aware of the passing of time.

Her husband does something really foolish. He gets remarried on the rebound to a woman who is a problem. She beats the children and abuses them in all kinds of ways. The husband becomes an alcoholic. How much of that tragedy is the first wife having to deal with? None of it, because she's asleep and knows nothing. Whatever troubles her kids go through, she does not have to deal with it until it's long over and God has taken care of it. You see why His way is really good news?

In my daughter's case, when she died, she was ready for it. She didn't want to go through the process of dying, but the thought of going to sleep sounded good, because she had been through way too much already in her fight with cancer. That sleep of death can be a welcome escape when people have suffered a lot.

And so, in a way, God gave us a sleep of escape to get us to the resurrection and the coming of Jesus.

Now we will play out the story of the fictional woman again, but this time with the false "Christian" teaching—the human tradition—that after death she goes straight up to heaven.

This time, after she dies, she's not in the casket unaware of anything, but rather she is up in heaven knowing everything. The tradition says that she is immortal like God. That is what the lie teaches. And so she watches events on earth. You have heard at a funeral that the loved one is looking down on us, right? I have— many times.

She observes her little girls and her husband crying, and she sees him lose it. He remarries right away, on the rebound, to a woman who is after his money and trying to destroy him while beating up on the kids and abusing them. The woman who died is stuck in heaven and can't do anything about her kids down on earth. What is heaven now like for her? It just became like hell. Have you thought about where that teaching leads? It is really terrible.

Jesus said, "Wide is the gate and broad is the way that leads to destruction, and there are many who go in by it. Because narrow is the gate and difficult is the way which leads to life, and there are few who find it" (Matthew 7:13, 14).

If we go straight to heaven or hell when we die, why do people always say at the funeral that the person is in heaven and not hell? It is obvious that tradition has wandered far from Bible truth.

The truth is that the dead rest quietly in the grave. They're not up in heaven being tortured by what they see, but are in their graves waiting for the resurrection when they can be reunited with loved ones. God will have already taken care of all the problems of the past.

Somebody may try to bring them up, and you say, "Oh, well, it's all history now. Praise the Lord that we are with Jesus. Thank You, Jesus."

Looking at the false teaching from the other direction, how much good news is there for somebody who thinks their loved one did not accept Christ before dying, which means they're roasting in hell right now? It is better to know that they're resting in the grave waiting for the final judgment to be done. I like Jesus' way of doing things.

I'm looking forward to the resurrection, because that is when I know that Satan has really been defeated. I have been in cemetery after cemetery, and I've helped put lots of people in the ground, including one living funeral director who accidentally slipped and fell in. (That was kind of funny. He climbed back up. But the rest have not come out yet.) When Jesus returns, I really want to be near a cemetery, because I want to see the redeemed emerge from the ground. That will be wonderful.

Three States of Being

Some might protest at this point, "Pastor Tim, 2 Corinthians 5 declares that to be absent from the body is to be present with the Lord." Does it say that? Kind of. But we should always take things in context. If we read the context in this case, we find that the Paul who wrote this statement is the same one who announced that we will be reunited at the resurrection and not before.

Christians who are following the devil's lie believe that there are two states of being—an earthly state and a heavenly one—and that as soon as we leave this earthly one, we go straight to heaven or hell. But are there just two? The text says that there are actually three states of being.

In 2 Corinthians 5 we find that there is not just an earthly life and a heavenly life, but there is also one that Paul calls "naked." "Earthly" means the present life, "heavenly" indicates the future life, and "naked" means without either life. The naked stage is the sleep of death.

"For we know that if our earthly house, this tent, is destroyed, we have a building from God, a house not made with hands, eternal in the heavens" (2 Cor. 5:1). That is God's promise to resurrect your body—to give you an immortal, incorruptible existence.

"For in this we groan, earnestly desiring to be clothed with our habitation which is from heaven" (verse 2). I assume you would rather have your heavenly existence than your earthly one. So would I.

"If indeed, having been clothed, we shall not be found naked" (verse 3). Paul would like to be in heaven, and he does not want that in-between state ("naked"), the one without the earthly life that does not yet possess the heavenly one.

"For we who are in this tent [body] groan, being burdened, not because we want to be unclothed, but further clothed, that mortality may be swallowed up by life" (verse 4). Paul is saying, "I want to go to heaven, but I don't really want to die." Can you understand that logic? "But further clothed" means he wants the better life and doesn't want to be without life! He is saying, "I'd like to go straight from this life to the next one, please."

But he suspects that he will have to die first and have the next life later. Remember, we're not immortal until Jesus comes back. Paul is saying here that in the future, mortality will be swallowed up by eternal life.

"Now He who has prepared us for this very thing is God, who also has given us the Spirit as a guarantee. Therefore we are always confident, knowing that while we are at home in the body we are absent from the Lord" (verses 5, 6). As long as I walk the streets of earth, I know that I'm not in heaven.

"For we walk by faith, not by sight. We are confident, yes, well pleased rather to be absent from the body and to be present with the Lord" (verses 7, 8). Where would you rather be—heaven or earth? That is all Paul is saying here: "I'd rather be in heaven!" As long as I'm here, I know that I'm not there, and I'd rather be there.

The Thief on the Cross

A comma in Luke 23:43 has led people to believe that Jesus said something He did not say. The thief hanging on the cross next to Jesus received a promise. First, look at this paragraph:

>*thenhesaidtojesuslordremembermewhenyoucomeintoyourkingdom*
>*andjesussaidtohimassuredlyisaytoyoutodayyouwillbewithmeinparadise*

That is an English version of how ancient Greek was often written—with no spaces or punctuation at all.

In Luke 23:43 Jesus says to the thief on the cross, "Assuredly, I say to you," and then the word "today," and then "you will be with Me in Paradise." So where does the comma go— before or after "today"?

It makes a huge difference where we put that comma. One way agrees with what we found to be taught in God's Word, and the other way appears to support the common Christian tradition that crept into the church later. The verses and punctuation were placed in the English Bible centuries after it was written. So which place do you think the comma went?

Translators placed it to reflect the later "Christian" tradition. So in your Bible you will probably see it as "Assuredly, I say to you, today you will be with Me in Paradise." This might make it appear that when they died, Jesus and the thief made it to heaven on Friday. If true, it opens a whole can of worms. We will get to that problem shortly.

Placing the comma the other way, "Assuredly, I say to you today, you will be with Me in Paradise" simply means that Jesus had the authority to tell the thief, "You are forgiven, and you will live with Me forever in Paradise." When Jesus comes back to earth, the thief will be resurrected and go with Him to heaven.

A Lutheran Bible, the Concordant Literal New Testament, puts the comma where I believe it should go. "Verily I say unto you today, you will be with me in paradise."

Remember that the translators could not go back to the original Greek to decide where the comma should go. It is not there. So they could either position it according to the context of the whole Bible, or they could place it using tradition. Most people go by tradition, unfortunately.

Here is a literal translation of the verse: "And he said to Jesus, 'Remember me, Lord, when You come in the kingdom of You.' And said to him Jesus, 'Truly I say unto you, today with Me you will be in paradise.' "

Or is it this way? "And said to him Jesus, 'Truly I say unto you today, with Me you will be in paradise.'" If I'm wrong on that, and the comma did go before "today," and Jesus promised the thief they would be in Paradise together that very day, I have a question about John 20:17.

In John 20 Jesus meets Mary on the Sunday after His death. She grabs hold of His feet, and He says to her: "'Do not cling to Me, for I have not yet ascended to My Father'" (verse 17).

Of course, God the Father is in heaven. If Jesus told the thief on Friday that they would both be in Paradise on Friday, then Jesus lied to the thief, because on Sunday He still had not gone to heaven yet.

Do you realize that if the comma in most Bibles is correct, it makes Jesus a liar? But if you understand the comma to have been placed by human tradition, not by the context of God's Word, you know that there's nothing wrong with placing the comma after "today." Suddenly Jesus' words make sense.

He was saying to the thief, "Verily I say unto you today, when I come back, you will be with Me in Paradise." Jesus could give that assurance while hanging on the cross, and the thief could relax and die in peace as far as possible.

Certainly it still hurt to be on the cross, but emotionally he could be at peace because he was no longer worried about eternity.

What about the people who have been taken to heaven? It is true that some are already there. For every one of them, the Bible tells us how they got there.

Genesis 5:24 says that Enoch walked with God and was no more. Why? Enoch kept walking with God until he became so in tune with Him that God said, "Let's go back to My house." They had become so close that God just took him with Him to heaven.

In 2 Kings 2 God told Elijah that he would be translated to heaven without seeing death. One day a fiery chariot/whirlwind came down and scooped him up. Elijah threw his mantle to Elisha, who became the next major prophet in Israel, and Elijah went to heaven.

Wouldn't that have been an awesome ride? We will get to do the same thing. Remember that Revelation says that Jesus' coming looks like lightning, so the clouds might have some fire around them too, just as with Elijah's chariot.

And then there is Moses. He was not translated without seeing death, but died on a mountaintop. According to Jude 9 and Matthew 17:3, 4, Moses was resurrected. Jude says that it was Michael, the archangel or commander of the angels, who came to resurrect him, the same one who brings resurrection to us. (Scripture mentions both Jesus and God as being involved in resurrection.)

So Moses was resurrected, and Satan argued with God about it. Michael just replied, "The Lord rebuke you." And He took Moses anyway and raised him to life.

Why would Satan resist? He knows very well that the wages of sin is death. Had Moses sinned? Sure, if murder counts (Exodus 2:12). So Moses was a sinner, and he died. Satan said, "He's mine! You can't have him!"

Jesus said, "Beat it!" and He raised Moses to life anyway. How did Jesus get away with it? In a way, He raised Moses on credit, because He had not yet died to remove the penalty for sin. Because Christ had not yet paid the price for human redemption, Satan naturally protested what the future Savior did.

Isn't it interesting that when Jesus was transfigured on the mountain into His heavenly glory (see Matt. 17:1-12), Elijah and Moses appeared and talked with Jesus? Can you picture the conversation they might have had with Him?

"Jesus, I'm Moses. If You don't go through with dying on the cross, Satan gets me back." And Elijah might have added, "You know, I have never died, but if You don't go through with the cross, Satan gets me, and You know what he's going to do to me."

Both of them realized what was on the line. God sent two human beings from heaven to make sure that Jesus understood the stakes involved with the cross. One of them, Elijah, represents those who are translated alive at the end of time, and Moses represents all the rest who have died and are waiting for the resurrection.

You may be wondering, "Is this just what Seventh-day Adventists teach?" Thankfully, the answer is no. I went to a Baptist funeral one day, and at most Baptist funerals I'm used to hearing that the person has gone straight to heaven and is now up there waiting. But in this one funeral, the preacher had the person sleeping in the grave waiting for the resurrection.

I thought, Wow! This guy is reflecting Scripture. So I waited until everybody had cleared out, and I walked up to the pastor and said, "Sir, I was listening to your presentation very closely. So did you just leave him sleeping in the grave, waiting for the resurrection?" You should have seen his expression. He bristled as he was getting ready to fight with me.

"Well, isn't that what the Bible says?" he replied. As a Baptist pastor, he got hit pretty hard every time he said that, I'm sure.

I said, "Brother," and I felt brotherly right then, "I'm just not used to hearing it. I agree with you, sir." As he relaxed, I added, "I'm just glad to hear it."

You see, it is good news. It is good news for somebody like me, who has lost a loved one. As I walked out of that hospital in Houston, Texas, after my daughter died, I looked up at the moon—it was daytime, but the moon was still out. Turning to my wife, I said, "Karen, from Jennifer's perspective, she's probably about passing the moon by now."

My wife looked at me strangely, so I added, "You know, because she goes to sleep in death, and the next thing she knows is the resurrection. So give her a few minutes after the resurrection, and we're all together on that cloud, going past the moon. Right now I want to think of it from her perspective, not mine."

When you die, you are asleep until Jesus rings the alarm, when He comes and blasts His trumpet. He shouts, we wake up and meet our loved ones, and finally we go home with Him.

Chapter 14

THE MILLENNIUM AND THE NEW EARTH

"At that time Michael shall stand up, the great prince who stands watch over the sons of your people; and there shall be a time of trouble, such as never was since there was a nation, even to that time. And at that time your people shall be delivered, every one who is found written in the book.

"And many of those who sleep in the dust of the earth shall awake, some to everlasting life, some to shame and everlasting contempt. Those who are wise shall shine like the brightness of the firmament, and those who turn many to righteousness like the stars forever and ever" (Daniel 12:1-3).

These verses in Daniel 12 are the basic outline for Revelation 20, 21, and 22. We have seen how God's people go through the plagues untouched and how, at the end of that time, Jesus returns to rescue them and resurrect those of His followers who have already died. In Revelation 20 we find two resurrections, one for the saved, and one for those who are not saved.

The first resurrection happens at the beginning of the 1,000-year period we call the millennium. You will not find the word "millennium" in a concordance, because it is not in the Bible. But Revelation does present the 1,000 years. The millennium begins with the second advent of Jesus.

The saved ones are happy when Jesus comes. "And it will be said in that day: 'Behold, this is our God; we have waited for Him, and He will save us. "This is the Lord; we have waited for Him; we will be glad and rejoice in His salvation'" (Isaiah 25:9). When we are God's people and Jesus arrives on His divine rescue mission, we will exclaim, "Yes! Finally! Jesus, I've been waiting for this day. Praise the Lord, You've come back to get us out of here." On the flip side, the lost are not so happy about it.

196

"Then the sky receded as a scroll when it is rolled up, and every mountain and island was moved out of its place. And the kings of the earth, the great men, the rich men, the commanders, the mighty men, every slave and every free man, hid themselves in the caves and in the rocks of the mountains, and said to the mountains and rocks, 'Fall on us and hide us from the face of Him who sits on the throne and from the wrath of the Lamb! For the great day of His wrath has come, and who is able to stand'" (Revelation 6:14-17)?

The choices we make in life are important. At the Second Coming we will be either praising the Lord or hiding and pleading for the rocks and mountains to fall on us. Everyone will have already made their decision.

"He who is unjust, let him be unjust still; he who is filthy, let him be filthy still; he who is righteous, let him be righteous still; he who is holy, let him be holy still" (Revelation 22:11).

From the moment Michael stands up, the judgment is over. From that time onward, there is no changing sides. By the time the plagues begin, every person has made their decision as to whether they are going to greet Jesus with joy or flee from Him when He comes.

The millennium commences with the Second Coming and the gathering of the saints at the first resurrection. "I saw thrones, and they sat on them, and judgment was committed to them. Then I saw the souls of those who had been beheaded for their witness to Jesus and for the word of God, who had not worshiped the beast or his image, and had not received his mark on their foreheads or on their hands.

"And they lived and reigned with Christ for a thousand years. But the rest of the dead did not live again until the thousand years were finished. This is the first resurrection. Blessed and holy is he who has part in the first resurrection. Over such the second death has no power, but they shall be priests of God and of Christ, and shall reign with Him a thousand years" (Revelation 20:4-6).

When does that resurrection happen? 1 Thessalonians 4 tells us: "I do not want you to be ignorant, brethren, concerning those who have fallen asleep, lest you sorrow as others who have no hope. For if we believe that Jesus died and rose again, even so God will bring with Him those who sleep in Jesus.

"For this we say to you by the word of the Lord, that we who are alive and remain until the coming of the Lord will by no means precede those who are asleep. For the Lord Himself will descend from heaven with a shout, with the voice of an archangel, and with the trumpet of God. And the dead in Christ will rise first. Then we who are alive and remain shall be caught up together with them in the clouds to meet the Lord in the air. And thus we shall always be with the Lord" (verses 13-17).

The Second Coming will be the time of the first resurrection and the start of the 1,000 years. The book of John confirms it: "Do not marvel at this; for the hour is coming in which all who are in the graves will hear His voice and come forth—those who have done good, to the resurrection of life, and those who have done evil, to the resurrection of condemnation" (John 5:28, 29). Notice that Daniel, John, and Revelation speak of two resurrections, but Revelation tells us of a 1,000-year period between them.

The glory of Jesus returning to earth is accompanied by a scene of dying and death. Revelation 19:11 and then verses 17 and following describe what we might call a fowls' feast: "Now I saw heaven opened, and behold, a white horse. And He who sat on him was called Faithful and True, and in righteousness He judges and makes war …

"Then I saw an angel standing in the sun; and he cried with a loud voice, saying to all the birds that fly in the midst of heaven, 'Come and gather together for the supper of the great God, that you may eat the flesh of kings, the flesh of captains, the flesh of mighty men, the flesh of horses and of those who sit on them, and the flesh of all people, free and slave, both small and great.'

"And I saw the beast, the kings of the earth, and their armies, gathered together to make war against Him who sat on the horse and against His army."

Jesus will return at the end of the plagues. At that time, Satan and a vast army gather to fight against God, and here He is, heading toward earth. "Then the beast was captured, and with him the false prophet who worked signs in his presence, by which he deceived those who received the mark of the beast and those who worshiped his image. These two were cast alive into the lake of fire" (Revelation 19:20).

"The lawless one will be revealed, whom the Lord will consume with the breath of His mouth and destroy with the brightness of His coming" (2 Thessalonians 2:8). The lawless one is the beast power, and he perishes in the lake of fire at the second advent of Jesus. We have a lake of fire for the beast and the false prophet.

What happens to all the people who followed the two false powers? Revelation 19:21: "And the rest were killed with the sword which proceeded from the mouth of Him who sat on the horse. And all the birds were filled with their flesh."

They are not destroyed in the lake of fire, but by the sword that comes from the mouth of Jesus Christ. Only the beast and the false prophet get thrown into the lake of fire when Jesus returns. The glory of His coming kills the rest.

2 Thessalonians 1:7, 8 says that at the return of Jesus, the brightness of His coming kills those who refused to follow Him.

"And to give you who are troubled rest with us when the Lord Jesus is revealed from heaven with His mighty angels, in flaming fire taking vengeance on those who do not know God, and on those who do not obey the gospel of our Lord Jesus Christ." The Second Coming will divide everyone into four groups:

1. The righteous who are still alive. They are changed to their perfect form in a moment, and they go up in the clouds to meet Jesus.

2. The righteous who have previously died. Resurrected, they ascend into the clouds to meet Jesus Christ, and He will take them to heaven with Him.

3. The wicked who are alive at the Second Advent. In terror they beg for the rocks and the mountains to bury them, only to perish from the brightness of His coming. The symbolic language of Revelation depicts them as being killed by the sword coming from Jesus' mouth—again the brightness of His coming. The living wicked all die.

4. The wicked who have previously died. Not resurrected yet, they are still asleep in death, waiting for the end of the 1,000 years.

The saints will live and rule in heaven during the millennium. "They lived and reigned with Christ for a thousand years ... Blessed and holy is he who has part in the first resurrection. Over such the second death has no power, but they shall be priests of God and of Christ, and shall reign with Him a thousand years" (Revelation 20:4-6).

"You shall rest," God said to Daniel, "and will arise to your inheritance at the end of the days" (Daniel 12:13). Daniel will receive his reward at the beginning of the 1,000 years.

Where will we be during that 1,000-year period? John 14:1, 2: "Let not your heart be troubled; you believe in God, believe also in Me. In My Father's house are many mansions; if it were not so, I would have told you. I go to prepare a place for you." God has promised us some time with Him in heaven. At His coming He takes us to be with Him.

The saints live and reign with Christ, but Revelation 20 tells us that they will also be judging, a role alluded to in 1 Corinthians 6:1, 2: "Dare any of you, having a matter against another, go to law before the unrighteous, and not before the saints? Do you not know that the saints will judge the world? And if the world will be judged by you, are you unworthy to judge the smallest matters?"

God's people do not judge anyone now. While God is conducting a judgment in heaven at the moment, His followers do not participate with Him.

But during the 1,000 years they will review the case of every person who has ever lived. We'll look more at why they do this later in this chapter.

Jesus brings His family into the New Jerusalem in heaven. It will be wonderful. I'm really not impressed so much by the streets of gold as by what the Bible says about having no more pain, suffering, or death. I could happily live on dirt streets in a world with no pain and death, no suffering at all. But God throws in the golden streets and all the rest of it as well.

What happens to Satan at the coming of Jesus and during the 1,000 years? One thing we can be sure of: Satan will not be in heaven to bother anyone.

"Then I saw an angel coming down from heaven, having the key to the bottomless pit and a great chain in his hand. He laid hold of the dragon, that serpent of old, who is the Devil and Satan, and bound him for a thousand years; and he cast him into the bottomless pit, and shut him up, and set a seal on him, so that he should deceive the nations no more till the thousand years were finished. But after these things he must be released for a little while" (Revelation 20:1-3).

Some have taught that the millennium has already begun, but that would mean Satan is already bound. I like Billy Graham's answer to that one: If Satan is already bound, it's by a rubber band that stretches from pole to pole.

The text makes clear that Satan is bound here on earth, and it will be desolate during the 1,000 years. The Greek word for bottomless pit, abussos, is the same word that the Septuagint, the Greek Old Testament, used to translate the Hebrew phrase "without form and void" in Genesis 1:2. Before Creation, when the earth was without life, it was "without form, and void."

When Jesus returns, the saved are either resurrected or transformed and then taken to heaven, while the wicked who rejected salvation will all die. No living people will remain on earth. The world goes back to its lifeless state, as it was in the beginning.

Jeremiah 25:33: "And at that day the slain of the Lord shall be from one end of the earth even to the other end of the earth. They shall not be lamented, or gathered, or buried; they shall become refuse on the ground."

If nobody is left alive on earth, no one will be around to bury the dead. Revelation uses the imagery of birds having a feast. So at this time the earth will be full of desolate, empty cities and piles of corpses. Satan is stuck on a lifeless planet with no one to tempt.

Satan had said earlier: "I will ascend into heaven, I will exalt my throne above the stars of God … I will be like the Most High" (Isaiah 14:13, 14).

He thought he could run the world better than God, so God says, "You cannot leave the world for 1,000 years, and nobody is left alive on it."

Satan will be stuck in solitary confinement on a totally ruined planet with no people on it, with plenty of time to think about what's he's done. Satan has read the prophecy. He knows what comes next, and it is not good for him.

The End of the Thousand Years

Satan is bound "that he should deceive the nations no more till the thousand years were finished. But after these things he must be released for a little while" (Revelation 20:3).

"When the thousand years have expired, Satan will be released from his prison and will go out to deceive the nations which are in the four corners of the earth, Gog and Magog, to gather them together to battle, whose number is as the sand of the sea" (verses 7, 8).

The devil immediately gathers a huge army. Where does it come from? All those who perished when Jesus returned at the beginning of the 1,000 years, and all those who had died in sin before He came back—all of the wicked from all time—are now resurrected. Once more Satan has people to deceive again.

Daniel 12:1, 2: "At that time your people shall be delivered, every one who is found written in the book. And many of those who sleep in the dust of the earth shall awake, some to everlasting life, some to shame and everlasting contempt."

Revelation 20 told us that we want to be in the first resurrection, because those who come back to life at the second resurrection face the lake of fire and the second death—everlasting contempt.

The Holy City Transfers to Earth

At this time the New Jerusalem descends to the earth from heaven. "Then I, John, saw the holy city, New Jerusalem, coming down out of heaven from God, prepared as a bride adorned for her husband."

"And he carried me away in the Spirit to a great and high mountain, and showed me the great city, the holy Jerusalem, descending out of heaven from God" (Revelation 21:2, 10).

The New Jerusalem is a huge city that may be half the size of the United States, and it is as tall as it is wide. In the description in Revelation 21, the wording in the original Greek may be depicting a city approximately 1,400 miles in total circumference, or it may be saying the city is 1,400 miles along each side. Either way, it is a large and beautiful city. Everyone who ever lived on earth could fit into a city that size. I'm expecting to enjoy the ride when God flies the New Jerusalem down to our world.

Revelation 20 describes what Satan will do next. "Now when the thousand years have expired, Satan will be released from his prison and will go out to deceive the nations which are in the four corners of the earth, Gog and Magog, to gather them together to battle, whose number is as the sand of the sea. They went up on the breadth of the earth and surrounded the camp of the saints and the beloved city" (verses 7-9).

As soon as the city is in place on earth, a vast army of soldiers from every era in history will immediately surround it. Perhaps they will try to assemble weapons, doing whatever they can to try to seize God's city that He brought down to our world. Satan with all his hosts prepares to attack.

Jesus said that there are more lost than saved. The leaders of the satanic armies know that they outnumber those inside the city. But because God the Father and Jesus are in the city, the city is safe—those two alone outweigh Satan's forces.

The hordes of the lost will advance to attack the city. Then fire will come down from God out of heaven and devour them all. Basically, God reveals Himself in His glory, which is a consuming fire in the presence of sin.

Some people ask me about Gog and Magog attacking the nation of Israel and the rebuilding of the Temple as the fulfillment of Ezekiel 38-48. Remember that for God's people who have accepted Christ and are His true Israel today, the promises for Israel keep getting bigger and better.

In Ezekiel 38-48, the enemies that would have attacked God's people if they had been faithful to God were Gog and Magog. That long-ago nation of Israel would have had a wonderful Temple if the people had been faithful after the Babylonian captivity, but they were not. Since the old Israel did not meet the conditions of the prophecy, the promise of Gog and Magog attacking ancient Jerusalem and of deliverance did not happen.

Instead, the attack of Gog and Magog has moved down to the end of time—to the New Jerusalem—in Revelation 20. There we find the promise of God raining fire down on the massive armies. He keeps the promise of Ezekiel 38-48 for His true Israel, for those who live by faith. His people in the old nation of Israel did not cash in on the promises. But God's people of faith from all time experience the fulfillment at the end of the 1,000 years.

In times past people kept claiming that God's ways were all based on the Temple—that it was His sole focus. But God said: "'Amend your ways and your doings, and I will cause you to dwell in this place. Do not trust in these lying words, saying, "The temple of the Lord, the temple of the Lord, the temple of the Lord are these"'" (Jeremiah 7:3, 4).

Today many look for a temple to be rebuilt in Jerusalem before Jesus returns. I believe this is the "lying words" again. A widespread contemporary prophetic viewpoint teaches things that do not match the Bible. As we have seen, these false teachings predict a seven-year tribulation after the return of Jesus, offer a second chance for people to choose Jesus during the seven years, teach that the beast is yet to come sometime in the future, and say that a third temple will be built in Jerusalem.

As we saw in chapter 12, if someone should erect a third temple and re-institute offering sacrifices again, they will be blaspheming, because Jesus was the sacrifice for all time. They would be denying that Jesus is already our Savior and the Lamb of God. I'm not saying there never will be a temple in Jerusalem again, but if there is, it will not be God's temple.

Revelation said that fire covers the face of the earth at this time. I have heard some people say the lake of fire is down in the center of the earth somewhere, but the Bible depicts it as on the face of the earth, and it calls it the second death.

"Death and Hades were cast into the lake of fire. This is the second death. And anyone not found written in the Book of Life was cast into the lake of fire" (Revelation 20:14, 15). With this fire God erases every trace of sin. He is cleaning up the mess made by sin forever.

We do not see the beast and the false prophet at the end of the 1,000 years. Consigned to the lake of fire at the beginning of the millennium, they are completely destroyed.Anything thrown into the lake of fire is never seen again. And now, at the end of the 1,000 years, Satan and all his followers also get cast into the lake of fire, and they will never appear again.

This is additional evidence that the beast and the false prophet are political/religious powers. If they were humans and not systems they would have been thrown into the fire with the rest at the end of the 1,000 years.

When He is finished burning up all traces of evil and sin, Jesus creates a new world for humanity. "I saw a new heaven and a new earth, for the first heaven and the first earth had passed away. Also there was no more sea" (Revelation 21:1).

I wasn't around the first time God created the world, but this time I plan to observe His acts of creation. Can't you just picture Him announcing, "Let there be grass and trees" and there they are? "Let there be birds in the sky," and they appear! "Lord, I want to be right where You're going to make that elephant. I want to see an elephant appear out of thin air. Thank You, Lord, that is great!"

It's going to be awesome to watch God create a new heaven and a new earth. The lion will lie down with the lamb, and there will be no suffering and no pain, for the former things have passed away. That's the promise God gave us.

Most awesome of all is that we will get to walk and talk with Jesus. The One who died to save us, the One who cleansed our record so that we could live forever with Him, the One who gave us the ability to do good works so that He could reward us according to what He Himself helped us to do—that is the One we get to walk and talk with forever and ever.

But you may wonder about the fate of the lost. "Pastor Tim, don't the wicked people burn forever and ever and ever? for millions and millions of years?" Let's look at the biblical evidence—and it is good news indeed.

As we've seen, fire comes down from God, something Scripture calls the second death. But where did the fire go? If flames spread across the face of the earth and now the earth is wonderfully remade, what happened to the fire?

I suggest that we go by the Bible's definition of eternal and unquenchable fire, not by the traditional explanation. It's better to follow Scripture. 2 Peter 2:9 declares: "The Lord knows how to deliver the godly out of temptations and to reserve the unjust under punishment for the day of judgment." This means that the wicked who died and are now sleeping in the grave are being held for the hellfire. They are not in hellfire yet. That happens at the end of the 1,000 years.

If people went straight to hell to burn and burn and burn for dying in sin, would that be fair? Imagine that I commit a murder now, while Cain murdered somebody 6,000 years ago, and neither of us asks God to forgive us. It would not be fair for Cain to suffer 6,000 years longer for the same crime.

But if we both die the sleep of death and are resurrected at the end of the 1,000 years, and we receive the same punishment at the same time, then God is fair and just. The Lord is reserving for punishment those who were unjust in times past. They are sleeping in death until He brings them forth at the second resurrection—the resurrection of damnation, as the Bible calls it.

Matthew 13:49, 50 explains that at the end of the world, God will do something just like fishermen sorting the good catch from the bad. The angels will separate the wicked from the just and cast them into the furnace of the fire, and there will be wailing and gnashing of teeth.

Is that happening now, or does it come at the end of the world? The Bible says that we do not have an immortal soul, so the wicked cannot be punished now, because the dead know nothing. The wicked never receive immortality. Only God's people do, and then only at the first resurrection.

The people of the second resurrection face the second death. They do not have immortality, and they cannot be punished forever because of that—which is a kindness on God's part.

Now take a look at what happens to Satan when he gets cast into the fire. Ezekiel 28:12 talks about the king of Tyre. "You were the seal of perfection, full of wisdom and perfect in beauty. You were in Eden, the garden of God."

Who was in Eden? Adam, Eve, God—and Satan. But not the king of Tyre. Rather, the king of Tyre serves as a metaphor for Satan as well as a representative of a neighboring people who afflicted Israel.

Satan had been an angel in heaven. "You were the anointed cherub who covers; I established you; you were on the holy mountain of God; you walked back and forth in the midst of fiery stones" (verse 14). He was the guardian cherub.

"You were perfect in your ways from the day you were created, till iniquity was found in you. By the abundance of your trading you became filled with violence within, and you sinned; therefore I cast you as a profane thing out of the mountain of God" (verses 15, 16).

Repeatedly in Scripture we have a description of Satan being cast or driven out of heaven. (Here Ezekiel shifts back more to the imagery of the king of Tyre, whose people were noted traders in the ancient world.)

"And I destroyed you, O covering cherub, from the midst of the fiery stones. Your heart was lifted up because of your beauty; you corrupted your wisdom for the sake of your splendor; I cast you to the ground, I laid you before kings, that they might gaze at you. You defiled your sanctuaries by the multitude of your iniquities, by the iniquity of your trading; therefore I brought fire from your midst; it devoured you, and I turned you to ashes upon the earth in the sight of all who saw you. All who knew you among the peoples are astonished at you; you have become a horror, and shall be no more forever" (verses 16-19).

What happens to Satan? He is reduced to ashes on the earth. He will be "no more forever."

Did you notice that this passage is written in the past tense? How would you like to be Satan and to hear God already talking about you in the past tense? If you had been kidnapped and became somebody's captive, for example, and they started talking about you in the past tense, would you consider that a good sign? Remember that when Satan reminds you of your past, you should remind him of his future. That is what God was doing in Ezekiel 28.

The last verse in that passage says Satan will "become a horror, and shall be no more forever." Does this leave him in charge of hell? No! Rather, he is no more. He is gone forever. That should give you a clue about what happened to the fire.

The soul of the sinner shall die, the Bible emphatically declares. We do not have immortal souls. There is only one way out of this dilemma, and that is to have our sins forgiven. After God pardons them, we do not have any sins on our record, so we are no longer sinners and will not die. But if our sins are not forgiven, we will die permanently and be no more.

Remember this famous verse? "God so loved the world that He gave His only begotten Son, that whoever believes in Him should not perish but have everlasting life" (John 3:16).

What are the options here? We either have everlasting life or perish. Did Jesus say you have a choice between everlasting life or punishment without end? No,

He has never presented the alternative to everlasting life as never-ending torture in a fire. Rather, He said that we would live or perish. Right there in John 3:16 you have a choice between living with Jesus forever or being reduced to ashes, as Satan will be.

"'Behold, the day is coming, burning like an oven, and all the proud, yes, all who do wickedly will be stubble. And the day which is coming shall burn them up,' says the Lord of hosts. 'That will leave them neither root nor branch. But to you who fear My name the Sun of Righteousness shall arise with healing in His wings; and you shall go out and grow fat like stall-fed calves. You shall trample the wicked, for they shall be ashes under the soles of your feet on the day that I do this,' says the Lord of hosts" (Malachi 4:1-3).

Here we have ashes again, this time under the soles of our feet. When the fire is over and the ashes have cooled, you can walk on them. God cleans up the world with fire, burning up all traces of sin. After the fire, God re-creates our planet.

"God will wipe away every tear from their eyes; there shall be no more death, nor sorrow, nor crying; and there shall be no more pain, for the former things have passed away" (Revelation 21:4).

Notice that this does not happen at the beginning of the 1,000 years, but at the end. I believe there is no pain or suffering in heaven, but I note with interest that God wipes away tears right after that final fire. I think it is because some of us on the inside of the New Jerusalem—perhaps all of us—will have a loved one out there on the wrong side of the wall. Perhaps that power of re-creation, watching God re-create, will help wipe away the tears.

Is there any good news in the fire? Yes. The wicked who have persistently refused to trust in Jesus Christ are put out of their misery and are no more. They will not be tortured eternally. God is love, and He is fair.

You might wonder where the teaching of eternal torture in hell came from. It emerged in the early church by at least the second century A.D. Several early Christian writers, such as Justin Martyr and Irenæus, wrote about the eternal punishment of the wicked, but asserted that the wicked would finally be destroyed.

Unfortunately, many converts to Christianity were educated in pagan concepts. Gradually, an idea from Greek mythology that the disembodied souls of the wicked would stay in Hades—put forward soon after the death of the apostle John—found a place in Christian thinking.

Sometime after A.D. 200, the Church Father Tertullian wrote plainly that the wicked would be tortured in hell forever. The view caught on and spread in later Christianity.[1] But the doctrine of eternal torture of the wicked does not appear in the Bible. The God of love does not torture people. He cleans up the earth and allows those who refuse to live in a perfect, sinless world to be no more.

What about the phrase that says the smoke ascends "forever and ever" (Revelation 14:11)? We need to find the truth about that kind of "forever" term.

More than 50 times the Bible employs the word "forever" for something that had an end. For example: "Then his master shall bring him to the judges. He shall also bring him to the door, or to the doorpost, and his master shall pierce his ear with an awl; and he shall serve him forever" (Exodus 21:6). In ancient Israel slaves were supposed to be set free after seven years.

But if a servant really liked his master and said, "I don't want to go free, and I want to be a servant for life," then the master would take an awl, and the servant would put his ear against the door frame of the master's house. The master would drive the awl through the servant's earlobe and into the doorframe, symbolizing that the servant was attached to the master's house for life.

The ritual did not, however, mean that the servant would stay with the master forever, but rather until he died. Again and again in the Bible the word "forever" indicates that something lasted until death.

People often said, "O king, live forever." It was not because they thought the king was never going to die. They meant, "O king, may you have a long and prosperous reign until you die."

When Jesus says to His people, "You will live forever" and "and you will never die,"[2] He means that God's people will not finally be overcome by death. The wicked are burned in the lake of fire, but there is an end to their life—the second death. It is not a fire burning them without end.

What about the unquenchable fire in Jeremiah 17:27? "If you will not heed Me to hallow the Sabbath day, such as not carrying a burden when entering the gates of Jerusalem on the Sabbath day, then I will kindle a fire in its gates, and it shall devour the palaces of Jerusalem, and it shall not be quenched."

---

1   *The outline of this historical change comes from Thomas B. Thayer,* The Origin and History of the Doctrine of Endless Punishment *(Boston: Universalist Publishing House, 1855), ch.. 6. Available online at www.tentmaker.org/books/OriginandHistory.html.*

2   *John 8:51, 10:28, 11:26.*

God would send unquenchable fire against Jerusalem if the people did not obey His commandment. They did not obey, and invaders destroyed their city. But I've been to Jerusalem, and it is not still in flames today.

If my house caught fire and the fire department could not extinguish the flames, does that mean that 100 years later my house would still be burning? No, the fire consumed all the fuel and left a pile of ashes. Once Satan and all of his people begin to burn, no one can put out that fire until they turn to ashes. Thus, once the fire starts, nothing can stop it until it has finished its work. This is the sense in which a fire "shall not be quenched." It burns until everything is gone.

Jude 7 compares the fate of the wicked with Sodom and Gomorrah: "As Sodom and Gomorrah, and the cities around them in a similar manner to these, having given themselves over to sexual immorality and gone after strange flesh, are set forth as an example, suffering the vengeance of eternal fire."

A similar thought comes from 2 Peter 2:6: "Turning the cities of Sodom and Gomorrah into ashes, condemned them to destruction, making them an example to those who afterward would live ungodly."

Archaeologists know that Sodom and Gomorrah existed because the records of other cities refer to them and even call them the "sin cities." They were located somewhere around the Dead Sea. But I have stood on Masada looking down into the Dead Sea basin, and no cities were on fire down there. These are examples of "eternal" fire, but where do we find them now? The cities are burned up and gone.

Satan will be a pile of ashes and no one will find him, just as happened with Sodom and Gomorrah. Sinners will be gone. Those who refuse God's forgiveness end up like those ancient cities and become ashes, and they will be no more. This is eternal punishment, not eternal punishing.

Once I was at a prayer breakfast, and a businessman came in and sat down at the table. "What do you do?" he inquired.

"I'm a pastor."

"Oh, which church?"

"Seventh-day Adventist Church."

"That's the church that doesn't believe in hell, isn't it?"

I smiled and said, "Oh, we believe in a hell, just a hotter one than you do."

Looking at me strangely, he asked, "What? What do you mean, 'a hotter one'?"

"We believe in one hot enough to do the job. It can reduce Satan and sinners into a pile of ashes and put an end to sin and suffering. You believe in a hell that's only partway hot enough and that God isn't really powerful enough to get rid of sin and suffering."

The Bible declares that God is strong enough, and that He reduces wickedness to ashes until it is no more.

Most people assume the existence of an eternal hell because of the belief that sinners have an immortal soul. But the Bible says that they do not. Only those who are forgiven receive immortality, and it begins at the return of Jesus.

The sinners thrown into the lake of fire perish because they are mortal. The fire is hot enough to do the job.

What would we say about God's character if He had a fire just hot enough to torture but not hot enough to destroy? Suppose you had a neighbor who tortures people, and he had a dungeon in the basement, and you could hear screaming coming from it.

 You would not think to yourself, my neighbor is actually kind and nice, because he only keeps people on the edge of death. He never lets anybody die. He tortures them year after year after year, and I can hear their constant anguish. Would you love that neighbor?

This is what people have taught about God. The teaching goes all the way back to Satan in the garden. "You won't really die," he lied. "You'll become like God—immortal." This teaching has made God look like a horrible being. The truth is that He allows sinners to have an end to their misery. Then He recreates the sinless earth, having gotten rid of the sin problem forever. He is big enough and loving enough to have a fire that's hot enough.

The question arises: Why does God go through all the trouble of bringing the wicked back to life a second time just to destroy them? Have you ever wondered that yourself?

One day a man asked, "Why didn't God just get rid of Satan when he had his first sinful thoughts? Why not just take him for a long walk and make sure he never came back?" After all, ultimately that's what God is going to do, isn't He? God will reduce Satan to ashes, and the devil will be no more.

I replied, "Would anybody want to go on a long walk with God after that? I mean, if people go on a long walk with Him and they never, ever come back, I wouldn't want to walk with Him at all."

The question to ask is this: What if God wiped out sin and suffering a little too early? If Satan got the message out that God is not fair, and then the Lord eliminated Satan, who would you think was right in the dispute? You would regard Satan as correct.

Thus God has to let the whole thing play out to the end in order to make sure that sin does not resurface and that all questions that might have come up will be answered by then.

Your Questions Answered

We said earlier in this chapter that we would talk about why God's followers, during the millennium, review the cases of everyone who has ever lived throughout history. Let's say that I am a man who died believing in Jesus. Resurrected, I rise to meet Jesus and my loved ones in the clouds, and then I am taken up to heaven. We go into the New Jerusalem, and God says, "You probably have some questions."

"I have a question. Why isn't my aunt here?"

"OK," God replies, "I'm going to open up the record books, and you can see for yourself. You can view all the records, and you can see all that I tried to do." Remember that the Bible tells us that we will judge everyone during the 1,000 years.

So I open up the books, and there I discover how God tried to reach my loved one and how she repeatedly spurned Him. I see when God used me to try to reach her, and she rejected what I sought to share about Jesus Christ.

By now I realize that God left no stone unturned to get her into salvation and to bring her into the New Jerusalem. But she would not accept. For 1,000 years God opens the records and answers all of our questions.

You know who is really on trial? God. Was He fair with that earlier judgment, the one that happened before Jesus returned to save His people? Was He fair when

He decided whom to resurrect to everlasting life and whom He did not? We now get to examine the records and see for ourselves the justice, mercy, and fairness of His decisions.

You might be thinking that if the rebellious ones could only see the New Jerusalem and what they were missing, they would change their minds and accept.

Just to make sure we know that He did not mess it up, what does God do at the end of the 1,000 years? "OK, let's go back down to earth," He announces, and He flies the whole city down there. He resurrects all the wicked, and they can see the New Jerusalem. What do they do? They follow Satan!

Satan rallies them together because he is their chosen leader, and they join him in a last attack on God. As they advance on the city, I look over the city wall and see my loved one, the very one about whom I had asked, "Why isn't she here?" My aunt looks up at me, and I realize that she is willing to kill me to seize the city.

That's what sin does. Sin makes us into hard, evil people when we reject the Holy Spirit and no longer allow Him to work in our hearts. Sinners become completely devoted to Satan. They are possessed, and in the end, they will kill all of us if they get the chance.

Finally, God says, "That is enough," and He reveals His glory as a consuming fire, something He calls His "strange act" (Isaiah 28:21). He does not want to do it—He loves sinners. But His glory destroys them, reducing them to ashes.

Now I turn to God and see tears in His eyes. The Lord has to wipe the tears from His own eyes, too. "Jesus, I understand," I tell Him. "Thank You for stopping them. Thank You." Never again will I question God about whether He was right. If He had pulled the plug too quickly, some people would still be wondering about His justice. Did He really give everyone every chance? But I have seen that the wicked are not interested in changing.

Don't wait for a second chance. It never comes. Now is the time to trust Jesus Christ, to let Him cleanse you from sin.

"Not everyone who says to Me, 'Lord, Lord,' shall enter the kingdom of heaven, but he who does the will of My Father in heaven" (Matthew 7:21). You have to do more than just say that you are a Christian—you have to actually live it.

To be truly Christian, you have to let Him be Lord and Savior, not just to forgive the past but to take over lordship of the present. As a result, you do whatever He asks you to do, and you won't let your boss, your family, or anyone else decide for you.

"Many will say to Me in that day, 'Lord, Lord, have we not prophesied in Your name, cast out demons in Your name, and done many wonders in Your name?'" (verse 22). Remember the false prophet that we said would appear at the end, performing miracles and wonders? It cast out demons in God's name and did many amazing things in His name. Jesus warned that there would be false signs and wonders and counterfeit miracles. God declares to those who did them: "I never knew you; depart from Me, you who practice lawlessness" (verse 23)!

If you break one of the commandments, you've dishonored them all, Jesus said. The Sabbath, adultery, lying—don't shrug off any of them. It doesn't matter how many good things you do. Your destiny depends on whether or not you are trusting Him.

"Therefore whoever hears these sayings of Mine, and does them, I will liken him to a wise man who built his house on the rock: and the rain descended, the floods came, and the winds blew and beat on that house; and it did not fall, for it was founded on the rock.

"Now everyone who hears these sayings of Mine, and does not do them, will be like a foolish man who built his house on the sand: and the rain descended, the floods came, and the winds blew and beat on that house; and it fell. And great was its fall" (Matthew 7:24-27).

God's Word is the authority. Have you surrendered your life to it? Trust Him completely. You don't have a second chance to change.

We are now in the "time of the end." Time could be very short. We have already entered what Daniel calls the whirlwind. Radical Islam will be destroyed, leading to the greatest opportunity of all time to share the gospel. For all who are trusting Jesus this is a wonderful time to be alive, trusting in Him and sharing His message.

Appendix A

CONTEXTUAL HERMENEUTICS: PRINCIPLES OF INTERPRETATION

There has been a discussion whether human powers that appear in the prophecy of Daniel 11 are literal/geopolitical, religious/ideological, or both geopolitical and religious/ideological. The internal context of Daniel gives us the answer. There is a change in the powers that appear in the prophecy. In Daniel 11:2-21, the powers referred to are literal/geopolitical.

In verse 22, however, the Prince of the Covenant, Christ, is introduced. He is a religious leader. In the following verses of the prophecy the king of the North is given the additional aspect of being religious while continuing as a geopolitical power. As a geopolitical power, the king of the North directs armies into combat in which large numbers die.

This is literal and geopolitical. However, the king of the North also attacks the covenant of God and God's people, making it a religious power as well.

This transition from literal/geopolitical to both geopolitical and religious takes place not just in Daniel 11, but also in Daniel 2, 7, and 8 at the same point in the flow of prophetic history. When the papacy takes power in the waning Roman Empire, a union of church and state results. So we have a geopolitical and religious combination.

In Daniel 7, the divided Roman Empire is represented by the 10 horns. The horns were geopolitical, but the little horn is religious. Once again, both geopolitical and religious powers are indicated since the little horn is among them and uproots three. Again we have a church and state union, or a geopolitical and religious combination.

In Daniel 8, the little horn starts out as Rome and changes to papal Rome. Both literally attack Israel from the northwest, pushing in a southeastern direction. Then it exalts itself into the place of the Prince of the Host (religious) and has an army support it (geopolitical). In Daniel 11, after the time of Christ the king of the North leads real armies into warfare (geopolitical) and it also attacks the covenant of God and the people of God (religious).

So the contextual evidence indicates that the king of the North in Daniel 11 will be both geopolitical and religious. As the enemy of the king of the North that counters its geopolitical and religious aims, the king of the South would also be both geopolitical and religious.

Another contextual issue is whether the powers represented by the king of the North or South can be changed during verses 23-45—or should they be the same beginning to end? In Daniel 7, 8, and 11, when you leave the focus of Imperial Rome, the kingly power switches to the papacy represented by the little horn. This power lasts from Rome to the coming of Christ's kingdom.

The parallel between these chapters indicates that the king of the North in Daniel 11:23-45 should be the same power (papacy) all the way through, and its antagonist to the south should be Islam all the way through—which, like the papacy is a geopolitical and religious power.

Daniel 11:29 also ties the conflict and players of verses 25-28 (the former) with verses 29-39 (the appointed time or "returns") and 40-45 (the latter or "time of the end"). This indicates that if the papacy is the king of the North at any point in Daniel 11:23-45, it should be the king of the North all the way through the whole section. In the same way, Islam should be the king of the South all the way through the whole section.

The parallel between Daniel 11:5-19 and verses 23-45 is striking. When the Greek empire divided, the same two powers (the Seleucids and the Ptolemies) were the kings of the North and South throughout their entire conflict, with Jerusalem caught in the middle.

The same thing happens in the divided Roman Empire. When this empire divides, the same two powers (papal-led Christianity and Islam) are the kings of the North and South throughout their entire conflict, with Jerusalem again caught in the middle.

The internal context of Daniel 11 indicates that the kings of the North and South should be both geopolitical and religious and that they start in the time of Rome and extend all the way to the end of the conflict of the North and South in verse 45. Only Rome and Islam match these criteria!

COMPARISON OF DANIEL 11:2 TO 12:4 WITH HISTORICAL EVENTS

For your reading ease, each table cell full of text on the left goes with the table cell on its right. This means pages in Appendix B may be different lengths so that the full text in each cell can stay together. So you may find white space at the bottom of some pages.

Prophecy (Daniel 11:2-22)	Historical/Projected Fulfillment
2 And now I will tell you the truth: Behold, three more kings will arise in Persia, and the fourth shall be far richer than them all; by his strength, through his riches, he shall stir up all against the realm of Greece.	**1.** Cambyses II (530-521 B.C.) **2.** Smerdis (521 B.C.) **3.** Darius I (521-485 B.C.) **4.** Xerxes (486-465 B.C.), excelling in wealth and power, launched an elaborate campaign against Greece and lost.
3 Then a mighty king shall arise, who shall rule with great dominion, and do according to his will. **4** And when he has arisen, his kingdom shall be broken up and divided toward the four winds of heaven, but not among his posterity nor according to his dominion with which he ruled; for his kingdom shall be uprooted, even for others besides these.	Alexander the Great (336-323 B.C.). Four lesser kingdoms emerged from the rubble of Alexander's Empire: Greece, Asia Minor, Syria, and Egypt, a four-part breakup indicated in Daniel 7:6 and 8:8. Daniel 11 describes world powers that would attack Israel from the northern or southern land invasion routes. If not specified, it is from the north.
5 Also the king of the south shall become strong, as well as one of his princes; and he shall gain power over him and have dominion. His dominion shall be a great dominion. **6** And at the end of some years they shall join forces, for the daughter of the king of the South shall go to the king of the North to make an agreement; but she shall not retain the power of her authority, and neither he nor his authority shall stand; but she shall be given up, with those who brought her, and with him who begot her, and with him who strengthened her in those times.	Greek kingdoms north **(N)** versus south **(S)**: **5 (S)** Egypt—Ptolemy I (305-283 B.C.); **(N)** Syria—Seleucus I (305-281 B.C.), who once served under Ptolemy as "one of his princes." **6 (S)** Ptolemy II (283-246 B.C.) gave his daughter Berenice in marriage alliance to his rival **(N)** Antiochus II (261-246 B.C.). Upon Ptolemy's death, Antiochus returned to his ex-wife Laodice (whom he had divorced in order to marry Berenice). Laodice then poisoned Antiochus and had Berenice and her child murdered so that *her* son Seleucus II could ascend the throne.

Prophecy (Daniel 11:2-22)	Historical/Projected Fulfillment
7 But from a branch of her roots one shall arise in his place, who shall come with an army, enter the fortress of the king of the North, and deal with them and prevail. **8** And he shall also carry their gods captive to Egypt, with their princes and their precious articles of silver and gold; and he shall continue more years than the king of the North. **9** Also the king of the North shall come to the kingdom of the king of the South, but shall return to his own land. **10** However his sons shall stir up strife, and assemble a multitude of great forces; and one shall certainly come and overwhelm and pass thgrough; then he shall return to his fortress and stir up strife. **11** And the knig of the South shall be moved with rage, and go out and fight with him, with the king of the North, who shall muster a great multitude; but the multitude shall be given into the hand of his enemy.	**7-9 (S)** Ptolemy III (246-222 B.C.), Berenice's brother ("branch of her root"), after Berenice's murder, launched a successful campaign against (N) Seleucus II (246-225 B.C.), who fled. Ptolemy took 40,000 talents' worth of silver, 4,000 talents of gold, and 2,500 idols from the Syrians back to Egypt. Seleucus II then recovered Syria. **10-11 (N)** Seleucus III (225-223 B.C.) succeeded Seleucus II, raised up an army, and launched a campaign against Attalus I of the Attalid dynasty. Seleucus III was assassinated after a brief two-year reign. His younger brother, **(N)** Antiochus III ("Antiochus the Great," 223-187 B.C.), succeeded him, amassed an army, and marched against **(S)** Ptolemy IV (221-205 B.C.) of Egypt. He was successful up until his defeat at Raphia in 217 B.C., a loss that nullified his previous gains.

Prophecy (Daniel 11:2-22)	Historical/Projected Fulfillment
12 When he has taken away the multitude, his heart will be lifted up; and he will cast down tens of thousands, but he will not prevail. **13** For the king of the North will return and muster a multitude greater than the former, and shall certainly come at the end of some years with a great army and much equipment. **14** Now in those times many shall rise up against the king of the South. Also, violent men of your people shall exalt themselves in fulfillment of the vision, but they shall fall. **15** So the king of the North shall come and build a siege mound, and take a fortified city; and the forces of the South shall not withstand him. Even his choice troops shall have no strength to resist. **16** But he who comes against him shall do according to his own will, and no one shall stand against him. He shall stand in the Glorious Land with destruction in his power. **17** He shall also set his face to enter with the strength of his whole kingdom, and uprights ones with him; thus shall he do. And he shall give him the daughter of women to destroy it; but she shall not stand with him, or be for him. **18** After this he shall turn his face to the coastlands, and shall take many. But a ruler [commander] shall bring the reproach against them to and end; and with the reproach removed, he shall turn back on him. **19** Then he shall turn his face toward the fortress of his own land; but he shall stumble and fall, and not be found.	**12 (S)** Ptolemy IV, his heart being lifted up after his victory in Palestine, sought to enter the Jewish Temple. The Jews resisted him, so he had "tens of thousands" put to death. **13-16 (N)** Antiochus III returned to wage ar against the (S) Ptolemies, and by 198 B.C., nearly 20 years after his defeat at Raphia, Antiochus had succeeded in taking possession of Palestine. The battle of Panium (198 B.C.) marked the end of Ptolemaic rule in Palestine. **17-19 (N)** Antiochus III gave his daughter Cleopatra in marriage to **(S)** Ptolemy V, hoping to use her to conquer Egypt through intrigue. To his dismay, **(S)** Cleopatra opposed her father. Antiochus then turned against Asia Minor ("the coastlands") but was turned back or defeated by the Roman commander Lucius Cornelius Scipio in 190 B.C. Antiochus III was killed while trying to plunder a pagain temple near Susa (187 B.C.) just a year following the peace accords with Rome (188 B.C.); thus he stumbled and fell and was found no more. The role of the king of the North switches to Rome at this point.

Prophecy (Daniel 11:2-22)	Historical/Projected Fulfillment
20 There shall arise in his place one who imposes taxes on the glorious kingdom; but within a few days he shall be destroyed, but not in anger or in battle.	**(N)** August Caesar (63 B.C. - 14 A.D.) is the first Roman emperor, whose taxing or census is recorded in Luke 2:1.
21 And in his place shall arise a vile person, to whom they will not give the honor of royalty; but he shall come in peaceably, and seize the kingdom by intrigue.	Through divorce, remarriage, and killings, Tiberius became the emperor (A.D. 14-17) but was never popular. During his rule Jesus, the price of the covenant, is broken/killed. The force of a flood is a reference to the Sanhedrin in a flood of emotion denying Jesus as king and claiming they had no king but Caesar.
22 With the force of a flood they shall be sweap away from before him and be broken, and also the prince of the covenant.	Here we have a clear anchor point. Verse **22** is a reference to the death of Jesus, so verse 22 is referencing A.D. 31.
23 And after the league is made with him he shall act deceitfully, for he shall come up and become strong with a small number of people. **24** He shall enter peaceably, even into the richest places of the province; and he shall do what his fathers have not done, nor his forefathers: he shall disperse among them the plunder, spoil, and riches; and he shall devise his plans against the strongholds, but only for a time.	**23** Rise of the papacy as the king of the North without its own army. The league is when Constantine the Great claims to be Christian and links with the church. This results in a blending of Christianity and paganism in the church **24** The pope, a "man of peace," will rule for a limited time. The 1,260 days/years of Daniel 7:25; 12:7; Revelation 12: 6, 14. The king of the North now enters its papal phase.

Prophecy (Daniel 11:2-22)	Historical/Projected Fulfillment
25 He shall stir up his power and his courage against the king of the South with a great army. And the king of the South shall be stirred up to battle with a very great and mighty army; but he shall not stand, for they shall devise plans against him. **26** Yes, those who eat of the portion of his delicacies shall destroy him; his army shall be swept away, and many shall fall down slain. **27** Both these kings' hearts shall be bent on evil, and they shall speak lies at the same table; but it shall not prosper, for the end will still be at the appointed time. **28** While returning to his land with great riches, his heart shall be moved against the holy covenant; so he shall do damage and return to his own land.	**25-30** Pagan Rome made no such invasion of Egypt/South after the death of Jesus. So this must be the papal-led Crusades against Islam initiated by Pope Urban II in 1095. Islam now controlled the area to the south of Israel. The king of the South is now in its Islamic phase. • Multiple major crusades and many minor ones • Armies large and casualties high • High intrigue within the armies • Both sides lied and broke agreements **28** The booty from the Crusades led to many relics and artifacts being taken to Western Europe.
29 At the appointed time he shall return and go toward the south; but it shall not be like the former or the latter.	"Former": The first conflict between Islam and Christianity, including Islamic conquest and Crusades (Daniel 11:25-28; cf. Revelation 9, first woe). Current or "appointed time": The second conflict between Islam and Christianity. This time against the Islamic Ottoman Empire during the time of the Reformation (Daniel 11:29-39, second woe of Revelation 9). "Latter": The future third and final conflict between Islam and Christianity (Daniel 11:40-45; possibly the third woe of Revelation 11:15-19 and 12:12). See appendix E, "The Appointed Time."

Prophecy (Daniel 11:2-22)	Historical/Projected Fulfillment
30 For ships from Cyprus [Kittim] shall come against him; therefore he shall be grieved, and return in rage against the holy covenant, and do damage. So he shall return and show regard for those who forsake the holy covenant. **31** And forces shall be mustered by him, and they shall defile the sanctuary fortress; then they shall take away the daily sacrifices, and place there the abomination of desolation.	Islamic naval victories in the battles of Preveza in 1538 and Dierba in 1560 led to decades of Islamic naval control until Pope Pius V organized the Holy League, which temporarily stopped Islam in the battle of Lepanto in 1571, one of the largest Middle Ages naval battles. Pope Pius V also reasserted the liturgical mass, Inquisition, and decrees of the Council of Trent. 31 Same themes as Daniel 8:11-13, the religious phase of the little horn.
32 Those who do wickedly against the covenant he shall corrupt with flattery; but the people who know their God shall be strong, and carry out great exploits. **33** And those of the people who understand shall instruct many; yet for many days they shall fall by the sword and flame, by captivity and plundering. **34** Now when they fall, they shall be aided with a little help; but many shall **join with them by intrigue. 35** And some of those understanding shall fall, to refine them, purify them, and make them white, until the **time of the end; because it is still for the appointed time.**	**32-34** This represents the Reformation, with many of the Reformers put to death and burned at the stake. **34** After it became safer to be a Protestant, many joined from false motives. **35** This suggests that verses 36-39 will be a summary of the evils of the rule of the papacy and a description of the Counter-Reformation.

Prophecy (Daniel 11:2-22)	Historical/Projected Fulfillment
36 Then the king shall do according to his own will: he shall exalt and magnify himself above every god, shall speak blasphemies against the God of gods, and shall prosper till the wrath has been accomplished; for what has been determined shall be done. **37** He shall regard neither the God of his fathers nor the desire of women, nor regard any god; for he shall exalt himself above them all. **38** But in their place he shall honor a god of fortresses; and a god which his fathers did not know he shall honor with gold and silver, with precious stones and pleasant things. **39** Thus he shall act against the strongest fortresses with a foreign god, which he shall acknowledge, and advance its glory; and he shall cause them to rule over many, and divide the land for gain.	**36** The Counter-Reformation and the stronger blasphemous statements of the authority of the papacy. **37** Speaking of celibacy? The pope as final authority. **38** Describes cathedrals and the veneration of Mary. **39** The papal practice of deciding who had the right to rule a country within the Holy Roman Empire.
40 At the **time of the end** the king of the South shall attack him; and the king of the North shall come against him like a whirlwind, with chariots, horsemen, and with many ships; and he shall enter the countries, overwhelm them, and pass through.	The king of the North continues as the papacy and its allies, and the king of the South continues as Islam, as in Daniel 11:25-39. The **time of the end** begins in the mid-1840s (end of the 2,300 days/years of Daniel 8:13-17, 26), and the battle is after the healing of the deadly wound of Revelation 13:3, because the papacy is able to mount a massive counterattack. It could be said that the developments from 1798 (the end of the 1,260-day/year prophecy) to the mid-1840s set up the time of the end. The military force comes from an alliance of the papacy with Europe (Revelation 17:12) and the United States (Revelation 13:11-17). After attacking the papacy and/or its allies (NATO), Islam is overwhelmed by the counterattack.

Prophecy (Daniel 11:2-22)	Historical/Projected Fulfillment
41 He shall also enter the Glorious Land, and many countries shall be overthrown;	The locations listed have both a geographical and religious worldwide application, i.e., both the papacy and Islam have also joined in worldwide religious struggle. **41** The papal alliance enters Israel. Many countries will also be overthrown.
but these shall **escape** from his hand: Edom, Moab, and the prominent people of Ammon. **42** He shall stretch out his hand against the countries, and the land of Egypt shall **not escape**. **43** He shall have power over the treasures of gold and silver, and over all the precious things of Egypt; also the Libyans and Ethiopians **shall follows at his heels**.	These verses suggest a three-way breakup of Islam. **Way 1.** Those who "escape" from the papal alliance are represented by modern Jordan, a friendly neighbor of Israel. Spiritually this may represent the Islamic "children of Abraham" from the line of Lot, Ishmael, and Esau who will accept Jesus (Hebrews 2:2, 3) and escape the mark of the beast (Revelation 13:8). **Way 2.** Those who do **not escape**—Egypt and many others. They are the radical center of Islam that will be defeated. **Way 3.** Those that **shall follow at his heels.** Libyans and Ethiopians may represent moderate or secular Islamic areas/people that will follow the papacy (Revelation 13:3, "all the world followed the beast," and verses 13-16, "mark of the beast").
44 But news from the **east** and the north shall trouble him; therefore he shall go out with great fury to destroy and annihilate many.	Just before Jesus comes from the east (Matthew 24:27) He speaks a final warning message known as the "loud cry" in Revelation 18:4-20. This will anger the papacy, and their alliance will enforce its mark (Revelation 13:13-17; see also Ezekiel 43:1-9 and 44:4-9).
45 And he shall plant the tents of his palace between the seas and the glorious holy mountain; yet he shall come to his end, and no one will help him.	The papal alliance will plant itself in or take control of Israel and/or spiritual worldwide Israel, the church. The papacy/king of the North will come to its end at the coming of Christ (Daniel 7:22, 27; 8:25; 2 Thessalonians 2:8; Revelation 19:20).

Prophecy (Daniel 11:2-22)	Historical/Projected Fulfillment
12:1 At that time Michael **shall stand up**, the great prince who stands watch over the sons of your people;	Michael (meaning "one who is like God"). Jesus is the prince who saves His people (Danial 9:25-27; 10:13, 21; 11:22). This is in harmony with Martin Luther and many others. The Archangel is not an angel, but over the angels or commander of the angels (Joshua 5:13-15). The pre-Advent judgment concludes when Jesus shall stand up. The judgment started when He sat down in Daniel 7:9, 10. The term "at that time" indicates it is simultaneous with the preceding verse.
And there shall be a time of trouble, such as never was since there was a nation, even to that time.	The seven last plagues of Revelation 16. Of interest if Revelation 15:8, in which the temple is filled with smoke and no man can enter. Once the plagues begin, no one changes sides during the plagues or after. God's people go through what Jeremiah 5:1-9 calls "Jacob's trouble."
And at that time your people shall be delivered, every one who is found written in the book. **2** And many of those who sleep in the dust of the earth shall awake, some to everlasting life, some to shame and everlasting contempt.	Jesus delivers and/or resurrects His followers at His return. There are two resurrections: one for the saved, at the beginning of the 1,000 years of Revelation 20, and the resurrection of the lost, at the end of the 1,000 years.
3 Those who are wise shall shine like the brightness of the firmament, and those who turn many to righteousness like the stars forever and ever.	The saved will live with God for eternity (Revelation 21:107, 27; and 22:1-5).
4 But you, Daniel, shut up the words, and seal the book until the time of the end; many shall run to and fro, and knowledge shall increase.	This verse is currently being fulfilled by the growing interest in and understanding of Daniel 11:1-12:4.

Appendix C

WHY I DO NOT BELIEVE THAT ATHEISTIC COMMUNISM IS THE KING OF THE SOUTH

Many believe that the king of the South in Daniel 11:40-45 is atheistic Communism. They remember that the atheistic perpetrators of the French Revolution attacked the Roman Catholic Church (the king of the North) and, like Pharaoh, said, "I don't know God."

According to such a view, the king of the South in Daniel 11:40-45 denies knowing God. Those who hold such a perspective go on to say that Communism, rooted in the French Revolution, took the place of the French Revolution as the king of the South.

Many also assume that the Roman Catholic Church overcame the king of the South in the late 1980s with the fall of Communism at the hands of the United States and the Vatican.

This leads them to conclude that Revelation 11 describes the French Revolution. I tend to agree with them in their understanding of Revelation 11, but I do not believe, for the following reasons, that the king of the South in Daniel 11 is the same power:

- Daniel 11 is literal/geopolitical from the beginning, so I would expect it to stay that way to the end. On the other hand, Revelation is symbolic, or "signified," from the beginning (Revelation 1:1). We should not apply the same rules to both Daniel 11 and Revelation 11. They are not alike.

- We have no reason to interpret the powers of Daniel 11 as only religious or only spiritual, because Daniel 11 already describes them as both geopolitical and religious.

- The historical fit of Islam as the king of the South from verses 25 to 43 is too great to ignore. It fits each of the details throughout the prophecy.

- We should not change the identity of the powers partway through the period between the Roman Empire and the second coming of Jesus Christ. Both viewpoints understand the king of the North to be the Roman Catholic papacy.

  Daniel 2, 7, and 8; 2 Thessalonians 2; and Revelation 13 all indicate that the king of the North covers the period from the fall of Rome to the second coming of Christ. If this is so, then the king of the South should also extend from the fall of the Roman Empire and last until just before the second coming of Christ.

  We would expect, based on Daniel 11:29, three eras of conflict between these same two powers in the time period between the collapse of Rome and the Second Advent. When we understand Islam to be the king of the South, we do not need to change the identity of the king of the South partway through the prophecy—Islam fits all the way through.

- Some have said that after Christ's death, the prophecies become symbolic or spiritual. If this is true of Daniel 11, why do we find such a good description of the Crusades and the Reformation, which are literal and geopolitical and yet occur after the time of Christ's death?

  It is not wise to spiritualize a prophecy when it makes sense literally. On the other hand, Revelation 11:8 does say that the power referred to as "spiritually called Egypt" is not literal, but symbolic. By not differentiating the styles of the writers, those of the atheistic Communism viewpoint have mixed apples and oranges.

- The context of Daniel 11:40-43 lends itself to interpreting the king of the South as Islam. When the king of North launches its final attack against the king of the South, it list nations by name. They are Egypt, Libya, Ethiopia, and western Jordan (Ammon, Edom, and Moab).

  What do these countries have in common? They are all predominantly Islamic, not Communist or atheistic. The question should be asked, How does the context of Daniel 11:40-45 indicate Communism? Answer: It doesn't. Those who believe this must find support for their view from outside Daniel 11:40-45.

- Geopolitical consistency: After the demise of the Roman Empire, the papacy takes the northern part of the empire, and Islam takes the southern part. For 1,400 years this has been true. Even today, you can see when you look at a map of Europe that it remains so, with Africa and Asia coded for Christian and Islamic-controlled countries.

Christian nations predominate to the north of Israel, and Islamic nations occupy lands predominately to the south of Israel. Those who believe that atheistic Communism is the king of the South find themselves forced to explain how the king of the South got so far north into Russia. In short, the atheistic Communism view is not geopolitically consistent with the prophecy.

Because the literal explanation fits so well, I am exceedingly reluctant to look for any other supposed meaning. So I firmly believe Islam to be the king of the South in Daniel 11:25-43.

This said, I will agree that some similarities do exist between Islam and atheistic Communism. As I mentioned in the chapter on Islam in prophecy, I believe Islam to be the king of the South, but I also believe that from about 1798 to 1990 Satan used the atheistic French Revolution/ Communism to keep Christianity in check.

In 1798, the French overthrew the papacy, and the Islamic Ottomans became a de facto protectorate of the British in 1840. That meant that the Protestant mission movement had its two major restrictions removed, and the mission and Bible societies flourished. With Islam down, Satan used the rising Communist movement to hold back the spread of Christianity.

At the same time that Communism was collapsing in the 1980s, Islam and Islamic terrorism was on the rise. It is interesting to note that the papacy and the United States apparently worked together to bring down Communism, and as I mention in the chapter on the United States in prophecy, I expect that they will crush Islam at the end. Now that Communism is not holding back Christianity as it was, Islam is once again strong and resisting Christianity in much of the world.

So I see Islam as the real king of the South, but atheistic Communism, as in Revelation 11, being a temporary substitute for the king of the South that took the leading role while Islam and the papacy were recovering from their wounds.

Since Daniel 11 describes the king of the North as both a geopolitical and religious power, as is Israel in the New Testament, I believe we should expect that the final conflict will have both localized geopolitical and worldwide religious application.

Appendix D

A GOSPEL APPEAL

As the primary part of this prophecy study, I need to make sure you understand what Jesus has done for you. It is of the highest importance to me, as I share prophecy, that people know Jesus Christ as their Lord and Savior. If I just tell you about prophecy, and it is just facts, I have made your condition worse than it was before.

But if you love Jesus Christ and recognize that He's the great prince who is watching over you, and you realize that no matter what happens, He is the one who died for you and took away your sins and is the center of Bible prophecy, then you have something to live for today! (And if you are already a Christian, please pray for those who might not be.)

Should somebody ask you how to become a Christian, could you answer? As a teenager, I was asked, "Do you know how to lead someone to Christ?" And I thought, *Hmmm, I'm a Christian, but I don't know. How would I lead someone to Christ?*

So he made a presentation, and I took notes on it. I went home and studied my Bible that week so that I could be ready to tell somebody how to become a Christian. Before the week was over, I was able to lead my first person to Jesus Christ—me.

I had thought I was a Christian, but I had somehow misunderstood what it really involved and was trying to do it all on my own. When I finally grasped that it was all about Jesus, I just gave myself to Him, and from then on I could have assurance that I would live forever.

Where to Start

To share the gospel with another, you could ask the question, "How does someone become a Christian?" You can expect all kinds of answers: by going to church, by giving offerings, by being a good person. But those aren't the real answers! If somebody tells you any of these answers, you've got good news for them!

How would you spend eternity if you were to die in your present spiritual condition? If you are like me before I understood what true Christianity was, I hoped vaguely that my good works somehow outweighed my bad works on the scales of divine justice. While I wished that would be the case, I really had no idea for sure. If you wonder where you stand with God, I have good news for you. You *can* know.

When you are ready to share that with someone, ask them, "Would you like me to show you?" If they don't want to hear and you try to present the gospel to them without getting their permission first, they're not going to listen. But if you request, and they say yes, you have a wide-open door to share the good news.

Should they respond negatively, then you can accept their answer and reply, "Tell me when you want to know." They might just get curious and say, "Oh, go ahead, tell me." I have had that happen.

Eternal Life Not Earned

Romans 6:23 tells us that we can't earn eternal life—it is a gift. "The wages of sin is death, but the gift of God is eternal life in Christ Jesus our Lord." You already merit death, and the only escape from that is through the gift of God.

How does He give us that gift? 1 John 1:10 says: "If we say that we have not sinned, we make Him a liar, and His word is not in us." But right before that verse comes this promise: "If we confess our sins, He is faithful and just to forgive us our sins and to cleanse us from all unrighteousness" (verse 9). How much sin does He cleanse? All of it!

You might say, "Well, there is something really horrible in my life!" So what? There is something really horrible in all of our lives. Jesus came to save sinners. That's what He announced and what He did. That horrible thing in your life is a sin that He came to forgive!

The only catch is one little word in the middle—the word "if." "*If* you confess your sins," you can be forgiven. But if you claim that you are not a sinner, you don't have a chance. You must admit to Jesus that you have sinned and need forgiveness.

As a kid, I broke into a house with a friend of mine. We took a few old antique bottles that we figured no one wanted anymore. If I'd said, "Lord, hey, we didn't steal anything of value; it wasn't any big deal," then I'd have been making an excuse for it. If I don't confess that I did something wrong, can I be forgiven? No.

Or I might have said, "My friend actually broke in through the door, so it's his fault, not mine, and I didn't really do anything wrong." Can God forgive me for taking things that were not mine? No, because I'm blaming my friend instead. As soon as I come to God and say, "God, I did it," He says, "Fine, you're forgiven." Whew! I'm free!

Now, imagine that a couple of days later Satan comes along and says, "Tim, remember when you broke into that house with your friend? You're a horrible person. You can't be a Christian." That's going to happen to you, and when it does, don't go back and ask Jesus to forgive you again. He has already forgiven.

Should you ask Jesus to forgive today what He forgave years ago? No, because if you do, it shows you don't believe that He has already forgiven and cleansed you. It will throw you into a cycle of doubt that will cause you to question God's forgiveness.

So when Satan tries to push the guilt button on you, here is what you do. If you have already asked Jesus to forgive you for something and Satan is claiming you're still guilty, say, "Jesus, thank You for already taking care of that for me." That gets rid of the guilt and messes up Satan's plan to ruin your life. I like spoiling Satan's plans.

We can be sure of salvation as long as we continue to trust Jesus. 1 John 5:11-13 declares, "And this is the testimony: that God has given us eternal life, and this life is in His Son. He who has the Son has life; he who does not have the Son of God does not have life. These things I have written to you who believe in the name of the Son of God, that you may know that you have eternal life, and that you may continue to believe in the name of the Son of God."

Can you know for sure that you have eternal life? If you trust in Jesus Christ, you will. If you choose not to trust Him, you will also know that you don't have eternal life. Are you trusting in Jesus? I hope so. If not, surrender to Jesus Christ, and you can be assured that you have eternal life. It is as simple as that.

In John 8:36 Jesus declared that He liberated us to live a new life, one free from sin. In John 14:15 He says: "If you love Me, keep My commandments." Here is an awesome thought: When He sets you free, you fall in love with Jesus, and because you love Him, you want to do the things that please Him.

If you start doing things that don't please Him, and please yourself instead, what does it say about your love for Him? If you were engaged to somebody and that person said, "I don't want to do anything to please you, only what pleases me," would you stay engaged to that person? It suggests a serious problem with their love, doesn't it?

If I do what pleases me and what is not pleasing to God, it indicates a problem in the relationship. Jesus said, "If you love Me, keep My commandments." Do it out of love and for no other reason.

Jesus becomes my Savior. He forgives my sin, and I let Him reign as my Lord. He leads me, and I follow in everything that He asks me to do. It's interesting that we need both a Lord and Savior. 1 John 2:1 tells us: "My little children, these things I write to you, that you may not sin. And if anyone sins, we have an Advocate with the Father, Jesus Christ the righteous."

Notice that Plan A is, Don't sin; follow Jesus. Plan B is, When you blow it and you're a Christian, ask Him to forgive you, and He will. When you have been following Him and you fail, don't give up. You go back to 1 John 1:9 ("If we confess our sins ... "), and then you are free.

Jesus continues as your Savior once you are a Christian. Satan will protest, "Oh, you claim to be a Christian, and you messed it up! It shows that you never were a Christian. Just give up!" He will do that to you again and again. But you probably knew that, right? Just don't give up!

After explaining these things to someone, you can ask, "Do you see what Christ wants for you? He wants to set you free and give you assurance of salvation. Have you ever thought of accepting Jesus Christ before? Maybe it is time for you, right now, to commit your life to Him. All you say is, 'Jesus, I blew it. Forgive me. Take control of my life.'" It is really not difficult.

Then you can pray with them. Teach them this prayer: "God, I have sinned. Please forgive me and cleanse me. I ask that You take over as Lord of my life. I ask this in the name of Jesus, and I thank You. Amen."

MINISTRY MAGAZINE, JUNE 1944

Application of Year-Day Principle, by Centuries, to Respective Trumpet Periods

KEY TO NATIONALITY OF WRITERS:
A—American; B—British; D—Dutch;
F—French; G—German; I—Italian;
S—Scottish.

TIME KEY:
391 days=360+30+1
396 days=365+30+1

No. Expositor	Nationality	Date of Pub.	Fifth Trumpet	Sixth Trumpet	Period Length Years	Days
I. Prior to Reformation						
1. Joachim of Floris	(I)	1190	5 months=150 yrs.			
(First to apply year-day principle and first to apply to Mohammedanism.)						
2. Brute of Britain	(B)	1391	5 months=150 yrs.			
3. Luther, Martin	(G)	1545		Sixth Trumpet is Mohammedanism		
II. Sixteenth Century						
1. Foxe, John	(B)	1586	606-756	1051-1573		
2. Napier, John	(S)	1593	1051-1201	1300-1696	396	
III. Seventeenth Century						
1. Downham	(B)	1603	630-780	1300-1696	396	
2. Brightman, Thomas	(B)	1609	830-930 (630-780)	1300-1696	396	
3. Pareus, David	(G)	1618	606-756	1300-1696	396	
4. Mede, Joseph	(B)	1627	830-980 (955-1055)	1057-1453	396	
5. Goodwin, Thomas	(B)	1639	830-980	1453-1849	396	
6. Huet, Ephraim	(A)	1644	606-756	1302-1695	395	
7. Parker, Joseph	(A)	1646		1259-1649 (1370-1859)	390	
8. de Launay, Pierre	(F)	1651	Saracens	Turkish Invasion		
9. Poole, Matthew	(B)	1666	839-980	1057-1453 (1300-1669)	396	
10. Jurieu, Pierre	(F)	1687	622-772	1300-1696	396	
11. Cressener, Drue	(B)	1689	637-787	1063-1453	391	
12. Knollys, Hanserd	(B)	1689	(150 Yrs.)	(391 "odd days")	391	
13. Lloyd, William	(B)	1690	(150 Yrs.)	1302-1698	396	
14. Newton, Isaac	(B)	1691	637-936 (300)	1063-1453	391	
15. Horchen, Heinrich	(G)	1697	622-1057	1057-1453	396	
16. Beverley, Thomas	(B)	1698		1055-1453	391	(+15 days)
IV. Eighteenth Century						
1. Fleming, Robert	(B)	1701	622-772	1067-1458	391	
2. Baxter, Richard	(B)	1701	(150 Yrs.)	1300-1696	396	
3. Brüssken, Conrad	(G)	1703	606-756	1057-1453	396	
4. Vitringa, C.	(D)	1705	Saracens (150)	(Turks)		
5. Whiston, William	(B)	1706	673-823	1301-1697 (1062-1453)	396	
6. Mather, Increase	(A)	1709		1300-1699	396	
7. Daubuz, Charles	(B)	1712	612-762	1386- (1356-)		
8. Henry, Matthew	(B)	1712	627-779	1075-1453	396	
9. Anonymous	(B)	1719	(150 Yrs.)	1057-1453	396	
10. Newton, Thomas	(B)	1758	612-762	1281-1672	391	
11. Durham, James	(B)	1764		(Period of Time)	391	
12. Gill, John	(B)					
13. Kershaw	(B)	1780	629-779	1301-1697	396	
14. Wood, Hans	(B)	1787	630-780	1030-		
15. Scott, Thomas	(B)	1791	612-762	1281-1672	391	(+15)
16. Osgood, Samuel	(A)	1794	622-772	997-1388 (1297-)	391	
17. Winthrop, James	(A)	1794	"150 yrs."	"391 years"	391+	
18. Woodhouse, J. G.	(B)	1794		1055-1453	391	
19. Bicheno, James	(B)	1799	606-756	1302-1697	391	(+16)
20. Kett, Henry	(B)	1799	612-762			
V. Nineteenth Century						
1. Mitchel	(B)	1800	622-772	1300-1696	396	
2. Evanson, Ed.	(B)	1802	632-782	1057-1453	396	
3. Priestly, Joseph	(B)	1804	612-762	1281-1672	391	
4. Barnes, Albert	(B)	1805	622-772 (629-779)	1057-1453	391	
5. Chamberlin, Richard	(A)	1805	(150 years)	1292-1683	391	(+14)
6. Faber, G. S.	(B)	1806	612-762	1281-1672	391	
7. Johnstone, Bryce	(B)	1807	606-756	699-1090	391	(+15)
8. French, Lawrence	(B)	1810	612-762	1065/68-1453 (1299-1685)	391	(+15)
9. Buck, Charles	(B)	1811		1453-1844	391	
10. Cunninghame, William	(B)	1813	612-662	1281-1672 (1057-1448)	391	(or 396)
11. Kinne, Aaron	(A)	1814	612-762	1281-1672	391	(+15)
12. M'Lleod, Alexander	(A)	1814	612-762	1281-1672	391	(+15)
13. Armstrong, Amzi	(A)	1815	612-762	1281-1672	391	(+15)
14. Brown, John	(B)	1815	610-760	1281-1672 (1302-1698)	391	
15. Frere, James H.	(B)	1815	612-762 (632-782)	1281-1692 (1063-1453)	391	
16. Holmes, James I.	(B)	1815	612-762	1281-1672	391	(+15)
17. Cornwallis, Mrs.	(B)	1820	612-762	1281-1672	391	(+15)

No. Expositor	Nationality	Date of Pub.	Fifth Trumpet	Sixth Trumpet	Period Length Years	Days
18. Gauntlett, Henry	(B)	1821	612-762	1281-1672	391	(+15)
19. Fry, John	(B)	1822	629-779	1453-1844	391	
			(612-762)			
20. Brown, J. A.	(B)	1823	(150 years)	1453-1844	391	
21. Cooper, Edward	(B)	1825	533 683	1301-1697	396	(or 391)
				(1327-1798)		
22. Park, J. R.	(B)	1825	612-762	1453-1844	391	
23. "Laicus"	(B)	1827	630-930	1299-1690	391	
			(300)	(1326-1717)		
24. Cox, John	(B)			1453-1844	391	
25. Keyworth, Thomas	(B)	1828	612-762	1281-1672	391	(+15)
26. Addis, Alfred	(B)	1829	786-936			
27. Homan, Ph.	(B)	1829		1453-1844	391	
28. Tudor, John	(B)	1829	622-762	391 yrs. & fraction	391	
29. Anonymous	(B)	1829	632-782	1062-1453	391	
30. Hales, William	(B)	1830	620-770	1281-1672	391	(+15)
			(632-782)	(1062-1453)		
31. MILLER, WILLIAM,	(A)	1831		1452-1843	391	(+15)
		1832	1298-1448	1448-1839	391	(+15)
		1839	1299-1449	1449-1840	391	(+15)
32. Keith, Alexander	(A)	1832	622-772	1057-1453	396	(+103)
33. Smith, Ethan	(A)	1833		1453-1818	360	
34. Habershon, Matthew	(B)	1834	612-762	1453-1844	391	(+15)
35. Bickersteth, Edward	(B)	1836	637-786	1453-1843/44	391	
				(1063-1453)		
36. Bogie, B. D.	(B)	1836	612-762	1300-1696	396	
37. Jenks, William	(A)	1838	612-762	1281-1672	391	(+15)
38. Litch, Josiah	(A)	1838	1299-1449	1449-1840 (Aug.)	391	(+15)
39. Wall	(A)	1840		1453-1849	396	
40. Whitaker & Thurston	(A)	1840		1453-1844	391	
41. Campbell, David	(A)	1840	612-762	1281-1692	391	(+15)
42. Crandall, A. I.	(A)	1841	606-756	1281-1672	391	
43. Fitch, Charles	(A)	1842	1299-1449	1449-1840	391	
44. Birks, T. R.	(B)	1843	632-682		391	
45. Stone, B. W.	(B)	1843	1299-1449	1449-1840	391	(+15)
46. Southard, Nath.	(A)	1843	1299-1449	1449-1840	391	(+15)
47. Anon. (Hyponia)	(B)	1844		1281-1672 (Aug.)	391	
48. Galusha, Elon	(A)	1844	1299-1449	1449-1840	391	(+15)
49. Elliott, E. B.	(B)	1844	612-762	1057-1453	396	(+130)
50. Gaussen, Louis	(F)	1844		1453-1844	391	
51. Guinness, H. G.	(B)	1844	622-762	1300-1699	396	
52. Junkin, George	(A)	1844	612-762	1281-1672	391	(+15)
53. Scott, James	(S)	1844		1453-1844	391	
54. Fysh, Frederick	(A)	1845	612-762	1301-1697	396	(+3 mos.)
			(607-757)	(1453-1849)		
55. Scott, Samuel	(A)	1848	622-922 (3	1059-1453	396	
56. Thom, Adam	(B)	1848	606-756	1062-1453	391	
57. Wickes, Thomas	(A)	1851	612-762	1281-1672	391	(+15)
58. Jenour, Alfred	(F)	1852	632-786	1062-1453	391	(+15)
59. Bliss, Sylvester	(A)	1853	622-762	1453-1844	391	(+15)
60. Jones, Joseph	(B)	1853	Saracens	Turkish Invasion	391	(+15)
61. Williams, Thomas	(B)	1853	612-762	1281-1672	391	(+15)
62. L'Hote, J. B.	(A)	1854	622-772	1057-1453	396	(+15)
				(1302-1698)		
63. Cumming, John	(A)	1855	612-762	1057-1453	396	
64. Slight, Benjamin	(Can.)	1855	629-779	1057-1453	396	
65. Lyon, J. C.	(A)	1859	612-762	1057-1453	365	(+106)
66. Butler, J. G.	(B)	1860	841-904	1057-1453	396	
67. Thomas, John	(A)	1861	632-782	1063-1453	391	(+30)
68. Royse, P. E.	(A)	1864		1250-1641	391	(+30)
69. Smith, Uriah	(A)	1865	1299-1449	1449-1840	391	(+15)
70. Gardner, J. P.	(A)	1867	Saracens	Turkish Invasion	391	(+15)
71. Hunt, E. M.	(A)	1870	612-762	1057-1453	396	
72. Steele, David	(A)	1870	612-762	1281-1672	391	
73. Pond, Enoch	(A)	1871	629-779	1062-1453	391	
74. De Pui, James	(A)	1873	728/30-879	1291-1682	391	
75. Simons, E. D.	(A)	1875	612-762	1057-1453	391	(+15)
				(1062-1453)		
76. Orr, John	(A)	1876	606-	Mohammedanism	396	
77. Johnson, B. W.	(A)	1881	632-782	1057-1453	396	(+3 mos.)
78. Kimball, I. E.	(A)	1897		1449-1840	391	(+15)
79. Moore, T. W.	(A)	1897	Mohammedanism	1070/71-1453	391	
				(1095-1478/79)		
80. Tanner, Joseph	(B)	1898	612-762	1062-1453	396	(15 or 30)
VI. Twentieth Century						
1. Hood, J. W.	(A)	1900	612-762	1281-1672	391	(+15)
2. Smith, F. G.	(A)	1908	Saracens	1281-1672	391	(+15)
3. Williams, H. C.	(A)	1917	612-672	1057-1453	396	
			(632-782)			

Appendix F

THE "TIMES" OF DANIEL 11 AND 12

The reader should note that part of the following information is a relatively new understanding of the time periods of Daniel 11 and 12. Further study and dialogue could result in modifications. Updated and expanded information with graphs are available upon request from newsletter@IslamAndChristianity.org or at www.IslamAndChristianity.org.

The visions of Daniel 7, 8, and 11 are each followed by an interpretation. It is in the interpretation that we are given added information and time elements. The vision in Daniel 11:2-12:4 tells us what will happen, while the interpretation in Daniel 12:5-13 gives us the time elements of the Daniel 11 prophecy. Note that in Daniel 12:6, the time element is the purpose of the interpretation "How long shall the fulfillment of these wonders be?" The prophecy of Daniel 11 has three "times" named that need further explanation regarding their time element.

"For a Time"

Daniel 11:24 says, "And he shall devise his plans against the strongholds, but only for a time." If Daniel 11 gives us the "what" and Daniel 12 gives us the "when," then we should find a corresponding time prophecy in Daniel 12, and we do.

The first time period is mentioned in Daniel 12:7 and is "time, times, and half a time." This is the same timeframe of "time, times and half a time," or 1,260 days, as Daniel 7. Both refer to the rise of the papacy and its 1,260-year time of supremacy from 538 to 1798 A.D. (See chapter 2 for more details.)

"The Appointed Time"

"The appointed time" of Daniel 11:29 appears to be more than just a point in time, because in verse 35 "the appointed time" or some aspect of it is still in the future. If the prophecy and history are correctly understood in this book, then "the appointed time" of Daniel 11:29-39 should be the time of the Reformation and the Ottoman Empire—the second Islamic-versus-Christian conflict.

The definition of "the appointed time" appears in its first use in Daniel 8:19. "Look, I am making known to you what shall happen in the latter time of the indignation; for at the appointed time the end shall be." This tells us that "the appointed time" is the end of something and is "in the latter time of the indignation."

Since Daniel 11:29 is definitely not the end of time, this must indicate the end of something else. It seems that the end of an appointed time would simply be the end of a time prophecy. The focus is the *end* of the time prophecy, not its duration.

"The appointed time" would be "in the latter time of the indignation." Since "the appointed time" is before "the time of the end," this would suggest that "the latter time of the indignation" is the latter part of the 1,260 days.

But what time prophecy would be ending in verse 29? We should look to chapter 12, which gives the time element for Daniel 11. The next time period is in Daniel 12:11, 12. This time starts from the "abomination of desolation" and extends to a blessing.

"The abomination of desolation" is the only starting point given for the 1,290 and 1,335 prophetic days, which implies that they both have the same starting point. In the same way, the blessing associated with the 1,335 days may apply to the 1,290 days as well.

The following points have led to the conclusion that the 1,290 and 1,335-day prophecies have parallel applications that serve as bookends of Daniel 11:29-39. The first application identifies the beginning of the Reformation and papal persecution. The second leads to the end of the papal persecution and "the time of the end."

1. There are two "abomination of desolations" (starting points) in Daniel. The first is in Daniel 9:27, which Jesus calls the "abomination of desolation" in Matthew 24:15. The second is in Daniel 11:31.

2. There are two endings of "the appointed time" in Daniel 11. In verse 29 "the appointed time" is present. However, in verse 35 "the appointed time" is once again future, suggesting that "the appointed time" comes to its end again after verse 29 (or for the second time).

3. In Daniel 8:13-19 "the appointed time" and "the abomination that brings desolation" are introduced, saying it is for both the sanctuary (the literal building in A.D. 70) and the host. (In Daniel 11:31, God's people, the host, are persecuted when the king of the North gets "the force of arms." Clovis, the Frank, gave military support to the papacy in A.D. 508 to eradicate opposition.)

What happens if we start the 1,290/1,335-day prophecies from both A.D. 70 and 508?

First, we start from A.D. 70: 70 + 1,290 = 1,360. In A.D. 1360 John Wycliffe began his work against the friars and became the "Morningstar," or "theoretician," of the Reformation. Also, 70 + 1,335 = 1,405. In 1405 A.D., the pope issued a decree that John Huss was to stop teaching from Wycliffe's writings. Huss ended up rebelling and becoming what some call "the first practicing Reformer."

Starting the 1,290/1,335-day prophecies from A.D. 70 brings us to a blessing—the beginning of the Reformation. Daniel 11:29-39 describes the time of the Reformation with "the appointed time" of 1360 A.D. as its starting point. At the same time the Ottoman Empire rose and conquered Constantinople in 1453 A.D.

Second, we start from A.D. 508, the second abomination, from Daniel 11:31. It looks like this: 508 + 1,290 = 1,798. This year, A.D. 1798, brings us to the blessing of the end of papal supremacy. Also, 508 + 1,335 = 1843 A.D.

This is the time of the prophetic movement based on the book of Daniel that introduces the beginning of the judgment. In this judgement in which the king of the North/little horn will would be judged and the kingdom of Christ will would be established.

Starting the 1,290/1,335-day prophecies from both of Daniel's abominations gives us the beginning and end of the Reformation, the Ottoman Empire, and leads into "the time of the end." Daniel 8:19 says "at the appointed time the end," and from 1360 to 1844 A.D., all the time prophecies relating to the papacy come to their end!

"The appointed time" as a time period runs from 1360 to 1844 A.D. This is compelling evidence that since Daniel has no future "abomination of desolation" in his sequential prophecies, there will be no future application of the 1,290/1,335-day prophecies. To start the prophecy from a future even of our choosing would not be true to the context of Daniel and would be a private interpretation, not a biblical one.

"The Time of the End"

Daniel 12 does not have a time prophecy for "the time of the end." However, Daniel 8:13-19 already tells us that the vision of 2,300 days and cleansing of the sanctuary refer to "the time of the end." So "the time of the end" would be 1844 A.D. and following. (For the calculations, see chapter 9.)

In Daniel 11:35 and 12:9, 10, "the time of the end" is related to God's people being made white or cleansed, which is what happens in the pre-Advent judgment following 1844. Daniel 12:4 says the prophecy will be understood "at time of the end."

From 1798 to 1844 there is a growing understanding of Daniel's prophecy. But it is not until after the disappointment of 1844 and the understanding of the pre-Advent judgment that it can be said that Daniel is understood. Also, it is only after 1844 that it can be said that the events connected to Jesus' return can now happen at any time. So we are now in "the time of the end."